First World War
and Army of Occupation
War Diary
France, Belgium and Germany

2 DIVISION
Divisional Troops
Royal Army Medical Corps
100 Field Ambulance
16 November 1915 - 22 June 1919

WO95/1339/1

The Naval & Military Press Ltd
www.nmarchive.com
Published in association with The National Archives

Published by

The Naval & Military Press Ltd

Unit 10 Ridgewood Industrial Park,

Uckfield, East Sussex,

TN22 5QE England

Tel: +44 (0) 1825 749494

www.naval-military-press.com

www.nmarchive.com

This diary has been reprinted in facsimile from the original. Any imperfections are inevitably reproduced and the quality may fall short of modern type and cartographic standards.

© Crown Copyright
Images reproduced by permission of The National Archives, London, England, 2015.

Contents

Document type	Place/Title	Date From	Date To
Heading	WO95/1339/1		
Heading	2 Div Troops 100 Field Ambs 1915 Nov To Dec		
Heading	33rd. Division 2nd. Div 100th F.A. Nov 15		
War Diary	Sliry Camp Salisbury	16/11/1915	16/11/1915
War Diary	Southampton	17/11/1915	17/11/1915
War Diary	Havre	18/11/1915	18/11/1915
War Diary	Sternleeque	19/11/1915	23/11/1915
War Diary	Busnes	23/11/1915	25/11/1915
War Diary	Fouquieres	26/11/1915	30/11/1915
Heading	33rd. Div 2nd Div 100th. F.A. Dec 1915 Vol 2		
Heading	War Diary No. 100 Field Ambulance From December 1st. To 31st. 1915 (Volume 2)		
War Diary	Fouquieres	02/12/1915	27/12/1915
War Diary	Gonnehem	29/12/1915	31/12/1915
Heading	2nd Division Medical 100 Field Ambulance Jan-Dec 1916		
Heading	33rd Div 100th. Field Ambulance Jan 1916 Vol 3		
Heading	War Diary Of 100 Field Ambulance From 1.1.16 To 31.1.16 Volume 3		
War Diary	Gonnehem	01/01/1916	17/01/1916
War Diary	Bethune	18/01/1916	31/01/1916
Heading	2nd Div No. 100 Field Ambulance Feb 1916 March 1916 April 1916		
Heading	War Diary Of 100 Field Ambulance From February 1st. To February 29th. (Volume 4)		
War Diary	Bethune	01/02/1916	19/02/1916
War Diary	Bourecq	19/02/1916	27/02/1916
War Diary	Bethune	28/02/1916	28/02/1916
War Diary	Barlin	29/02/1916	29/02/1916
Heading	War Diary Of 100 Field Ambulance From March 1st. To March 31st. Volume 5		
War Diary	Barlin	01/03/1916	22/03/1916
War Diary	Bruay	22/03/1916	31/03/1916
Heading	War Diary Of 100 Field Ambulance From April 1st. To April 30th. Volume 6		
War Diary	Chateau De Boismont (France 36B 3rd. Ed D.10.B.4.8)	01/04/1916	02/04/1916
War Diary	Chateau De Boismont	02/04/1916	17/04/1916
War Diary	Barlin	18/04/1916	30/04/1916
Heading	War Diary Of 100 Field Ambulance From May 1st. To May 31st. Volume 7		
War Diary	Barlin	01/05/1916	11/05/1916
War Diary	Bruay	11/05/1916	25/05/1916
War Diary	Gauchin-Legal	25/05/1916	25/05/1916
War Diary	Gauchin	25/05/1916	31/05/1916
Heading	War Diary Of 100 Field Ambulance From June 1st. To June 30th. 1916 Volume 8		
War Diary	Gauchin Legal	01/06/1916	02/06/1916
War Diary	Estree Cauchie	02/06/1916	30/06/1916
Heading	War Diary Of 100 Field Ambulance From July 1st. To July 31st. Volume 9		

War Diary	Estree Cauchie	01/07/1916	17/07/1916
War Diary	Ourton	17/07/1916	20/07/1916
War Diary	Dieval	20/07/1916	20/07/1916
War Diary	Longeau	21/07/1916	21/07/1916
War Diary	Morlancourt	22/07/1916	22/07/1916
War Diary	Dive Copse	22/07/1916	31/07/1916
Heading	War Diary 100 Field Ambulance August 1st. To August 31st. 1916 Volume 10		
War Diary	Dive Copse J.24.B. Map (62D)	01/08/1916	05/08/1916
War Diary	Dive Copse	06/08/1916	11/08/1916
War Diary	Mericourt	12/08/1916	13/08/1916
War Diary	St. Sauveur	13/08/1916	16/08/1916
War Diary	Wargnies	16/08/1916	17/08/1916
War Diary	Macfer	17/08/1916	18/08/1916
War Diary	Vauchelles	18/08/1916	19/08/1916
War Diary	Couin	20/08/1916	31/08/1916
Heading	War Diary Of 100 Field Ambulance From September 1st. To September 30th. 1916 Volume 11		
War Diary	Couin	01/09/1916	30/09/1916
Heading	2nd. Div 100th. Field Ambulance Oct 1916		
Heading	War Diary Of 100 Field Ambulance October 1st. To October 31st. 1916 Volume 12		
War Diary	Couin	01/10/1916	02/10/1916
War Diary	Acheux	02/10/1916	31/10/1916
Heading	2nd. Div 100th. Field Ambulance Nov 1916		
Heading	War Diary Of 100 Field Ambulance November 1st. To November 30th. 1916 Volume 13		
War Diary	Acheux	01/11/1916	20/11/1916
War Diary	Beauval	20/11/1916	20/11/1916
War Diary	Gorges	21/11/1916	22/11/1916
War Diary	Ribeaucourt	23/11/1916	23/11/1916
War Diary	Gapennes	24/11/1916	24/11/1916
War Diary	Caours	25/11/1916	26/11/1916
War Diary	Conteville	27/11/1916	30/11/1916
Heading	2nd. Div 100th Field Ambulance Dec 1916		
Heading	War Diary Of 100 Field Ambulance December 1st. December 31st. 1916 Volume 14		
War Diary	Conteville	01/12/1916	31/12/1916
Heading	2nd Division War Diaries 100th. Field Ambulance January To 31st. December 1917		
Heading	War Diary Of 100 Field Ambulance January 1st. To January 31st. 1917 Volume 15		
War Diary	Conteville	01/01/1917	09/01/1917
War Diary	Le Meillard	10/01/1917	11/01/1917
War Diary	Puchevillers	12/01/1917	12/01/1917
War Diary	Aveluy	13/01/1917	31/01/1917
Heading	War Diary Of 100 Field Ambulance February 1st. To February 28th. 1917 Volume 16		
War Diary	Aveluy	01/02/1917	28/02/1917
Heading	War Diary Of 100 Field Ambulance March 1917 Vol 17		
War Diary	Aveluy	01/03/1917	09/03/1917
War Diary	Pozieres	10/03/1917	22/03/1917
War Diary	Aveluy	23/03/1917	24/03/1917
War Diary	Vadencourt	25/03/1917	26/03/1917
War Diary	Gezaincourt	27/03/1917	27/03/1917

War Diary	Sericourt	28/03/1917	28/03/1917
War Diary	Siracourt	29/03/1917	30/03/1917
War Diary	Pernes	31/03/1917	31/03/1917
Miscellaneous	B.E.F. Summary Of Medical War Diaries For 100th. F.A. 2nd. Divn 13th. Corps 1st. Army		
War Diary	Headquarters		
War Diary	Moves	09/04/1917	10/04/1917
War Diary	Transfers	10/04/1917	10/04/1917
War Diary	Moves Detachment	12/04/1917	12/04/1917
War Diary	Moves	12/04/1917	12/04/1917
War Diary	Transport	13/04/1917	13/04/1917
War Diary	Transfer	13/04/1917	13/04/1917
War Diary	Medical Arrangements	14/04/1917	14/04/1917
War Diary	Accomodation	27/04/1917	27/04/1917
Miscellaneous	100th F.A. 2nd Divn. 13th Corps.	01/04/1917	01/04/1917
War Diary	Casualties	28/04/1917	28/04/1917
War Diary	Assistance	28/04/1917	28/04/1917
War Diary	Transport	28/04/1917	28/04/1917
Miscellaneous	100th F.A. 2nd Divn. 13th Corps.	01/04/1917	01/04/1917
War Diary	Casualties	29/05/1917	29/05/1917
War Diary	Casualties R.A.M.C.	29/05/1917	29/05/1917
War Diary	Casualties	29/05/1917	29/05/1917
War Diary	Headquarters		
War Diary	Moves	09/04/1917	10/04/1917
War Diary	Transfer	10/04/1917	10/04/1917
War Diary	Moves Detachment	12/04/1917	12/04/1917
War Diary	Moves	12/04/1917	12/04/1917
War Diary	Transport	13/04/1917	13/04/1917
War Diary	Transfer	13/04/1917	13/04/1917
War Diary	Medical Arrangements	14/04/1917	14/04/1917
War Diary	Accomodation	27/04/1917	27/04/1917
Miscellaneous	100th F.A. 2nd Divn. 13th Corps.	01/04/1917	01/04/1917
War Diary	Assistance	28/04/1917	28/04/1917
War Diary	Transport	28/04/1917	28/04/1917
Miscellaneous	100th F.A. 2nd Divn. 13th Corps.	01/04/1917	01/04/1917
War Diary	Casualties	29/05/1917	29/05/1917
War Diary	Casualties R.A.M.C.	29/05/1917	29/05/1917
War Diary	Casualties	29/05/1917	29/05/1917
Heading	War Diary Of 100 Field Ambulance April 1917 Vol 18		
War Diary	Pernes	01/04/1917	08/04/1917
War Diary	Bajus	09/04/1917	09/04/1917
War Diary	Bajus (Lens II) 1/100000	10/04/1917	10/04/1917
War Diary	Marceuil	11/04/1917	12/04/1917
War Diary	Anzin	13/04/1917	30/04/1917
Miscellaneous	Monthly Strength Return Of The Ranks		
Miscellaneous	Wounded Admissions Evacuations This Out April Daily For 24 Hours Ending 9 a.m.		
Miscellaneous	B.E.F. Summary Of Medical War Diaries For 100th F.A. 2nd. Divn. 13th. Corps 1st Army		
War Diary	Medical Arrangements Evacuation Cont	30/05/1917	30/05/1917
Miscellaneous	100th F.A. 2nd Divn. 13th Corps.	01/05/1917	01/05/1917
War Diary	Casualties	03/05/1917	03/05/1917
War Diary	Moves Detachment	04/05/1917	04/05/1917
War Diary	Medical Arrangements	04/05/1917	04/05/1917
War Diary	Moves	04/05/1917	04/05/1917
War Diary	Casualties	05/05/1917	05/05/1917

War Diary	Moves	06/05/1917	06/05/1917
War Diary	Operations R.A.M.C.	06/05/1917	22/05/1917
War Diary	Moves Detachment	23/05/1917	23/05/1917
War Diary	Moves	23/05/1917	24/05/1917
War Diary	Accomodation	24/05/1917	24/05/1917
War Diary	Evacuation Medical Arrangements	24/05/1917	24/05/1917
War Diary	Medical Arrangements Evacuation	30/05/1917	30/05/1917
Heading	War Diary Of 100 Field Ambulance May 1st. To 31st. 1917 Vol 19		
War Diary	Anzin-St. Aubin (51B 1/40000) G.7.C.8.7	01/05/1917	03/05/1917
War Diary	Anzin	04/05/1917	04/05/1917
War Diary	Ecoivres	05/05/1917	06/05/1917
War Diary	Rocourt	06/05/1917	24/05/1917
War Diary	Roclincourt	24/05/1917	31/05/1917
Miscellaneous	Appendix I		
Heading	War Diary Of 100 Field Ambulance June 1st. To June 30th. 1917 Vol 20		
War Diary	Roclincourt	01/06/1917	14/06/1917
War Diary	Cambigneul	15/06/1917	19/06/1917
War Diary	Bethune	20/06/1917	20/06/1917
War Diary	Locon	21/06/1917	30/06/1917
Heading	War Diary Of 100 Field Ambulance July 1st. To July 31st. 1917 Vol 21		
War Diary	Locon	01/07/1917	31/07/1917
Heading	War Diary Of 100 Field Ambulance August 1st. To August 31st. 1917 Vol 22		
War Diary	Locon Mesplaux Farm X.14.B.9.6 Ref. Map Bethune (Combined Sheet) Edition 6	01/08/1917	10/08/1917
War Diary	Locon Mesplaux Farm X.14.B.9.6 Ref. Map 36d S.E.	10/08/1917	16/08/1917
War Diary	Locon (Mesplaux Farm)	17/08/1917	31/08/1917
Miscellaneous	Return Of Sick & Wounded Admissions Evacuations Etc During Month Of August 1917		
Miscellaneous	Notes On 2nd. Division Diet Records By Instruction In Catering First Army	15/08/1917	15/08/1917
Miscellaneous	Report by Instructor In Catering First Army	04/08/1917	04/08/1917
Heading	War Diary No. 100 Fd Amb Volume 23 Sept 1917		
War Diary	Locon (Mesplaux Fm) X.14.B.9.6	01/09/1917	07/09/1917
War Diary	Locon	08/09/1917	13/09/1917
War Diary	Locon (Mesplaux Farm)	14/09/1917	17/09/1917
War Diary	Merville (XI Corps Rest Station)	18/09/1917	23/09/1917
War Diary	Merville	24/09/1917	30/09/1917
Miscellaneous	Appendix. 1.		
Heading	War Diary Of 100 Field Ambulance For October 1917 Volume 24		
War Diary	XI Corps Rest Station Merville (K29)	01/10/1917	06/10/1917
War Diary	Auchel C.27.B.6.4 (Hotel De Ville)	07/10/1917	17/10/1917
War Diary	Auchel	18/10/1917	31/10/1917
Heading	No. 100 Field Ambulance Appendix "A" To Vol 24 Oct 1917 Movement Orders During Month		
Miscellaneous	2nd Division Medical Arrangements No. 22	07/10/1917	07/10/1917
Miscellaneous	2nd Division Medical Arrangements No. 22	04/10/1917	04/10/1917
Miscellaneous	O's. C. Nos. 5.6.100 Field Ambulance	04/10/1917	04/10/1917
Operation(al) Order(s)	2nd Division R.A.M.C. Order No. 83	04/10/1917	04/10/1917
Miscellaneous	Table To Accompany 2nd. Division R.A.M.C. Order No. 83 Of 4.10.17	04/10/1917	04/10/1917

Heading	No. 100 Field Ambulance Appendix "B" Vol 24 Oct 1917		
Miscellaneous	List Of Surgical & Medical Equipment Required For An Advanced Dressing Station In War Time		
Miscellaneous	A.D.M.S. 2nd Division		
Heading	No. 100 Field Ambulance Appendix "C" To Vol 24 Oct 1917		
Miscellaneous	C Appendix To War Diary October 1917		
Heading	War Diary Of No. 100 Field Ambulance For November 1917 Volume 25		
War Diary	Auchel (C.27.B.7.3)	01/11/1917	04/11/1917
War Diary	Busnes Sheet 5A 1/100,000 Square 56	05/11/1917	05/11/1917
War Diary	Estaires Map 5A Square 5I	06/11/1917	06/11/1917
War Diary	Eecke	07/11/1917	07/11/1917
War Diary	Herzeele Area	08/11/1917	08/11/1917
War Diary	Herzeele Area (D.17.C.8.6)	09/11/1917	23/11/1917
War Diary	On The Train	24/11/1917	24/11/1917
War Diary	Beaumetz Lez-Cambrai (J.20.C)	25/11/1917	26/11/1917
War Diary	Hermies (J.29.A.3.0)	27/11/1917	28/11/1917
War Diary	Hermies	29/11/1917	30/11/1917
Miscellaneous	Appendix To War Diary Summary Of Admissions & Evacuations Etc For November 1917		
War Diary	Hermies J.29.A.3.0	01/12/1917	04/12/1917
War Diary	Velu Wood P.1.B.0.9	05/12/1917	11/12/1917
War Diary	Hermies J.29.A.3.0	12/12/1917	26/12/1917
War Diary	Velu Wood (P.1.B.9.9)	27/12/1917	31/12/1917
Heading	2nd Division No. 100 Field Ambulance 1918 Jan-1919 June		
Heading	War Diary No. 100 Field Ambulance For January 1918 (Volume 27)		
War Diary	Velu Wood France 57C (Edition 2) P.1.A.9.9	01/01/1918	03/01/1918
War Diary	Lechelle P.25.C.5.5	04/01/1918	04/01/1918
War Diary	Lechelle 57C P.25.C.5.5	05/01/1918	11/01/1918
War Diary	Lechelle	12/01/1918	31/01/1918
Heading	War Diary Of No. 100 Field Ambulance From 1st. Feby 1918 To 28th. Feby 1918 (Volume 28)		
War Diary	Lechelle France 57C P.25.C.5.5	01/02/1918	11/02/1918
War Diary	Lechelle P.25.C.5.5	12/02/1918	28/02/1918
Heading	War Diary Of No. 100 Field Ambulance From 1st. March 1918 To 31st. March 1918 (Volume 29)		
War Diary	Lechelle P.25.C.5.5	01/03/1918	13/03/1918
War Diary	Metz Q.19.C.9.1	14/03/1918	19/03/1918
War Diary	Rocquigny Q.27.C.9.4	20/03/1918	22/03/1918
War Diary	Courcelette M.25.b.9.3.	23/03/1918	24/03/1918
War Diary	Beaumont Hamel H.5.-75.03	25/03/1918	25/03/1918
War Diary	Louvencourt (5.F.95.10)	25/03/1918	25/03/1918
War Diary	Arqueves 6.F.65.87	26/03/1918	31/03/1918
Miscellaneous	(Appendix A) Reference G.R.O. 3472 D/-25.2.18 List Of Articles Of Equipment For A Field Ambulance Recommended To Be Dispensed With	25/02/1918	25/02/1918
Heading	War Diary Of No. 100 Field Ambulance From 1st. April 1918 To 30th. April 1918 (Volume 30)		
War Diary	Arqueves (6.F.6.9)	01/04/1918	01/04/1918
War Diary	Orville 5.E.93.42	02/04/1918	02/04/1918
War Diary	Rebreuve (3.E.05.15)	03/04/1918	09/04/1918
War Diary	Canettemont 3.E.40.35	10/04/1918	10/04/1918

War Diary	Warluzel 4.F.65.75	11/04/1918	11/04/1918
War Diary	Grincourt 5.F.93.99	12/04/1918	13/04/1918
War Diary	Larbret 4.G.70.52	14/04/1918	14/04/1918
War Diary	Le Bac Du Sud Q.32.A.5.0	15/04/1918	30/04/1918
Heading	War Diary Of No. 100 Field Ambulance From 1st. May 1918-31st. May 1918 (Volume 31)		
War Diary	Le Bac Du Sud Q.32.A.5.0	01/05/1918	10/05/1918
War Diary	Warluzel Q.27.C.8.8	11/05/1918	31/05/1918
Heading	War Diary Of No. 100 Field Ambulance From 1st. June 1918 To 30th. June 1918 (Volume 32)		
War Diary	Warluzel Q.27.C.8.8	01/06/1918	06/06/1918
War Diary	Ransart X.7.B.8.2	07/06/1918	07/06/1918
War Diary	Ransart	08/06/1918	09/06/1918
War Diary	Ransart (X.7.B.8.2)	10/06/1918	23/06/1918
War Diary	Ransart	24/06/1918	30/06/1918
Heading	War Diary No. 100 Field Ambulance Appendix "A"		
Miscellaneous	Totals S & W Officers & Other Ranks		
Heading	War Diary No. 100 Field Ambulance From 1st. July 1918 To 31st. July 1918 (Volume 33)		
War Diary	Ransart (X.7.B.8.2)	01/07/1918	31/07/1918
Miscellaneous	Appendix To Vol 33		
Heading	War Diary No. 100 Field Ambulance From 1st. August 1918 To 31st. August 1918 (Volume 34)		
War Diary	Ransart (X.7.B.8.2)	01/08/1918	06/08/1918
War Diary	W.13.D.9.7	07/08/1918	17/08/1918
War Diary	Ransart (X.7.B.8.2)	18/08/1918	22/08/1918
War Diary	A.15.A.1.1 (Courcelles)	23/08/1918	23/08/1918
War Diary	A.15.A.1.1	24/08/1918	31/08/1918
Heading	War Diary Of No. 100 Field Ambulance From 1st. Sept 1918 To 30th. Sept 1918 (Volume 35)		
War Diary	A.15.A.1.1	01/09/1918	02/09/1918
War Diary	B.20.B.3.7	02/09/1918	02/09/1918
War Diary	B.29 Cont	03/09/1918	03/09/1918
War Diary	Morchies	03/09/1918	03/09/1918
War Diary	Morchies (I.11.B.5.2)	04/09/1918	04/09/1918
War Diary	Morchies	05/09/1918	08/09/1918
War Diary	Ervillers B.19.D.7.4	08/09/1918	30/09/1918
Heading	War Diary Of No. 100 Field Ambulance From October 1st. 1918 To October 31st. 1918 (Volume 36)		
War Diary	Ervillers B.19.D.7.4	01/10/1918	03/10/1918
War Diary	Beaumetz J.13.B.2.1	04/10/1918	04/10/1918
War Diary	Beaumetz Lez-Cambrai (J.13.B.2.1)	05/10/1918	05/10/1918
War Diary	Beaumetz J.13.B.2.1	06/10/1918	13/10/1918
War Diary	Novelles (L.11.B.2.8)	14/10/1918	14/10/1918
War Diary	La Targette (H.15.C.2.2)	15/10/1918	23/10/1918
War Diary	St Python (V.30.C.7.4)	24/10/1918	30/10/1918
War Diary	Vertain W.15.A.9.8	31/10/1918	31/10/1918
Heading	War Diary Of No. 100 Field Ambulance From 1st. Nov 1918 To 30th. Novr. 1918 Volume 37		
War Diary	Vertain W.15.A.9.8	01/11/1918	07/11/1918
War Diary	Villers-Pol L.34.D.6.6	08/11/1918	17/11/1918
War Diary	La Longueville 3.K.24.50	18/11/1918	19/11/1918
War Diary	Elesmes 3.A.15.71	20/11/1918	23/11/1918
War Diary	Ressaix I.C.30.00	24/11/1918	24/11/1918
War Diary	Marchienne Au-Pont E.2.75.88	25/11/1918	27/11/1918
War Diary	Chatelet (2.G.35.83)	28/11/1918	28/11/1918

War Diary	Sart-St. Laurent 2.I.90.83	29/11/1918	30/11/1918
Heading	War Diary Of No. 100 Field Ambulance From 1-12-18 To 31-12-18 (Volume No. 38)		
War Diary	Sart-St Laurent 2.I.90.83	01/12/1918	03/12/1918
War Diary	Marche-Les-Dames I.L.55.78	04/12/1918	05/12/1918
War Diary	Seilles 6.A.93.00	05/12/1918	05/12/1918
War Diary	St Vitu I.E.20.82	06/12/1918	06/12/1918
War Diary	Oneux 1.H.17.68	07/12/1918	08/12/1918
War Diary	Johuster 1.J.37.72	09/12/1918	10/12/1918
War Diary	Ster 1.L.47.47	11/12/1918	11/12/1918
War Diary	Lager Elsenborn 1.F.	12/12/1918	12/12/1918
War Diary	Eicherscheid 10.H.	13/12/1918	13/12/1918
War Diary	Boich 7.J.	14/12/1918	18/12/1918
War Diary	Birkes Dorf 5.J.	19/12/1918	20/12/1918
War Diary	Oberembt	21/12/1918	21/12/1918
War Diary	Oberembt 1.J.	22/12/1918	26/12/1918
War Diary	Glessen 1.N.	27/12/1918	31/12/1918
Heading	War Diary Of No. 100 Field Ambulance From January 1st. 1919 To January 31st. 1919 (Volume 39)		
War Diary	Glessen 1.N.	01/01/1919	31/01/1919
Heading	War Diary Of No. 100 Field Ambulance From February 1st. 1919 To February 28th. 1919 (Volume 40)		
War Diary	Glessen 1.N.	01/02/1919	28/02/1919
Heading	War Diary Of No. 100 Field Ambulance From March 1st. 1919 To March 31st. 1919 (Volume 41)		
War Diary	Glessen	01/03/1919	31/03/1919
Heading	War Diary Of No. 100 Field Ambulance From April 1st. 1919 To April 30th. 1919 (Volume 42)		
War Diary	Glessen	02/04/1919	30/04/1919
Heading	War Diary Of No. 100 Field Ambulance From 1st. May 1919 To 31st. May 1919 (Volume 43)		
War Diary	Glessen	01/05/1919	31/05/1919
Heading	War Diary Of No. 100 Field Ambulance From June 1st. To June 22nd. 1919 Volume 45		
War Diary	Glessen	01/06/1919	20/06/1919
War Diary	Glessen To Sinner Dorf	21/06/1919	21/06/1919
War Diary	Sinners Dorf	22/06/1919	22/06/1919

WO 95/3301

2 DIV

100 Field Amb

1915 Nov & Dec

Box 1012

33 Act Zimmern 22 nov. 00 100 k F.a. / rol I

12/7656

Nov 1915

Nov. 15.

WAR DIARY
or
INTELLIGENCE SUMMARY
(Erase heading not required.)

Army Form C. 2118

Instructions regarding War Diaries and Intelligence Summaries are contained in F. S. Regs., Part II. and the Staff Manual respectively. Title Pages will be prepared in manuscript.

Place	Date	Hour	Summary of Events and Information	Remarks and references to Appendices
Sling Camp Salisbury.	Nov. 16th	5.30 am	100th Field Ambulance left Camp & marched to Amesbury Station & proceeded thence by Train to Southampton - orders received from E.B.O. to send transport with 2 Officers & 115 men (including ASC) & horses by H.M.T. Bellerophon, the troopship left for Havre at 5 pm. The remainder of the Officers & other ranks of the unit were billeted at Southampton for the night.	Muster major RAMC
Southampton	17th	4.30 pm	Remainder of Unit proceeded to Havre on H.M.T. "Thomas Green"	Enemy
Havre	18th	7 am	Disembarked & marched to Entraining Station to wait till 4.30 when the Transport etc joined us. Unit entrained & left Havre at 7.30 pm.	Enemy
Steenbecque	19th	6 pm	Detrained & unit marched to billets, where we stayed until the 23rd inst	Enemy
"	23rd	9.15 am	left Steenbecque & marched with 99th Brigade to Busnes. Proceeded to billets in the village of La Pierrière	Enemy
Busnes.	23rd	8.15 pm	Received instructions from A.D.M.S. 2nd Division to detail two Officers to proceed to 2nd Division for instruction - Lieuts Okell & Rigby were	

Army Form C. 2118

WAR DIARY
INTELLIGENCE SUMMARY
(Erase heading not required.)

Instructions regarding War Diaries and Intelligence Summaries are contained in F. S. Regs., Part II. and the Staff Manual respectively. Title Pages will be prepared in manuscript.

Place	Date	Hour	Summary of Events and Information	Remarks and references to Appendices
Buire	23	10.45 p.m.	detailed. Received instructions from H.Q. 33rd Division to detail two Officers to proceed to 4th Division for instruction. Lieuts Garrod & Murray were detailed.	Appendix
"	24	7.30 a.m.	The two Officers mentioned above left to proceed to Bethune.	Appendix
"	24	3 p.m.	Attended a conference at the Office of the A.D.M.S. 33rd Division.	Appendix
"	25	8.15 a.m.	Unit proceeded with 99th Brigade & marched to Verdrel by Bethune & thence to Fouquières where I took over the Site & Buildings previously occupied by the 19th Field Ambulance & proceeded to make preparation for the reception of patients.	Appendix
Fouquières	26	—	The A.D.M.S. 2nd Div. visited 100th Field Ambulance & gave instructions that I was to form the 2nd Division Rest Station & make preparations accordingly.	Appendix
"	27	—	First patient received. 10th F.A. from 1st Division.	Appendix
"	28	—	49 patients were transferred from No 5 & No 6 Field Ambulances.	Appendix

Army Form C. 2118

WAR DIARY
INTELLIGENCE SUMMARY
(Erase heading not required.)

Instructions regarding War Diaries and Intelligence Summaries are contained in F. S. Regs., Part II. and the Staff Manual respectively. Title Pages will be prepared in manuscript.

Place	Date	Hour	Summary of Events and Information	Remarks and references to Appendices
Fromgines	28th	8.15 a.m	Made instructions from A.D.M.S. 2nd Division. Lieut R.A. Paton R.A.M.C, 1 N.C.O. & six stretcher Bearers proceeded to the Advanced Dressing Station of No 5 Field Ambulance for instructions. Lieut Hennessy reported to No 15 F.A.	
"	29th	-	Lieut K.M. Coote R.A.M.C., 1 N.C.O & 6 Bearers proceeded to No 6 F.A. for instruction. Lieut Skell & Party reported to No 15 F.A. Received visit from C.R.E. 2nd Division with reference to line repair of line & staff. Other infirm horses building of lean to's for ten quarters 37 & 39 horses, putting up of field bath etc.	
"	30th	10.30 a.m	A.D.M.S. visited 105th F.A & examined patients & also stretcher P.B. here.	Verwey Verwey

J. Williford.
Majr. R.A.M.C.
O.C. 105th Field Ambulance

133 H.Q. 2nd Div

100 B F.A.
Vol: 2

131
7910

Dec 1915

WAR DIARY

INTELLIGENCE SUMMARY

(Erase heading not required.)

Army Form C. 2118

CONFIDENTIAL

WAR DIARY
OF
No. 100 FIELD AMBULANCE
from December 1st to 31st 1915.
(VOLUME 2)

Army Form C. 2118

WAR DIARY
or
INTELLIGENCE SUMMARY
(Erase heading not required.)

Place	Date	Hour	Summary of Events and Information	Remarks and references to Appendices
FOUQUIÈRES	3/12/15		CAPTAIN S.D. LARGE R.A.M.C. joined 100 Field Ambulance from 1st ROYAL BERKSHIRE Regiment, for duty.	
"	4/12/15		Lieut. C.C. OKELL, R.A.M.C. (T.C.) was transferred from 100 Field Ambulance to 6 Field Ambulance for duty. Lieut. J. RIGBY. R.A.M.C. (T.C.) proceeded to 2nd Div. R.E. (for temporary duty) Lieut. A.N. GARROD R.A.M.C.(T.C) transferred as a temporary measure to 22nd Royal Fusiliers for duty vice Lieut. A. MACINTYRE R.A.M.C. (T.C.) who reported here for duty. No 74405 Pte. BOND. J.H. R.A.M.C. admitted to Hospital one of the Officers' riding horses died yesterday from pneumonia. Lieut.-Colonel DELVAS reported his arrival, & taken on the strength of the Unit.	Stafford Mackintyre
"	6/12/14		D.D.M.S 1st Corps and C.R.E. 2nd Div. visited 100 Field Ambulance; now billeted on 2nd Div. Rest Station with reference to the question of expansion. It was postponed until a School room by church be taken on for the purpose, but as authority was not obtainable	

1875 Wt. W593/826 1,000,000 4/15 J.B.C. & N. A.D.S.S./Forms/C. 2118.

Army Form C. 2118

WAR DIARY
or
INTELLIGENCE SUMMARY
(Erase heading not required.)

Instructions regarding War Diaries and Intelligence Summaries are contained in F. S. Regs., Part II. and the Staff Manual respectively. Title Pages will be prepared in manuscript.

Place	Date	Hour	Summary of Events and Information	Remarks and references to Appendices
FOUQUIÈRES	6/12/15		It was decided to keep two huts - each to hold 24 patients - in the field near Blue Rest Station -	Appendix
"	7/12/15		The building of the new huts commenced today.	Appendix
"	9.12.15.		No 64754 Pte DAVISON. W.T. RAMC were admitted to Hospital. Captain B.W. ARMSTRONG RAMC (TC) reported for duty from No 6.FA. Lieut. J.H. MURRAY RAMC (TC) was transferred to No 6.FA. for duty.	Appendix
"	10-12-15.		No.7842. Pte. GRAY. C.W. RAMC reported for duty from No 6 FA. No. 66507 Pte. COTTER. W.T. RAMC transferred to No 6 FA.	Appendix
"	11-12-15.		Hearing that the Rest Station was to be handed over to 12th Div. at an early date I accompanied D.A.D.M.S. 2nd Div. & an Officer on to A.A. & Q.M.G. Offices to GONNEHEM to look for a suitable place for 2nd Division Rest Station - no place was suitable.	Appendix
"	12-12-15		Lieut. S.J. COWELL. RAMC. (TC) proceeded to 2nd Division Train for temporary duty.	Appendix
"	14-12-15.		Lieut. P.J. LANE RAMC (TC) proceeded to 34th Brigade R.F.A. for temporary duty.	Appendix

Army Form C. 2118

3

Instructions regarding War Diaries and Intelligence Summaries are contained in F. S. Regs., Part II. and the Staff Manual respectively. Title Pages will be prepared in manuscript.

WAR DIARY
or
INTELLIGENCE SUMMARY
(Erase heading not required.)

Place	Date	Hour	Summary of Events and Information	Remarks and references to Appendices
FOUQUIÈRES	15.12.15		Took over temporary charge of 2nd Divisional Rest Station from MAJOR E.H.M. MOORE R.A.M.C. who has proceeded to ENGLAND on 10 days' leave.	e.Charge Capt.Keane.
"	16.12.15		Received officers riding horse to replace the one that died on 5.12.15.	edr. Capt. R.A.M.C. Keane
"	17.12.15		Received correspondence from ENGLAND saying that Sgt. F.S. WEBB had fraudulently enlisted. Forwarded the correspondence to be completed pending further proceedings.	edr.
"	18.12.15		LIEUT. RIGBY R.A.M.C. detailed for duty with 2nd Bn. R.E. and struck off strength of this unit accordingly	edr.
"	19.12.15		CAPT. T. BOURNE-PRICE R.A.M.C. joined this unit for duty, and was taken on the strength accordingly	edr.
"	21.12.15		LIEUT. COATES R.A.M.C. proceeded to 2nd D.A.C. for temporary duty	edr.
"	22.12.15		No 64700 Pte Mc MANUS R.A.M.C. detailed for duty with 11th Corps, and struck off strength accordingly	edr.
"	23.12.15		LIEUT. COWELL returned to this unit from temporary duty	edr.
"	24.12.15		MAJOR E.H.M. MOORE R.A.M.C. returned from leave	e.Charge Capt.Keane

WAR DIARY / INTELLIGENCE SUMMARY

Army Form C. 2118

Instructions regarding War Diaries and Intelligence Summaries are contained in F.S. Regs., Part II. and the Staff Manual respectively. Title Pages will be prepared in manuscript.

(Erase heading not required.)

Place	Date	Hour	Summary of Events and Information	Remarks and references to Appendices
FOUQUIÈRES	26-12-15		Lieut A.N. GARROD. R.A.M.C. (T.C.) rejoined 100 F.A. for duty from 2nd Royal Fusiliers.	
			No. 47419 Corpl. ANDERSON. C.H. and No. 37630 Pte. POORTON. W.J. R.A.M.C. reported for duty with this unit from 9th H.L.I where they were employed as stretcher bearers.	Appendix
	27-12-15		Captain T. BOURNE-PRICE. R.A.M.C (T.C.) proceeded to 7th Br. R.G.A. for temporary duty.	Appendix
GONNEHEM	9-12-15		100 F.A. having handed over Buildings, Patients etc to 36 F.A. at WITTES. proceeded by road to GONNEHEM & took over the Billets occupied by No 99 F.A. Two huts are reserved for the reception of Sick & wounded, the rest being accommodation for about 50 cases. During the period the Division is in reserve, the Personnel of 100 F.A. in addition to their ordinary duties will undergo course of training in all subjects connected with field Ambulance Work.	Appendix

Army Form C. 2118

WAR DIARY
or
INTELLIGENCE SUMMARY
(Erase heading not required.)

Instructions regarding War Diaries and Intelligence Summaries are contained in F. S. Regs., Part II. and the Staff Manual respectively. Title Pages will be prepared in manuscript.

Place	Date	Hour	Summary of Events and Information	Remarks and references to Appendices
GONNEHEM	30.12.15		Corporal ANDERSON & Pte POULTON, RAMC proceeded to England on 7 days' leave.	[signature]
"	31.12.15		Training of RAMC Personnel proceeded according to syllabus.	[signature]

John Wood
Major RAMC
O.C. 100 Field Ambulance

1875 Wt. W593/826 1,000,000 4/15 J.B.C. & A. A.D.S.S./Forms/C. 2118.

2ND DIVISION
MEDICAL

100 FIELD AMBULANCE

JAN - DEC 1916

33rd Div
10th Field Ambulance
Vol. 3

File II

Jan 1916

Army Form C. 2118

WAR DIARY
INTELLIGENCE SUMMARY
(Erase heading not required.)

CONFIDENTIAL

WAR DIARY
OF
100 FIELD AMBULANCE

From 1.1.16. to 31.1.16.
Volume 3

WAR DIARY

INTELLIGENCE SUMMARY

(Erase heading not required.)

Army Form C. 2118

Instructions regarding War Diaries and Intelligence Summaries are contained in F. S. Regs., Part II. and the Staff Manual respectively. Title Pages will be prepared in manuscript.

Place	Date	Hour	Summary of Events and Information	Remarks and references to Appendices
BONNEHEM	1-1-16	—	Message received from A.D.M.S. 2nd Division - giving instructions for a Medical Officer to visit 2nd Div Mounted Troops at CANTRAINNE daily. Lieut. A. MACINTYRE. R.A.M.C. was detailed for this duty. See C/side etc.	Previous Major RAMC
"	3-1-16	—	During the last three days the ordinary training whilst in reserve has been proceeding, but nothing of importance has happened.	January February
"	4-1-16	—	Lieut. R.A. PETERS. R.A.M.C. (SR) to 1st ROYAL BERKS for temporary duty	February
"	6-1-16	—	Lieut. V.M. COATES. R.A.M.C. (TC) proceeded to 17th ROYAL FUSILIERS as Medical Officer to that Regiment & is accordingly struck off the Strength of 100 Field Ambulance.	January
"	7-1-16	—	Lieut. A. MACINTYRE R.A.M.C. (T.C.) to 2nd OX & BUCKS for temporary duty. Lieut. P.J. LANE. R.A.M.C (T.C) to visit 2nd Div. Mounted Troops vice Lieut. A. MACINTYRE.	January
"	9-1-16	.	Received ordr from A.D.M.S. 2nd Division to proceed the next day to Dismounted Cavalry Division as temporary D.A.D.M.S.	January
"	10-1-16	.	Handed over to Capt H. [illegible] A.D.S.S. A.D.M.S.	January February

Army Form C. 2118

WAR DIARY
or
INTELLIGENCE SUMMARY

(Erase heading not required.)

Instructions regarding War Diaries and Intelligence Summaries are contained in F.S. Regs., Part II. and the Staff Manual respectively. Title Pages will be prepared in manuscript.

Place	Date	Hour	Summary of Events and Information	Remarks and references to Appendices
GONNEHEM	10.1.16		Took over temporary charge of 100 F.A. from MAJOR E.H.H. MOORE, who is acting as D.A.D.M.S. DIS. CAVALRY DIVISION.	L.D. Large Captaine
GONNEHEM	14.1.16		Took over craft & horse of V.180 2.7. which is to be used as an hospital for sick from the division in rest. Began work on it and drew material from R.E.	ditto
GONNEHEM	15.1.16		Received orders to move to CIVIL & MILITARY HOSP. BETHUNE, with advanced dressing station at LONE-FARM, GIVENCHY F12.c.8.7. CAPTAIN S.D. LARGE awarded Military cross.	ditto
GONNEHEM	16.1.16		Inspected LONE FARM and CIVIL and MILITARY HOSP. LIEUT. S.V. COWELL detailed for temporary duty with 4th bde R.F.A.	ditto
GONNEHEM	17.1.16		LIEUT. A. MACINTYRE returned to duty. LIEUT. AN. GARROD admitted to OFFICER'S HOSPITAL, BETHUNE, suffering from laryngitis. Party of 2 N.C.Os and 20 men under CAPT. T. BOURNE PRICE proceeded to advanced dressing station at F.12.c.8.7. at 10 a.m. advance for 5 O.R. N.C.O. & 10 men proceeded to CIVIL and MILITARY HOSP. BETHUNE at 10 a.m. LONE FARM (F.12.c.8.7.) has been fairly heavily shelled lately. I have ordered CAPT. BOURNE-PRICE to evacuate it if shelling is continued, and use new advanced dressing station on embankment on S.bank of canal at canal junction F.10.d. 7.75. arranged to get R.B. man complete with 6 horses and 6 hanging camps from R.E. LIEUT. D.S. CASSIDY joined for duty and is taken on the strength accordingly.	All mat. returned to BETHUNE. CONSIGNED-SHEETS 40,000
BETHUNE	18.1.16		Moved to CIVIL & MILITARY HOSP BETHUNE and took over from 58 F.A. admitted 5 wounded O.R.	ditto
BETHUNE	19.1.16		Evacuated 3 wounded. Handed over to MAJOR E.H.M. MOORE	L.D. Large Captaine

1875 Wt. W503/826 1,000,000 4/15 J.B.C. & A. A.D.S.S./Forms/C. 2118.

Army Form C. 2118

WAR DIARY

INTELLIGENCE SUMMARY

(Erase heading not required.)

Place	Date	Hour	Summary of Events and Information	Remarks and references to Appendices
BETHUNE	19/1/16	—	Returned to 100 Field Ambulance for duty & took over charge from Captain S.D. LARGE RAMC. In this Hospital the French Authorities have given us the use of two large wards which accommodate in the ordinary way 50 patients, on stretchers or mattresses on floor space in time of stress however, but it will be possible to provide floor space in time of stress for 150 patients in the two wards. In addition, there are 3 small rooms which could accommodate a further 20 patients. There is also a very good room which is used as an operating theatre. The RAMC personnel are billeted in the Old Hospital Buildings in which also there are rooms which can be utilized for pack store, steward store, clothing store etc. The latrine accommodation is not good but I am making arrangements for a new one to be put up. Captain S.D. LARGE RAMC proceeded on leave to England for 8 days. Wounded admitted 6. Evacuated 6.	Jermy

WAR DIARY
INTELLIGENCE SUMMARY

(Erase heading not required.)

Army Form C. 2118

Place	Date	Hour	Summary of Events and Information	Remarks and references to Appendices
BETHUNE.	20/1/16	—	Lieut. A.N. GARROD. R.A.M.C. (T.C.) discharged Hospital & returned for duty. Wounded admitted – 17. " Evacuated 2.	
"	21/1/16	—	Visited the advanced dressing Station of the Field Ambulance. It is a farm house – "Lone Farm" situated hors. BETHUNE Contoured Sheet. 1:40,000. F.12.a.8.7. It is a very good accommodation for reception of wounded in a large cellar under the house – at present there are 2 Officers, & 16 men doing duty there. A "advanced bearers" are at a Regimental aid post". Visited this aid post which is situated hors (as above) A.8.b.4.6. This advanced dressing station has been also has a good cellar. A good deal shelled of late – but it has not been hit since it was taken on by this Unit. A red cross flag is erected just outside the farm house. Whether this is really a protection or not remains	[signature]

WAR DIARY
or
INTELLIGENCE SUMMARY

(Erase heading not required.)

Army Form C. 2118

Instructions regarding War Diaries and Intelligence Summaries are contained in F.S. Regs., Part II. and the Staff Manual respectively. Title Pages will be prepared in manuscript.

Place	Date	Hour	Summary of Events and Information	Remarks and references to Appendices
BETHUNE	21/1/16	–	Blue Cross! Wounded admitted. 4.	Stormy
"	22/1/16	–	5 " wounded 6. Extract from London Gazette of 19/1/16. "Major b.p. bear Colonel while in charge of a field Ambulance - E.H.M. MOORE. RAMC." Wounded admitted 10. " 6.	Stormy
"	23/1/16	–	Lieut R.A. PETERS. RAMC (SR) returned to flee wait for duty. Wounded admitted 2. " " 5. " Evacuated 5. Lieut. G.N. GARROD RAMC (TC) to Advanced Dressing Station vice Capt T BOURNE-PRICE, RAMC (TC) who returned to duty at H/Q. 100TA.	Breezy
"	24/1/16	–	Capt R.O ARMSTRONG RAMC (TC) returned from leave. Lieut A. MACINTYRE RAMC (TC) went to England on leave on receiving a mid Statist Service When of his father. Wounded admitted 11. Lt RA PETERS RAMC (SR) promoted Captain after 6 months motorised Service.	Stormy

WAR DIARY
INTELLIGENCE SUMMARY
(Erase heading not required.)

Army Form C. 2118

Instructions regarding War Diaries and Intelligence Summaries are contained in F. S. Regs., Part II and the Staff Manual respectively. Title Pages will be prepared in manuscript.

Place	Date	Hour	Summary of Events and Information	Remarks and references to Appendices
BETHUNE	25/7/16	1.30 pm	Received an urgent message from Lieut. P.J. LANE RAMC (TC) from "LONG FARM" saying that Lieut. A.N. GATROD RAMC (TC) had been killed. I proceeded immediately to the advanced Dressing station & found that he had been hit by a shell in the right chest, probably causing instantaneous death. His body was found about 400 yards from "LONG FARM" near "WINDY CORNER" Map. BETHUNE (Canadian Sheet) 1 - 40,000. A.7.d.8.7. Apparently there was no enemy fire about GATROD 15 be at the spot for at the time he was killed – 12:30 pm for x – "WINDY CORNER" was being rather heavily shelled. I made arrangements for his body to be brought into BETHUNE boat evening. Capt. T. BOURNE PRICE proceeded to "LONG FARM" for duty. Lieut. J. LYONS RAMC (TC) reported for duty who too T.A. from CALAIS Wounded admitted 3 (wounded - 7.	Appendix

Army Form C. 2118

WAR DIARY
INTELLIGENCE SUMMARY
(Erase heading not required.)

Instructions regarding War Diaries and Intelligence Summaries are contained in F. S. Regs., Part II. and the Staff Manual respectively. Title Pages will be prepared in manuscript.

Place	Date	Hour	Summary of Events and Information	Remarks and references to Appendices
BETHUNE	26/1/16	—	The late Lieut CARROD was buried in BETHUNE Cemetery — Position of Grave "BETHUNE TOWN Cemetery Grave 9 Row 12". Lieut & Quarter. Master. E. SNOWDEN. RAMC (T.C) Joined this unit for duty from No 36 field Ambulance, on receiving his Commission. Wounded admitted. 11. Evacuated. 6.	Powery
"	27/1/16	—	Lieut & QM E. SNOWDEN proceeded on leave to England for 7 days, to get necessary kit & do business in connection with his promotion. Wounded admitted 2. Evacuated 8.	Powery
"	28/1/16	—	Wounded admitted 9. Evacuated 7.	Powery
"			Lieut. J. L. W.S. RAMC (TC) proceeded to 36th Brigade R.F.A. at Lt. PREOL for temporary duty.	Powery

Army Form C. 2118

WAR DIARY
INTELLIGENCE SUMMARY

(Erase heading not required.)

Instructions regarding War Diaries and Intelligence Summaries are contained in F. S. Regs., Part II. and the Staff Manual respectively. Title Pages will be prepared in manuscript.

Place	Date	Hour	Summary of Events and Information	Remarks and references to Appendices
BETHUNE	29/1/16	—	Lieut. S. J. COWELL ROWE (T.C.) proceeded to 22nd Royal Fusiliers having been posted as permanent Medical Officer & is consequently struck off the Strength of this Unit.	Army
			Wounded admitted. 1.	
			" evacuated. 8.	
"	30/1/16	—	Wounded admitted. 1.	Army
			" evacuated. 4.	
"	31/1/16	—	Captain S. D. LARGE. R.A.M.C. returns to duty from leave.	Army
			Wounded admitted 4	
			" evacuated 4.	

Bruceford
Lt.Col. R.A.M.C.
O.C. 100 Field Ambulance

Feb 1916
March 1916   No. 100. Field Ambulance   (?)   2nd Division
April 1916

Army Form C. 2118

WAR DIARY

~~INTELLIGENCE SUMMARY~~

(Erase heading not required.)

CONFIDENTIAL

WAR DIARY
of
100 Field Ambulance

From February 1st to February 29th.

(Volume 4.)

Army Form C. 2118

WAR DIARY
or
INTELLIGENCE SUMMARY
(Erase heading not required.)

Instructions regarding War Diaries and Intelligence Summaries are contained in F.S. Regs, Part II. and the Staff Manual respectively. Title Pages will be prepared in manuscript.

Place	Date	Hour	Summary of Events and Information	Remarks and references to Appendices
BETHUNE.	Feb 1st 1916.	3.p.m.	Visited the Advanced Dressing Station at "LONE FARM" A,7,d, 1.3., and found all arrangements were going on satisfactorily. Application has been made to the R.E's for help to reinforce the ceiling of the 1st floor with struts & sandbags, which (?) in order to render the cellar more proof against shells which fall freely round the dressing station.	Map ref of Dressing Station 36 100.7A 1/10,000.
"	Feb 2nd	—	Wounded admitted 1 " evacuated 4.	Hamilton West R.A.M.C. 36 100.7A.
"	"	—	Lieut. D.S. CASSIDY. R.A.M.C. (T.C.) proceeded to 23rd ROYAL FUSILIERS for temporary duty.	Germany
"	Feb 3rd	—	Wounded admitted 2 " evacuated 0	Germany
"	"	—	Wounded admitted 6. " evacuated 4.	Germany
"	Feb 4th	—	Wounded admitted 6. " evacuated 6.	Germany

1875 Wt. W593/826 1,000,000 4/15 J.B.C. & A. A.D.S.S./Forms/C. 2118.

Army Form C. 2118

WAR DIARY

INTELLIGENCE SUMMARY

(Erase heading not required.)

Instructions regarding War Diaries and Intelligence Summaries are contained in F.S. Regs., Part II. and the Staff Manual respectively. Title Pages will be prepared in manuscript.

Place	Date	Hour	Summary of Events and Information	Remarks and references to Appendices
BETHUNE	Feb 5th	—	Wounded admitted. 1 " Evacuated. 3.	Summary
"	Feb 6th	—	Lieut. & Qrmr. Lieut. E. B. SNOWDEN RAMC, returned from leave to the United Kingdom & took over the duties of Quarter Master to 100 Field Ambulance. Orders from A.D.M.S. to hand over charge temporarily to Capt. S.D. LARGE RAMC from 9th to 18th inst, when I am to act as A.D.M.S. 2nd Division during the absence of Lt. Col. A.D.M.S. Wounded admitted. 6 " Evacuated. 1.	Summary
"	Feb 7th	—	Lieut. A. MACINTYRE RAMC (T.C.) proceeded to 17th MIDDLESEX Regt. for temporary duty. Wounded admitted. 2 " Evacuated. 4	Summary

1875 Wt. W593/826 1,000,000 4/15 J.B.C. & A. A.D.S.S./Forms/C. 2118.

Army Form C. 2118

WAR DIARY
or
INTELLIGENCE SUMMARY
(Erase heading not required.)

Instructions regarding War Diaries and Intelligence Summaries are contained in F. S. Regs., Part II. and the Staff Manual respectively. Title Pages will be prepared in manuscript.

Place	Date	Hour	Summary of Events and Information	Remarks and references to Appendices
BETHUNE	Feb 8th	—	Handed over Charge of 100 Field Ambulance temporarily to Captain S.D. LARGE. R.A.M.C. in accordance with orders of 6th inst. Lieut J. LYONS. R.A.M.C. (T.C.) returned to duty with 100 F.A. from 36th Brigade R.F.A. Wounded admitted. 5 " Evacuated. 3	January
"	Feb 9th	—	Advanced Dressing Station at "LONE FARM" shelled in the afternoon, one horse was killed & one injured. no other casualties	January
			Wounded admitted. 5. " Evacuated. 7.	January
"	Feb 10th	—	Wounded admitted. 5. " Evacuated. 6.	January
"	Feb 11th	—	Wounded admitted. 20. " Evacuated. 9.	January

Army Form C. 2118

WAR DIARY
or
INTELLIGENCE SUMMARY
(Erase heading not required.)

Instructions regarding War Diaries and Intelligence Summaries are contained in F. S. Regs., Part II. and the Staff Manual respectively. Title Pages will be prepared in manuscript.

Place	Date	Hour	Summary of Events and Information	Remarks and references to Appendices
BETHUNE	Feb. 12th	—	Lieut. D.S. CASSIDY. RAMC (TC) returned to no 7A. for duty. Captain R.H. PETERS. RAMC (SR) proceeded on leave to England. Wounded admitted 2. " evacuated 6.	Fenny
"	Feb 13th	—	Lieut. P.J. LANE. RAMC (TC) proceeded on leave to Ireland. Orders received from A.D.M.S. 2nd Division for 100 Field Ambulance to proceed to BOUREC?, U.1.c.q.2. on the 18th inst., & to leave a holding party at the Civil & Military Hospital in BETHUNE. Wounded admitted. 4. " evacuated 7.	Map reference FRANCE. Sheet 36A. 2nd Edition 1:40,000. Fenny
"	Feb. 14th	—	Wounded admitted 4. " evacuated 7.	Fenny
"	Feb 15	—	Wounded admitted. 6 " evacuated 4.	Fenny

Army Form C. 2118

WAR DIARY
or
INTELLIGENCE SUMMARY
(Erase heading not required.)

Place	Date	Hour	Summary of Events and Information	Remarks and references to Appendices
BETHUNE	Feb 16	—	Capt. S.D. LARGE, R.A.M.C. & party proceeded to BOURECQ to take over billets &c. party left there to find billets. Wounded admitted 1. " Evacuated 4. " Evacuated 4.	Summary
"	Feb 17	—	Capt. W.B. PURCHASE, R.A.M.C. (T.C) sent for duty to 100 Field Ambulance vice Capt. S.D. LARGE R.A.M.C. who is to report to D.A.D.M.S. Trains, H.Qrs. I.C.C. Lieut. A. MACINTYRE R.A.M.C. (T.C) rejoined went from 17th Middlesex Regt. Move order for 18th inst postponed for 24 hours. Wounded admitted 0. " Evacuated 3.	Summary
"	Feb 18	—	Last night at 10 p.m. a shell hit a house at A.C.C.8.3 in which advanced R.A.M.C. Bearers & Regimental Bearers were sleeping killing No 64190 Cpl G.H. MILLER, R.A.M.C. 100 Field Ambulance & " No H.J. HALL " wounding No 64795 " H.J. HALL " in the right hand causing he to go further, besides these, nine(9)	Map of Battle line, Cambrai Sheet Edition 6 & hereto

WAR DIARY
INTELLIGENCE SUMMARY

Army Form C. 2118

Place	Date	Hour	Summary of Events and Information	Remarks and references to Appendices
BETHUNE	Feb 18th (cont)	—	Other men were injured, the shell that hit the house was the first to come over, & the occupants had no warning. The work at "LONE FARM" has been going on well, a part of the old floor ceiling has been strutted & strengthened with sandbags & bricks & when the work is completed, the cellar below should be quite safe. — The advanced Dressing Station was handed over today to 129 Field Ambulance, 38th Division. Wounded admitted 14. " Evacuated 13.	Neuville
"	Feb 19th	—	A & B Sections, 100 Field Ambulance proceeded to BOURECQ at 10.25 a.m. arriving there at 11.45 p.m. There are two huts for the reception of sick & wounded accommodating 20 in each. Corporal MILLER buried in BETHUNE TOWN Cemetery, Grave No 21 Row "O".	

Army Form C. 2118

WAR DIARY
INTELLIGENCE SUMMARY
(Erase heading not required.)

Instructions regarding War Diaries and Intelligence Summaries are contained in F.S. Regs., Part II. and the Staff Manual respectively. Title Pages will be prepared in manuscript.

Place	Date	Hour	Summary of Events and Information	Remarks and references to Appendices
BOURECQ	Feb 19th 1916	5 pm	Lt. Col. E.H.M. MOORE, RAMC. rejoined 100 Field Ambulance.	Spamy
	Feb 20th	—	Lieut. S.J. COWELL, RAMC (TC) posted to 100 Field Ambulance from 2/2nd Royal Fusiliers	
			Lieut. J. LYONS, RAMC (T.C.) 100 Field Ambulance posted to No 6 Field Ambulance	
			Lieut. S.J. COWELL, R.A.M.C. (TC) proceeded to 2nd South Staffords Regt. for temporary duty.	Spamy
	Feb 21st 1916	—	Captain R.A. PETERS RAMC (SR) returned unit from leave to England.	Spamy
	Feb 23rd	—	Captain S.D. LARGE, RAMC proceeded to ABBEVILLE to report to DADMS Ambulance train, in accordance with order from ADMS 2nd Division.	Spamy

Army Form C. 2118

WAR DIARY
INTELLIGENCE SUMMARY
(Erase heading not required.)

Instructions regarding War Diaries and Intelligence Summaries are contained in F. S. Regs., Part II. and the Staff Manual respectively. Title Pages will be prepared in manuscript.

Place	Date	Hour	Summary of Events and Information	Remarks and references to Appendices
BOURECQ	Feb 23rd 1915	5 p.m.	Wired 2nd Division for all units to be ready to move at short notice - all preparations made. Wagon packed & all patients evacuated to No 6 Casualty Clearing Station at LILLERS.	Stacey
		10 p.m.	Lieut. P. J. LANE R.A.M.C. (T.C.) rejoined unit from leave to England. No further orders.	Stacey
	Feb 24.	—	No further orders for move. Lieut. D. S. CASSIDY. R.A.M.C. (T.C.) proceeded on leave to England.	Stacey
	Feb 25th	—	No 6449 Private W. D. FORREST joined unit & taken on strength - seen here of 1st Royal Berks Regt wounded by bomb accident. No further news of move. Wire from 2nd Division stopping all leave.	Stacey
	Feb 26th	—	Awaiting further orders.	Stacey
	Feb 27th	1 p.m.	Orders from A.D.M.S. 2nd Division for A. & B. Sections, No 5 Field Ambulance to proceed forthwith to Civil & Military Hospital, BETHUNE. Arrived at 6.15 p.m.	Stacey

Army Form C. 2118

WAR DIARY
INTELLIGENCE SUMMARY
(Erase heading not required.)

Instructions regarding War Diaries and Intelligence Summaries are contained in F.S. Regs., Part II. and the Staff Manual respectively. Title Pages will be prepared in manuscript.

Place	Date	Hour	Summary of Events and Information	Remarks and references to Appendices
BETHUNE	Feb 28.	—	Instructions received from A.D.M.S. 2nd Division that 100 Field Ambulance will take over buildings occupied by No 3/a French Ambulance at BARLIN. K. 33. a. 7. 4. Proceeded to BARLIN & reconnoitred & found the French still in occupation & also that they had had no orders to evacuate.	Map ref Bethune Environs Sheet 51. 6 1/20000 Gywww
BARLIN	Feb 29th	—	Orders received at 11.45 a.m. to proceed forthwith to BARLIN. Arrived at BARLIN 4.20 p.m. The French evacuated last buildings here at 7.30 am the morning. Have accommodation for Wounded & Sick in the "Circle Catholique" & a Boys' School & should be able to take from 200 to 400 patients if necessary.	

E.W.Wood
Lt. Col R.A.M.C.
O.C. 100 Field Ambulance

Army Form C. 2118

WAR DIARY

INTELLIGENCE SUMMARY

(Erase heading not required.)

33rd Div

100 F Amb
Vol 5
2nd Div

COMMITTEE FOR THE
MEDICAL HISTORY OF THE WAR
Date 9 - JUN 1915

CONFIDENTIAL

WAR DIARY
of
100 FIELD AMBULANCE

from MARCH 1st to MARCH 31st

Volume 5.

March 1918

WAR DIARY
INTELLIGENCE SUMMARY
(Erase heading not required.)

Army Form C.2118

Instructions regarding War Diaries and Intelligence Summaries are contained in F.S. Regs., Part II. and the Staff Manual respectively. Title Pages will be prepared in manuscript.

Place	Date	Hour	Summary of Events and Information	Remarks and references to Appendices
BARLIN	March 1st	—	Owing to the buildings being still occupied by infantry it is still impossible to take more than a few patients. Captain J. BOURNE PRICE RAMC, one Sergeant & 4 men proceed to the "Malterie" at NOULETTE, R.22.a.3.6, to take over the advanced dressing station from the French, & an aid post at NOULETTES. No.64707 Corpl MOORE M. No.66543 Corpl BUTTLE.S., cooks of this Field Ambulance reputed to rank with rank of Private, being unable to carry out their duties efficiently - they were both reprimanded & unfit for their appointments. No.1327 Pte FARROW.H. promoted acting Lance Corpl.	MAP reference FRANCE Sheet 36 B 3rd Edition 1:40,000
	2nd	—	Orders received from A.D.M.S. to make preparations for the treatment of all scabies cases of the 2nd Division. Lieut. P.J. LANE RAMC & A.B. men proceeded below advanced dressing station for duty. Wounded admitted 5.	Shellfire Machine gun fire Enemy

WAR DIARY
INTELLIGENCE SUMMARY

(Erase heading not required.)

Army Form C. 2118

Instructions regarding War Diaries and Intelligence Summaries are contained in F. S. Regs., Part II. and the Staff Manual respectively. Title Pages will be prepared in manuscript.

Place	Date	Hour	Summary of Events and Information	Remarks and references to Appendices
BARLIN	March 3rd		I visited the Advanced Dressing Station. There is splendid accommodation in cellars under the Brewery. There cellars could take 200-300 cases, which I visited if necessary. The advanced post is smaller & can only take 2 or 3 cases at a time, but the cellar is "good" one & its chief use is to shelter S.R.A.M.C. bearers who take over the wounded from the Regimental Aid post & carry them to the advanced Dressing Station. The Infantry Report been left the huts at the Main Clearing Station, the Club, Shed & the School are now take 200 patients. No 66207 Pte HICKMAN. R. R.A.M.C. No 66482 " BRADNER. A. R.A.M.C. } appointed acting Lance Corpl. No 66152 " ELFORD. F. R.A.M.C. } Wounded admitted. 3. " Evacuated. 5	

Army Form C. 2118

WAR DIARY
or
INTELLIGENCE SUMMARY
(Erase heading not required.)

Instructions regarding War Diaries and Intelligence Summaries are contained in F. S. Regs., Part II. and the Staff Manual respectively. Title Pages will be prepared in manuscript.

Place	Date	Hour	Summary of Events and Information	Remarks and references to Appendices
BARLIN	March 4th	—	Wounded admitted. 0. " Evacuated. 3.	Fine
"	5th	—	G.O.C. 2nd Division & ADMS inspected this Field Ambulance Wounded admitted 4. " Evacuated 1.	Stormy
"	6th	—	A.D.M.S visited Hill Ambulance today & informed me there was a possibility of the Unit being moved to "The Chateau" COUPIGNY Q.11.a.6.5. I went over to see the place & found there was only room for 50 to 100 patients in the Chateau itself, but others could be used to accommodate wounded. No ground in outhouses, if necessary. Awaiting further orders. Wounded admitted 1. " Evacuated 3.	Map reference FRANCE Sheet.36B 3rd Edition 1-40,000. Showery

Army Form C. 2118

Instructions regarding War Diaries and Intelligence Summaries are contained in F. S. Regs., Part II. and the Staff Manual respectively. Title Pages will be prepared in manuscript.

WAR DIARY
or
INTELLIGENCE SUMMARY

(Erase heading not required.)

Place	Date	Hour	Summary of Events and Information	Remarks and references to Appendices
BARLIN	March 7th	—	Rode over from A.D.M.S. 1 Sergeant & 2 men proceeded to COUPIGNY to show H.Q. Canteen & where it was to be further ordered.	
"	8th	—	No 7843 Pte QRAK, a. w. Rt. a c awarded 21 days Field Punishment No 1 for "Drunkenness on active Service"	
			I was informed by A.D.M.S. that it was not probable that this Field Ambulance would go to COUPIGNY, but that the party there would remain to last January. The cold & wet weather is producing much sickness & many cases of "trench foot". Wounded admitted 6.	
"	9th	—	Pte QRAK Sen. & APM in division to undergo Field Punishment. Went to AIX NOULETTE & NOULETTE to visit the advanced dressing posts of the Field Ambulance. Also visited the Regimental aid posts of the 2nd Royal Inniskilling & of the 17th Royal Fusiliers, which	

WAR DIARY or INTELLIGENCE SUMMARY

Army Form C. 2118

(Erase heading not required.)

Instructions regarding War Diaries and Intelligence Summaries are contained in F. S. Regs., Part II. and the Staff Manual respectively. Title Pages will be prepared in manuscript.

Place	Date	Hour	Summary of Events and Information	Remarks and references to Appendices
BARLIN	March 9th (cont)		Our wounded is due, not to be trenches about 1½ miles, it takes little time from the Advanced R.A.M.C. Reserve Post; it is a long carry & we had our full hard work at night. The work being carried on at the Advanced dressing station is very satisfactory. Wounded admitted. 3. Evacuated. 5. Dich. 1	Johnson
"	10th		Case of Cerebro Spinal Meningitis evacuated to No 7 General Hospital. Wounded admitted 14. " Evacuated 4. " Dich 1	
"	11th		No 66354 Pte DUTTON A.R.A.M.C. appointed acting Lance Corpl. No 64425 Pte CUTHBERT W. R.A.M.C. returned from 7A for duty.	Johnson

1875 Wt. W.503/826 1,000,000 4/15 J.B.C. & A. A.D.S.S./Forms/C. 2118.

WAR DIARY

INTELLIGENCE SUMMARY

Place	Date	Hour	Summary of Events and Information	Remarks and references to Appendices
RAWIN	May 11th 1918		No 14581 Pte DAVIES. H. R.A.M.C Evacuated sick to N.I.F. Whitley. "66340 Pte. FLINT. J.W. R.A.M.C Evacuated to C.C.S. for dental treatment. Wounded admitted. 2. Evacuated 7.	Greeny
"	12th		Lieut. S.T POWELL. R.A.M.C. (T.R.) rejoined Hd. Field Ambulance on temporary duty with 2nd South Stafford Regt. Wounded admitted. Evacuated.	Greeny
"	13th		No M2 132046 Pte PETTITT. A.S.C (motor ambulance driver) proceeded to Base on duty. Wounded admitted. Evacuated.	Greeny

Army Form C. 2118

WAR DIARY
or
INTELLIGENCE SUMMARY
(Erase heading not required.)

Instructions regarding War Diaries and Intelligence Summaries are contained in F. S. Regs., Part II. and the Staff Manual respectively. Title Pages will be prepared in manuscript.

Place	Date	Hour	Summary of Events and Information	Remarks and references to Appendices
BARLIN	March 14th	—	Visited advanced dressing station – found everything satisfactory.	Appendix
			(1) Wounded admitted. 9	
			" evacuated. 6.	
		10	D.M.S. 1st Army paid a surprise visit between 11 & 12. Interviewed	appendix
			& inspected New Hospital & Barbrite.	
			Received Operation Orders from A.D.M.S. 2nd Division for the	
			Field Ambulance to proceed to BRUAY at 10·30 a.m. on the	
			22nd inst & take over buildings etc. occupied at present	
			by No 11 Field Ambulance.	
			Wounded admitted. 5	
			" evacuated. 4.	appendix

Army Form C. 2118

WAR DIARY

INTELLIGENCE SUMMARY

(Erase heading not required.)

Place	Date	Hour	Summary of Events and Information	Remarks and references to Appendices
BARLIN	March 16th	—	Proceeded to BRUAY to see the site I am to take over from 7 Field Ambulance. There was large recreation room (or hut) which would accommodate about 40 patients, a hut in the grounds of a school closely accommodating about 30 patients & a home about 1/2 a mile away which accommodated about 40 patients — all arrangements in connection with there places were in my opinion very unsatisfactory for the treatment of sick. I have reported the matter to the A.D.M.S. 2nd Division who informs me that he is trying to obtain another place. Wounded admitted. 10. " evacuated. 5	January
BARLIN	17th	—	M.A. F.S. LANE R.A.M.C has proceeded to PERNES to act as medical officer to the Divisional School of Instruction. Wounded admitted. 8. Evacuated. 11 Died 1	January

Army Form C. 2118

WAR DIARY
INTELLIGENCE SUMMARY
(Erase heading not required.)

Instructions regarding War Diaries and Intelligence Summaries are contained in F. S. Regs., Part II. and the Staff Manual respectively. Title Pages will be prepared in manuscript.

Place	Date	Hour	Summary of Events and Information	Remarks and references to Appendices
BARLIN	March 18th	—	Wounded admitted 4. Evacuated 2. died 1.	Journey
"	19th	—	Wounded admitted 0. " " Evacuated 6.	Journey
"	20th	—	A.D.M.S. 2nd Division visited the Field Ambulance. Receives orders from him for the Unit to go to lu Ecole ÉMILE LOUBET at BRUAY (J.10.c.5.3.) on the 22nd Inst instead of the ECOLE, the building occupied by the 7/8th Field Ambulance. Captain T. BOURNE PRICE R.A.M.C. (T.F.) proceeded on leave to England. Wounded admitted 12. " " Evacuated 12	Map reference FRANCE Sheet 36B 3rd edition
				Journey

Army Form C. 2118

WAR DIARY
INTELLIGENCE SUMMARY
(Erase heading not required.)

Place	Date	Hour	Summary of Events and Information	Remarks and references to Appendices
BARLIN	March 21st	—	Captain R.A. PETERS R.A.M.C. (CR) proceeded to BRUAY to make arrangements for his taking over the École EMILE LOUBET. This school was recently occupied by No 9 French Ambulance, and is now a Section of 71 Field Ambulance in formation late yesterday. An advanced party from this Field Ambulance proceeded to BRUAY & there Lt Col Loubet is to hold his other buildings occupied by 71 Field Ambulance. An advanced party arrived at BARLIN from 71 Field Ambulance to take over huts & huts occupied by 100 Field Ambulance. Huts taken over the A.D.M.S. 2nd Division. No 64449 Pte FORREST W D R.A.M.C. & No 64512 Pte LEVI J. R.A.M.C were transferred to No 33 Casualty Clearing Station for duty. Wounded admitted 1, evacuated 9.	January

Army Form C. 2118

WAR DIARY
INTELLIGENCE SUMMARY
(Erase heading not required.)

Instructions regarding War Diaries and Intelligence Summaries are contained in F. S. Regs., Part II. and the Staff Manual respectively. Title Pages will be prepared in manuscript.

Place	Date	Hour	Summary of Events and Information	Remarks and references to Appendices
BARLIN	March 22nd	10.30am	100 Field Ambulance marched from BARLIN en route for BRUAY.	Bruay
BRUAY	"	11.45am	Arrived at Ecole EMILE LOUBET.	
			The school is splendidly situated & the arrangements made by the French for reception & treatment of sick & wounded are excellent. The school will accommodate 180 patients comfortably, (or if necessary 300 or more could be accommodated in the School buildings, & huts & tin outbuildings). Whilst the 2nd Division is in the back area, it is improbable that the Field Ambulance will receive any wounded.	
			N.S.6.69 Pte BOYLE T. & M2.13122 Pte ROGERS L. A.S.C. M.T. arrived with two Daimler Cars for duty yesterday.	
"	23rd	—	Lieut. A. MACINTYRE, R.A.M.C. (T.C.) proceeded to 2nd Dx. & Bucks Regt. for temporary duty. Interpreter DERKAS, M. to PERNES for temporary duty.	Pernes

1875 Wt. W593/826 1,000,000 4/15 J.B.C. & A. A.D.S.S./Forms/C. 2118.

Army Form C. 2118

WAR DIARY
or
INTELLIGENCE SUMMARY
(Erase heading not required.)

Instructions regarding War Diaries and Intelligence Summaries are contained in F. S. Regs., Part II. and the Staff Manual respectively. Title Pages will be prepared in manuscript.

Place	Date	Hour	Summary of Events and Information	Remarks and references to Appendices
BRAY	March 23rd cont	—	No 66173 L.Cpl. WILLIS. W. evacuated to 5 Field Ambulance returned to No 4 Stationary Hospital, sick.	per lorry
"	24th	—	No 61 Capt. ELLIS. B.Q. RAMC " 169. Pte. BONNER. A.H " " 7455 " HUMPHRIES. T.F. " } arrived & reported for duty with this Field Ambulance, on reinforcements.	
			No 66304. Pte FLINT. J.W. RAMC reported this unit for duty. Medical Board held on Capt Surgeon GALLAGHER. Royal Engineers to fitness for commission in Regular Army.	lorry
"	25th	—	A.D.M.S. visited & inspected the Field Ambulance.	lorry
"	26th	—	Lieut A. MACINTYRE. RAMC (T.C.) reported unit for duty. Orders received to move A.D.M.S. 2nd Division to detail bus Bearer Division & this Field Ambulance to be ready to move tomorrow at short notice.	lorry

Army Form C. 2118

WAR DIARY
or
INTELLIGENCE SUMMARY
(Erase heading not required.)

Instructions regarding War Diaries and Intelligence Summaries are contained in F.S. Regs., Part II. and the Staff Manual respectively. Title Pages will be prepared in manuscript.

Place	Date	Hour	Summary of Events and Information	Remarks and references to Appendices
BRAY	March 27th	—	Medical Board held on No 9310 Pte FRIEND. F. 2nd South Staffords, as his mental condition — this man is a deserter — found not to be suffering from mental disability.	
			No 9643. Pte Q.R.A.K.C.W. R&m.C. rejoined this unit for duty from A.P.M. 2nd Division, at his expiration of his 21 days Field Punishment No 1.	Appendix
	28th	—	A.D.M.S. 2nd Division visited the Field Ambulance & inspected the Horse & Motor Transport.	Appendix
	29th	—	Handed over Command of this Field Ambulance temporarily to Captain B.W. ARMSTRONG R&m.C, whilst I am away on leave. Signature Nicolarne O.C. 6th F.A.	
			Took over command of this Field Ambulance during the temporary absence of Lt Colonel Moore on leave. B.W. Armstrong Capt RAMC	
			Major T. Bowring Price. R.A.M.C. (T.C.) reported sick for duty from leave to U.K.	Appendix

Army Form C. 2118

WAR DIARY
INTELLIGENCE SUMMARY
(Erase heading not required.)

Instructions regarding War Diaries and Intelligence Summaries are contained in F. S. Regs., Part II. and the Staff Manual respectively. Title Pages will be prepared in manuscript.

Place	Date	Hour	Summary of Events and Information	Remarks and references to Appendices
BRUAY	March 29th		39251 Sergt Major REASON.F. & 39908 Sergt-FORMAN.D. admitted to hospital & evacuated for dental treatment	A.D.M.S
	30th		This morning received instructions from A.D.M.S. 2nd DIV. that the Ambulance would have to vacate ECOLE EMILE LOUBET the following day so the School is required for educational purposes in the near future. A section of the Ambulance to proceed to Chateau de BOISMONT (C.10.b.4.8) & there to form hospital ready for patients on April 2nd & B & C sections to BAJUS (0.22) to 11.st. billets. To be clear of ECOLE EMILE LOUBET by 2 p.m.	Maisnières FRANCE Sheet 36 B 3rd Edition
	31st		This morning instructions were received from A.D.M.S. 2nd DIV. that the Rev. J. FITZPATRICK is to report for duty to O.C. 22nd C.C.S., BRUAY,	B.M.A.

Army Form C. 2118

WAR DIARY
or
INTELLIGENCE SUMMARY
(Erase heading not required.)

Instructions regarding War Diaries and Intelligence Summaries are contained in F. S. Regs., Part II. and the Staff Manual respectively. Title Pages will be prepared in manuscript.

Place	Date	Hour	Summary of Events and Information	Remarks and references to Appendices
BRUAY	March 5th		His pleasure it the Ambulance to be taken by the Rev N. COONEY — Roman Catholic Chaplain 4th Class for duty with the 99th Bde. The latter reported his arrival at noon today	
		1.30pm	The Ambulance greeted ECOLE EMILE LOUBET at 1.30pm. to proceed to above named destinations. Move completed by about	
		4.30pm	4.30pm. B & C Sections at BAVIUS (at 0.22) under Command of (Capt) W.R. PURCHASE R.A.M.C.	

1875 Wt. W593/826 1,000,000 4/15 J.B.C. & A. A.D.S.S./Forms/C. 2118.

Army Form C. 2118

WAR DIARY
INTELLIGENCE SUMMARY
(Erase heading not required.)

32nd Div.

100 F Amb
Vol 6

Confidential

WAR DIARY
of
100 Field Ambulance
from April 1st to April 30th
Volume 6

COMMITTEE FOR THE
MEDICAL HISTORY OF THE WAR
Date 9 - JUN -

Army Form C. 2118

WAR DIARY
INTELLIGENCE SUMMARY
(Erase heading not required.)

Instructions regarding War Diaries and Intelligence Summaries are contained in F. S. Regs, Part II. and the Staff Manual respectively. Title Pages will be prepared in manuscript.

Place	Date	Hour	Summary of Events and Information	Remarks and references to Appendices
Chateau de BOISMONT (FRANCE 36J - 3rd O.N.V.45)	April 1st		There are two in the Chateau to large rooms which are now transformed into wards — the rest of one being turned off to form a dispensary & operating theatre. The wards accommodate some 30 stretcher cases, but in the event of more space being needed, it will be possible to transform one of the rooms till the role is heard. Total accommodation reported EADAC at 50 patients. Of personnel there are tents room 120 including A.S.C. (H+M.T) etc. non-skilled in stables & barns but the exception of some 25 R.A.M.C. who are under canvas. Most of the lorries & transport have been ------, two sections (B+C) of the Ambulance are at BAJUS (O.22) the remaining two sections (B+C) of the Ambulance are at BAJUS (O.22) under command of Capt. W.B. FAIRHAIR E. RAMC. Under instructions of A.D.M.S 2nd Div., No 61 (Lt ELLIS. B.Q. + the 169 McDONNER.A.N. Sur. Mr. No) set off for duty to the 49F (W.R.) Divisional Sanitary Section. Inspected billets occupied at BAJUS (O.22) by B+C sections. There is plenty of accommodation & we could if necessary arrange further more men & horses.	Map reference FRANCE 36 B 1/50,000
	2nd			

WAR DIARY
INTELLIGENCE SUMMARY
(Erase heading not required.)

Army Form C. 2118

Instructions regarding War Diaries and Intelligence Summaries are contained in F.S. Regs., Part II. and the Staff Manual respectively. Title Pages will be prepared in manuscript.

Place	Date	Hour	Summary of Events and Information	Remarks and references to Appendices
Lillers BOISNON	9/4		S.D.M.S. of F. Corps inspected hospital this morning. An A.D.M.S. 2nd Div had a meal in the afternoon	A.M.S.
	4/4	11.30am	The entire ambulance was inspected this morning by G.O.C. 2nd Division on large pasture close to Château. 175 (all ranks) on parade. The G.O.C. afterwards inspected hospital. Lt. R. PETERS & Capt W.B. PURCHASE R.A.M.C. attended lectures today at AIRE by the Gas Expert.	A.M.S.
	5/4		Lt. PETERS & Capt. PURCHASE again attended lectures at AIRE R.A.M.C. visited hospital this afternoon	A.M.S.
	6/4		Capt. W.B. PURCHASE R.A.M.C. detailed for temporary duty with the 1st Highlanders Regt for the instruction from 2 D.M.S.	A.M.S.
	7/4		A.D.M.S. visited hospital today. Two grams received from A.A. & R.M.S. 2nd Division for list of patients & personnel.	A.M.S.

Army Form C.2118

WAR DIARY
or
INTELLIGENCE SUMMARY
(Erase heading not required.)

Instructions regarding War Diaries and Intelligence Summaries are contained in F.S. Regs., Part II. and the Staff Manual respectively. Title Pages will be prepared in manuscript.

Place	Date	Hour	Summary of Events and Information	Remarks and references to Appendices
CHATEAU DE BOISMONT	April 8th		RAMC No 38362 L/Cpl WINTER.R.O. admitted to hospital & evacuated to C.C.S. suffering from LARYNGITIS	
	9th		ADMS 2nd Div inspected hospital	
	11th		S.M. REASON returned to unit for duty from No 4 Stationary Hospital where he has been undergoing dental treatment	
	12th		In accordance with instructions received from ADMS 2nd Div - Lieut A. MACINTYRE detailed to assume medical charge of 47 Fd. Supply Column at VALHUON (N.6. Central) in addition to his other duties	Map reference from 365 2nd Edition
			T/02387 A/w T. PARKIN ASC & T5/7941 Driver D. SCOTT ASC admitted to No 6 F.A. suffering from Scabies.	

1875 Wt. W593/826 1,000,000 4/15 J.B.C. & A. A.D.S.S./Forms/C. 2118.

Army Form C. 2118

WAR DIARY
or
INTELLIGENCE SUMMARY
(Erase heading not required.)

Instructions regarding War Diaries and Intelligence Summaries are contained in F. S. Regs., Part II. and the Staff Manual respectively. Title Pages will be prepared in manuscript.

Place	Date	Hour	Summary of Events and Information	Remarks and references to Appendices
CHATEAU DE BOISNGHT	April 15th		The following men joined unit today for duty: 66304 Pte W. THOMAS R.M.C. 69662 " H. ROLFE " 79505 " J. RODGERS " 83620 " F.J. ROBERTS " 7311 " J.W. RANSON " 16242 " A. PORTER " Under instructions from A.D.M.S. 2nd Bri. Lieut. S.J. POWELL R.A.M.C. proceeded to the 2nd South Staffordshire Regt. today for Railway duty. 1st of R.A.M.S. for afternoon. Received orders instructions regarding evening man. The Ambulance is returning to BARLIN in its entirety. Dressing station at AIRONSMETTE (K.22.a.6.5.) Cbse section to move to BARLIN on 16th & report to O.C. No 69 F.A. for accommodation at Ecole des Mines (K.33.b.1.4) & to send forward early next day leaven	map of france FRANCE 36 B 3rd Edition

1875. Wt. W593/826 1,000,000 4/15 J.B.C. & A. A.D.S.S./Forms/C. 2118.

Army Form C. 2118

WAR DIARY
or
INTELLIGENCE SUMMARY
(Erase heading not required.)

Instructions regarding War Diaries and Intelligence Summaries are contained in F.S. Regs., Part II. and the Staff Manual respectively. Title Pages will be prepared in manuscript.

Place	Date	Hour	Summary of Events and Information	Remarks and references to Appendices
CHATEAU DE BOISMONT-17	April		party to AIX-NOULETTE to relieve party of No 69 F.A. who will hand over A.B.S. & advanced Bearer post on night of 17/4/16. 2 tack-up section of No 69 F.A. to report here on 16/4/16. Remainder of ambulance & cars on 18/4/16 to Ecole des Mines. BARLIN to replace No 69 F.A.	
	14th		Proceeded to BARLIN this morning to inspect Ecole des Mines & found there splendid accommodation for at least 600 patients & for personnel. Visited ADMS office at BRUAY in the afternoon to report to him in person.	AAA
	15th		No 17594 Cpl E. McCHRISTALL RAMC joined unit today for duty from No 5 F.A. Act/L/Cpl HICKMAN returned to general duty having previously been in charge of patients cook house & rations to permanent rank of Pte. T3/023537 D.T. PARKIN. A.SC. T3/7941 Pte B. SCOTT +C discharged from No 6 F.A. as ground unfit	BBB

1875 Wt. W593/826 1,000,000 4/15 J.B.C. & A. A.D.S.S./Forms/C. 2118.

WAR DIARY or INTELLIGENCE SUMMARY

Army Form C. 2118

(Erase heading not required.)

Instructions regarding War Diaries and Intelligence Summaries are contained in F.S. Regs., Part II. and the Staff Manual respectively. Title Pages will be prepared in manuscript.

Place	Date	Hour	Summary of Events and Information	Remarks and references to Appendices
CHATEAU DE BOISRINET	April 16th		B Section under Capt T. BOURNE-PRICE RAMC with Lieut S.D. CASSIDY RAMC + Lieuts C W SNOWDEN RAMC left for BARLIN Fd Ambulance under instructions from ADMS detailed above. Section of No 69 F.A. [Regiment] under Lieut ORCHARD RAMC reported to our RAMC accommodated at BAJUS.	NWA
	17th		64080 Pte S.D. TURNER RAMC transferred to No 7 General Hospital suffering from MEASLES, + was struck off the strength accordingly. Bearer Sub-division of B section under Capt T. BOURNE-PRICE RAMC with Lieut S.R. CASSIDY RAMC moved up to AIX-NOULETTE + took over MDS at the "Malmer" (R.22 & 2.5) + advanced horse post at NOULETTE (R.29 & 4.9) the evening. At the former place there are enormous cellars capable of accommodating several hundred cases — at the latter there is a cellar holding a few stretcher bearers + a dug out taking four upon stretcher beds.	Map Reference France 36B 3rd Edition NWA

Army Form C. 2118

WAR DIARY
or
INTELLIGENCE SUMMARY
(Erase heading not required.)

Place	Date	Hour	Summary of Events and Information	Remarks and references to Appendices
BARLIN	April 18th	8.45 am	A & C sections left Chateau at BUISMONT at 8.45 am & reached Ecole des Mines BARLIN at 12.30 pm. (K.33.f.14). Capt R A PETERS	Map Reference Transvers 1/40,000 2nd Edition
		2.30pm	R.A.M.C. proceeded in an hour in order to assume medical charge of hospital as soon as No 69 F.A. had quitted it. Accommodation of the hospital reported to A.D.M.S. as 150 in rooms. At present there are two large wards & a small operating theatre in use for the surgical cases & two smaller wards also holding about 30 British cases for medical cases. As other large rooms is now in use so is having beds but but will later converted into another medical ward. There are several small rooms one of which is converted into a dispensary & another but an officers ward holding two cases. The personnel are all billeted in large lofts above the hospital's while we have quarters starting in the houses on a large field behind the hospital	

Army Form C. 2118

WAR DIARY
or
INTELLIGENCE SUMMARY

(Erase heading not required.)

Instructions regarding War Diaries and Intelligence Summaries are contained in F. S. Regs., Part II. and the Staff Manual respectively. Title Pages will be prepared in manuscript.

Place	Date	Hour	Summary of Events and Information	Remarks and references to Appendices
BARLIN	April 18th		No 64735 Pte. C.E. LEESON RAMC is this day posted to H.Q. 2nd Bn (A.D.M.S. Office) & struck off strength from 16/4/16	AMA
	19th		A.D.M.S. found sick this morning but did not inspect hospital. Under instructions of A.D.M.S. Pte J.M. HERRING RAMC departed to day to S.O.N.E.R. to report to OC 28th Bn LONDON Regiment & was struck off the strength of this unit. Wounded admitted 10 evacuated 7	AMA
	20th		No 1327 L/Cpl (A/Cpl) FARROW A. (unpaid) reported act/L/Cpl with pay from today's date. Wounded evacuated 1 - no admissions	AMA
	21st		Field of A.D.M.S. this morning who did not know myself isolated No 1908 Pte D. FOREMAN RAMC this day reported sick from No 4 Stationary Hospital where he has been undergoing dental treatment. Reverted admitted 5 evacuated 5 7 2	AMA

Army Form C. 2118

WAR DIARY
or
INTELLIGENCE SUMMARY
(Erase heading not required.)

Instructions regarding War Diaries and Intelligence Summaries are contained in F.S. Regs., Part II. and the Staff Manual respectively. Title Pages will be prepared in manuscript.

Place	Date	Hour	Summary of Events and Information	Remarks and references to Appendices
BARLIN	April 23rd		Under instruction of ADMS Capt. L.W. BAIN RAMC (Temporary) joined unit today for temporary duty. Wounded admitted 1 evacuated 2	RMA
	24th		I visited ADS at Rubbra AIX-NOULETTE (R.2.a.2.5) & found everything there in good order & all arrangements working correctly. Wounded admitted 5 evacuated 3. ADMS D.D.M.S. inspected hospital this afternoon. Wounded admitted 6 evacuated 5	Ref-reference FRANCE 36 B 3rd letter
	25th 26th		Under instruction of ADMS Lieut A. MACINTYRE RAMC proceeded to the 1st Kings (Liverpool Regiment) for temporary duty today. Wounded admitted 11 evacuated	RMA RMA RMA
	27th		ADMS inspected Ambulance this morning. Lieut Colonel & Mr Moore RAMC ♦of♦ joined unit this evening from sick leave in H.K. Wounded admitted 4 evacuated 4 64. 6 8 6. Pte. S.D. TURNER reported sick today From No 7 9.R. was taken on strength accordingly	RMA

1875 Wt. W593/826 1,000,000 4/15 J.B.C. & A. A.D.S.S./Forms/C. 2118.

WAR DIARY
or
INTELLIGENCE SUMMARY

(Erase heading not required.)

Army Form C. 2118

Instructions regarding War Diaries and Intelligence Summaries are contained in F.S. Regs., Part II. and the Staff Manual respectively. Title Pages will be prepared in manuscript.

Place	Date	Hour	Summary of Events and Information	Remarks and references to Appendices
BARLIN	April 28	9.30 a.m.	Lieut Colonel E.H.M. MOORE departed this morning for temporary duty.	MMM
	29		2nd ADMS 9th Div. Admitted 20. Evacuated 13. Wounded — A.D.M.S. inspected hospital this morning & made arrangements from Mr. le Directeur of the Ecole des Mines to take possession of two small outhouses attached to school for patients bathroom. Visited ADS at AIX-NOULETTE this afternoon in company of DADMS 2nd Div. inspecting in the way & new French hut which is being made by us for the evacuation of wounded from the Regimental Aid Posts & one Advance Dressing post at R. 21. d. 2. 5. Some of our horses at A.B.P. slightly gassed this morning. Interpreter ELVAS departed on leave this morning. Lieut S. J. Powell reported here this morning from temporary duty with 2nd N.S. Staff Regt.	Map reference FRANCE 36 B. 5 2nd Ed.

1375 Wt. W503/826 1,000,000 4/15 J.B.C. & A. A.D.S.S./Forms/C. 2118.

Army Form C. 2118

WAR DIARY
or
INTELLIGENCE SUMMARY
(Erase heading not required.)

Instructions regarding War Diaries and Intelligence Summaries are contained in F.S. Regs., Part II. and the Staff Manual respectively. Title Pages will be prepared in manuscript.

Place	Date	Hour	Summary of Events and Information	Remarks and references to Appendices
BARLIN	April 19th		Surgeon General Sir Anthony Bowlby inspected Hospital this afternoon. Wounded admitted 6. Evacuated 11.	MA.
	20th		30 men (including NCOs) of "A" Section sent up to AIX NOULETTE this evening to replace corresponding number of men of "B" Section who returned to BARLIN. 2 Cpl W. O'BRIEN (54422) R.A.M.C. reported wounded for duty today from leave in the strength accordingly. Wounded admitted 1. Evacuated 3.	MA

WAR DIARY
INTELLIGENCE SUMMARY
(Erase heading not required.)

Army Form C. 2118

32/u • 2nd Div 100 F A amb

Vol 7

May 1916

Confidential

WAR DIARY
of
100 Field Ambulance
from May 1st to May 31st

Volume 7.

Army Form C. 2118

WAR DIARY
or
INTELLIGENCE SUMMARY
(Erase heading not required.)

Instructions regarding War Diaries and Intelligence Summaries are contained in F.S. Regs., Part II. and the Staff Manual respectively. Title Pages will be prepared in manuscript.

Place	Date	Hour	Summary of Events and Information	Remarks and references to Appendices
BARLIN	May 1st		The D.G.M.S. inspected buildings & enquired by F.A. this morning with a view to accommodation for a C.C.S. Wounded admitted 13 evacuated 4	Motor ambulance personnel
"	2nd		Colonel ENSOR A.M.S. took Lieut Colonel NORMAN (O.C. No. 6 C.C.S.) round hospital this morning & inspected the buildings from point of view of suitability for a C.C.S. Wounded admitted 15 Evacuated 7.	R.A.M.C
"	3rd		D.D.M.S. visited hospital this afternoon. Wounded admitted 14 evacuated 15	R.A.M.C
"	4th		A.D.M.S. 23rd Div. inspected hospital this afternoon. The following joined 16 Ambulance today for duty from base into the strength 26167 Cpl T.C. MACKEY R.A.M.C 10881 Pte A. COLEMAN R.A.M.C 74440 Pte E.C. ALLARD R.A.M.C Wounded admitted 23 Evacuated 16	R.A.M.C

1875 Wt. W593/826 1,000,000 4/15 J.B.C. & A. A.D.S.S./Forms/C. 2118.

Army Form C. 2118

WAR DIARY
or
INTELLIGENCE SUMMARY
(Erase heading not required.)

Instructions regarding War Diaries and Intelligence Summaries are contained in F. S. Regs., Part II. and the Staff Manual respectively. Title Pages will be prepared in manuscript.

Place	Date	Hour	Summary of Events and Information	Remarks and references to Appendices
BARLIN	May 5th		A.D.M.S. visited hospital today & gave me verbal instructions regarding coming move. Been out admitted 13 evacuated 12.	MA
BARLIN	6th		Lt Colonel NORMAN R.A.M.C. commanding No. 6 C.C.S. arrived here this morning & informed me that he had instructions to take over the Ecole des Mines for a C.C.S. He left behind two officers & during the day a party of men & 7 lorry loads of stores arrived. In the afternoon I visited Ecole Marmotta BRUAY which is an auxiliary hospital taking over from No. 70 F.A. & inspected the billeys & staff. Wounded admitted 4. Evacuated 4. 74067 Sgt R.G. HUMES R.A.M.C. admitted to hospital suffering from DEBILITY & DENTAL CARIES. During enemy's recent bombardment from A.D.M.S. to be in readiness to march Ecole des Mines on Monday morning May 8th	MA MA

1875 Wt. W593/826 1,000,000 4/15 J.B.C. & A. A.D.S.S./Forms/C. 2118.

WAR DIARY
or
INTELLIGENCE SUMMARY
(Erase heading not required.)

Army Form C. 2118

Place	Date	Hour	Summary of Events and Information	Remarks and references to Appendices
BARLIN	May 7th		In accordance with instructions received from ADMS. Lieut S.A. CASSIDY R.A.M.C. was detailed for temporary medical charge of 2nd H.L.I. & proceeded thither this morning. Capt L.W. BAIN R.A.M.C. proceeded this morning to No 6 F.A. for temporary duty. Capt W.B. PURCHASE returned from leave in U.K. & resumed command this evening. Wounded admitted 6. Evacuated 7.	
			Special instructions received from ADMS today to take effect on May 8th one section of No 100 F.A. will change with one section of No 9 F.A. at Maroc to BRUAY) Each ½ section (BRUAY) to move today to No 100 F.A. to premises at BRUAY (Ecole Maronite). Starting point test crossing K26c. not g a.m. AFS at AIX-NOULETTE to be handed over to advance section of No 7 F.A. on night of 9th–10th May. Later in the day messages received from ADMS postponing the above moves by 24 hours.	Map reference France 36A B Edition 1 in 40,000

Army Form C. 2118

WAR DIARY
or
INTELLIGENCE SUMMARY

(Erase heading not required.)

Instructions regarding War Diaries and Intelligence Summaries are contained in F. S. Regs., Part II. and the Staff Manual respectively. Title Pages will be prepared in manuscript.

Place	Date	Hour	Summary of Events and Information	Remarks and references to Appendices
BARLIN	May 8/15	9 am	All hands vacated places and to No 6 C.C.S. Wounded admission and evacuation (including transfers) 10.	
BARLIN	May 9th	—	Lt. Col. E.H.M. MOORE R.A.M.C. rejoin'd col. 100. 7.0. from temporary duty as A/A.D.M.S. 2nd Division, & resumed command of 11th Field Ambulance. C. Sectn. 100 F/A. proceeded to Ecole MARMOTTAN, BRUAY (J.22.a.3.8) taken over building to be occupied by No 70 Field Ambulance, 23rd Division.	Map ref. France Sheet 36B 1:40,000 instead of 1:100,000 A.Moore Lt Colonel
BARLIN	May 10.	—	Lt.S.J. COWELL R.A.M.C. (T.C) proceeded to PERNES (H.11) for temporary duty as M.O. IV Corps School of Instruction. No 66331 Sergt. F.S. WEBB R.A.m.c. evacuated to No7 General Hospital, Advanced Dressing Station at AIX NOULETTE (R.22.a.7.8.) handed over to No 70 Field Ambulance. Lieut. L.W. BAIN R.A.M.C (T.C) proceeded on leave to U.K.	A.Moore

Army Form C. 2118

WAR DIARY
INTELLIGENCE SUMMARY
(Erase heading not required.)

Instructions regarding War Diaries and Intelligence Summaries are contained in F. S. Regs., Part II. and the Staff Manual respectively. Title Pages will be prepared in manuscript.

Place	Date	Hour	Summary of Events and Information	Remarks and references to Appendices
BARLIN	May 11th	1.45 pm	100 Field Ambulance (Lieut C Section) left BARLIN.	Appendix
BRUAY	"	3.15 pm	" " arrived BRUAY - & occupied Buildings at Ecole MARMOTTAN. Accommodation for 150-200 cases. — Orders from A.D.M.S. Further arrangements to treat Divisional Ill cases & to form Divisional Rest Station.	Appendix
BRUAY	May 12th	—	Orders from A.D.M.S. to Detail one Officer & 40 Other Ranks to proceed to the front of NIEPPE for trench cutting etc tomorrow.	Appendix
BRUAY	May 13th	9 a.m	Capt. W. B. PURCHASE, R.A.M.C (TC) & 40 Other ranks left in lorries from the front of NIEPPE.	Appendix
BRUAY	May 14th	—	No 94321 Pte. T. W. HODGKISS R.A.M.C, Specially enlisted as Dispenser, arrived from No 8 Stationary Hospital for duty with 100 Field Ambulance - admitted acting Sergeant	Appendix

1875 Wt. W593/826 1,000,000 4/15 J.B.C. & A. A.D.S.S./Forms/C. 2118.

WAR DIARY
INTELLIGENCE SUMMARY
(Erase heading not required.)

Army Form C. 2118

Place	Date	Hour	Summary of Events and Information	Remarks and references to Appendices
BRUAY	May 15th	-	No 64450 Sergt. P.T. CLARKE R.A.M.C. proceeded to No 6 Stationary Hospital for duty.	Appx. 2.
BRUAY	May 16th	-	No M2/133664 Pte T. HONOUR A.S.C. M.T. proceeded to Divn. for temporary duty as dispatch rider. Vice No 64739 Pte PARK R.A.M.C. who rejoined this unit. A.D.M.S. orders. Capt. L.W. BAIN. R.A.M.C. (T.C.) posted to No 5 Field Ambulance & is struck off the strength of No 100 Field Ambulance.	Appx.
BRUAY	May 18th	-	Lieut. D.S. CASSIDY. R.A.M.C. (T.C.) rejoined unit from temporary duty with 2nd H.L.I. Captain. B.W. ARMSTRONG R.A.M.C. (T.C.) proceeded on leave to U.K. No 64667 Pte. D.S. GRANT. R.A.M.C. awarded 7 days field punishment No 2.	Appx.

Army Form C. 2118

WAR DIARY

INTELLIGENCE SUMMARY

(Erase heading not required.)

Instructions regarding War Diaries and Intelligence Summaries are contained in F.S. Regs, Part II. and the Staff Manual respectively. Title Pages will be prepared in manuscript.

Place	Date	Hour	Summary of Events and Information	Remarks and references to Appendices
BRUAY	May 19th	—	No 15494 Corporal F. McCRISTALL RAMC permitted to re-engage to complete 21 years. No T4/042153 acting Sergeant HODGE & No T4/042058 acting Sergt FAIRCLOUGH A.S.C. (HT) confirmed in their rank of Sergeant.	Signed
BRUAY	May 20th	—	Under orders from A.D.M.S. 2nd Division — the following departures took place — No 66402 Pte W. JAMES RAMC Transferred to No 6 Field Ambulance. No T4/042085 Sgt. FAIRCLOUGH A.S.C. (HT) } to be 2nd Divl Train for duty. No T4/043291 Driver J. JONES ASC (HT) } No M2/133899 Pte BOULTWOOD ARC MT. to Base Depot ROUEN. and were struck off strength of 100 Field Ambulance. also 1 Riding Horse, 1 light draft horse & 1 heavy draft horse were sent to No 3 Mobile Veterinary Section. and 1 hsstr [?] horse sent to 2nd Divl Supply Column. On account of reduction in establishment in Horse & Mule Transport.	Signed

1875 Wt. W593/826 1,000,000 4/15 J.B.C. & A. A.D.S.S./Forms/C. 2118.

Army Form C. 2118

WAR DIARY
INTELLIGENCE SUMMARY
(Erase heading not required.)

Instructions regarding War Diaries and Intelligence Summaries are contained in F.S. Regs., Part II. and the Staff Manual respectively. Title Pages will be prepared in manuscript.

Place	Date	Hour	Summary of Events and Information	Remarks and references to Appendices
BRUAY.	May 22nd	—	No 66331 Sergt. F.S. WEBB, R.A.M.C. rejoined unit from No 7 Gen. Hosp.	Hosp. at France. Sheet 360 . 1 woman
	"	6.30am.	Orders received from A.D.M.S. 2nd Division for Field Ambulance (less one Complete Section) to be prepared to move at one hours notice - Preparations made accordingly.	
	"	4pm.	Warning order from A.D.M.S. two Ambulance Cars & 16 stretcher bearers proceed to FRESNICOURT (Q.19.d.) for temporary attachment to No 6 Field Ambulance	Germany Prisoners
BRUAY.	May 23rd	—	A.D.M.S visited 100 F.A.	
"	24th	—	Orders received from A.D.M.S for 100 F.A. to evacuate Ecole Mamottan BRUAY Tomorrow & proceed to & take on site, occupied by No 7th London Field Ambulance, 47th Division, at GAUCHIN-LE-GAL (P.30.d.0.3) and CHOCQURT (V.S.6.S.6). Captain W.D. PURCHASE R.A.M.C. (T.C.) & 40 other ranks rejoined unit from FOREST OF NIEPPE -	Germany

Army Form C. 2118

WAR DIARY or INTELLIGENCE SUMMARY

Place	Date	Hour	Summary of Events and Information	Remarks and references to Appendices
BROAY	May 24 (cont)		No. 64687 Pte D.S. GRANT. R.A.M.C. rejoined unit from A.P.M. 2nd Div.	Appendix
BROAY	May 25th	2 pm	No. 7.A. Wkshp BROAY.	
GAVRINCOURT	"	4.15 pm	1 D.D.T.H. arrived. Captain W.B. PURCHASE (R.A.M.C.) (T.C.) & B Section proceeded to CAUCOURT. Buildings & huts taken over. To receive Sick. ADS Care of QAUCHIN & to form Divisional Rest Station at CAUCOURT. Accommodation at GAVRINCOURT for patients 60 in a boys' hut. 140 in sheds & outbuildings of Nunnery. at CAUCOURT - normally 150 in huts. possible accommodation 240.	Keep up FRANCE SHEET 36B 1:40,000
"	"	6 pm	Indts or Men from A.D.M.S. Capt. T. BOURNE-PRICE (R.A.M.C.) (T.C.) and Lieut. D.S. CASSIDY. R.A.M.C. (T.C.) & 34 Other ranks proceeded to ESTREE-CAUCHIE (H.2.b.) to be attached to 6 Field Ambulance for temporary duty	
QAUCHIN	May 26th		No. 66451 Pte W. KEATES. R.A.M.C. rejoined unit from No 7 [General] Hospital	Appendix
"	27th		A.D.M.S. visit	Appendix

WAR DIARY
INTELLIGENCE SUMMARY

Army Form C. 2118

Place	Date	Hour	Summary of Events and Information	Remarks and references to Appendices
GAUCHIN	May 28th	—	ADMS (DADMS 2nd Div. visited HQ Qrs 100 F.A. and Rest Station at GAUCOURT	Breezy
"	29th	—	No 79605 Pte. RODGERS(L)RAMC joined unit from APM 2nd Div. for 21 days P.P. No 1	
			Captain R.A. PETERS. RAMC (S.R) proceeded to 1st K.R.R. Corps for temporary duty as Medical Officer to that Regiment.	Breezy
GAUCHIN	May 30th	—	No 45248 Serjeant W.C. KIRBY. RAMC proceeded to No 113 Field Ambulance for duty Vice No 35343 Serjeant A.W. HAMLINGTON RAMC who reported to 150 Field Ambulance for duty.	
			No 86196 Pte FRETWELL RAMC } evacuated to No 1 Cavalry Hospital. " 64690 Pte T. JAMIESON RAMC }	
RAVELIN	May 31st	—	No 66168 Pte L/C HALL RAMC evacuated to No 7 General Hospital.	

Lieut Colonel
ADMS 2nd Div

Army Form C. 2118

WAR DIARY
2nd Armoun
INTELLIGENCE SUMMARY
(Erase heading not required.)

1007 amb Vol 8

CONFIDENTIAL

WAR DIARY
of
100 Field Ambulance
from June 1st to June 3
Volume 8

COMMITTEE FOR THE
MEDICAL HISTORY OF THE WAR
Date 5 AUG. 1915

Place	Date	Hour	Summary of Events and Information	Remarks and references to Appendices
	Jun/16			

WAR DIARY

INTELLIGENCE SUMMARY

Army Form C. 2118

Place	Date	Hour	Summary of Events and Information	Remarks and references to Appendices
GAUCHIN LE GAL	June 1st	—	A.D.M.S. 2nd Division visited 100 Field Ambulance and the Rest Station at CAUCOURT (V.S.b.s.3)	Map refs France Sheet 36B in use
"	"	4 pm	Orders received from A.D.M.S. to evacuate premises at GAUCHIN LE GAL (P.s.o.d.o.3) and take over premises occupied by N° 6 Field Ambulance at ESTRÉE CAUCHIE — To open for reception of Sick & Dis. in rid Section Cara. * (V.S.a.a.7.) Move to be completed by 11 am. Premises at GAUCHIN to be handed over to IV Corps & holding party to be left behind for the purpose. The one Section of N° 6 Field Ambulance to stand fast at CAUCOURT & continue as Divisional Rest Station. Lieut. A. MACINTYRE. R.A.M.C. (T.C.) proceeded on leave later in the P.m.	Brunton W.Col.A.D.M.S. O.C. 100 F.A.
GAUCHIN LE GAL	June 2nd	10.30 am	100 Field Ambulance (less one Section) moved from premises at GAUCHIN.	
ESTRÉE CAUCHIE	"	11 am	" arrived at ESTRÉE CAUCHIE, & opened for reception of Sick etc. There are 5 huts, accommodating roughly 200 patients.	
"	"	3.30 pm	Visited Divisional Rest Stn. at CAUCOURT.	Brunton

Army Form C. 2118

WAR DIARY
—or—
INTELLIGENCE SUMMARY
(Erase heading not required.)

Instructions regarding War Diaries and Intelligence Summaries are contained in F. S. Regs., Part II. and the Staff Manual respectively. Title Pages will be prepared in manuscript.

Place	Date	Hour	Summary of Events and Information	Remarks and references to Appendices
ESTREE (AVENUE)	June 2nd	11 pm	Orders received from A.D.M.S. 2nd Division to O.C. 100 F.A. Bearer over a house at MONT ST ELOY (Y.E.d.3.4. Map 51c) from O.C. 6 F.A. Captain T. BOURNE PRICE R.A.M.C. (T.C.) put in charge with an R. & Bearer Subdivision in formed. This have the was as an advanced dressing station to wounded evacuated from her Battalion on its right of the right Sector taken over by the 2nd Division. All wounded from their Battalion to be evacuated to No 6 Field Ambulance at LES QUATRES VENTS (W.9 Central. Map 36 c).	[signature]
"	June 3rd	—	Visited Advanced Dressing Station & made arrangements reporting st Bearers etc. Captain. R.A. PETERS. R.A.M.C. (S.R.) posted as Medical Officer to 1st R.R.R. & struck off the strength of 100 F.A. Lieut. S. T. Cowell R.A.M.C. (T.C.) returned 100 F.A. for duty from temporary duty with IV Corps School of Infantry	[signature]

1875 Wt. W593/826 1,000,000 4/15 J.B.C. & A.   A.D.S.S./Forms/C. 2118.

WAR DIARY / INTELLIGENCE SUMMARY

Army Form C. 2118

Place	Date	Hour	Summary of Events and Information	Remarks and references to Appendices
ESTRÉE (AUCHY)	July 4	—	Visited Advanced Dressing Station on MONT ST. ELOY & the following posts in connection with it. 1. Dug out at F.4.a.3.3. (map 57c) where 2 bearers are posted for relay work 2. Dug out at S.29.d.2.4. (map 36 ⊕) " " " " " 3. Dug out at S.25.6.7.5. (map 36c) which is used as the advanced bearer post of the A.D. Dressing Stn & where 1 N.C.O. & 16 bearers are kept. 4. Regimental aid post S.20.6.77. (map 36c) where 6 bearers are kept. Considerable amount of work requires to be done in all the dug outs.	[illeg]
	5th	—	Nothing of importance has taken place since above entry – routine work. Lieut & Q.M. W.D. E.B. SNOWDEN R.A.M.C. (T.C.) departed on leave to U.K.	[illeg]
	6th	—	Visited Advanced Dressing Stn – work proceeding satisfactorily. No. 64765 Pte. E.A. COKER. R.A.M.C. rejoined 600 ypc for duty from Hospital	

Army Form C. 2118

WAR DIARY
or
INTELLIGENCE SUMMARY
(Erase heading not required.)

Instructions regarding War Diaries and Intelligence Summaries are contained in F. S. Regs., Part II. and the Staff Manual respectively. Title Pages will be prepared in manuscript.

Place	Date	Hour	Summary of Events and Information	Remarks and references to Appendices
ESTRÉE CAUCHY	July 9	11 am	Acted as President to Medical Board on Pte. HARDING, 1st K.R.R.C. who being tried by F.G.C.M. for desertion pleaded "wandering mania". Opinion of the Board was that he was non mentale fit.	Appendix
"	10 "	—	Lieut. A. MACINTYRE R.A.M.C (T.C) returned from leave.	Appendix
			No 66196 Pte. T. FRETWELL R.A.M.C } reported for duty from No 64690 Pte. T. JAMIESON R.A.M.C } Hospital.	Appendix
"	11 "	—	ADMS 2nd Div visited & in Prewarned 60 men Spa new draft to 2nd H.L.I.	Appendix
			Visited Advanced Dressing Sta — satisfactory.	
"	12 "	11 am	G.O.C. 2nd Division inspected the Field Ambulance & the Divisional Rest Station at CAUCOURT.	Appendix
"	13 "	—	No 35467 Pte B.W. THORNE R.A.M.C rejoined unit from Hospital & the No 66166 Pte. G.H. HALL R.A.M.C rejoined unit from No 7 General Hospital.	Appendix

Army Form C. 2118

WAR DIARY
INTELLIGENCE SUMMARY
(Erase heading not required.)

Place	Date	Hour	Summary of Events and Information	Remarks and references to Appendices
ESTREE CAUCHIE	Aug 14th	—	D.D.M.S. IV Corps inspected the Field Ambulance.	[initials]
"	15th	—	Orders received from A.D.M.S. 2nd Div. to detail an Officer for Medical Charge of 41st Brigade R.F.A. Capt. W.B. PURCHASE R.A.M.C. (T.C.) detailed.	[initials]
"	16th	—	Lieut & Qrmr Mastr E.B. SNOWDEN R.A.M.C. (T.C.) returned unit from leave to U.K.	[initials]
"	17th	—	Captain W.B. PURCHASE R.A.M.C. (T.C.) proceeded to 41st Brigade R.F.A. as Medical Officer in charge & struck off the strength of this Company. Visited Adv. Dressing Stn —	[initials]
"	18th	—	Routine —	
"	19th	—	Lieut R H WILSON R.A.M.C. (T.C.) posted to this Unit for duty & taken on the strength.	
"	20th	—	No 66462 Pte. A.J. BRABNER R.A.M.C. transferred to C.C.S. & struck off this Unit.	[initials]

1875 W.J. W 593/826 1,000,000 4/15 J.B;C.& A. A.D.S.S. Forms/C. 2118.

WAR DIARY

INTELLIGENCE SUMMARY

(Erase heading not required.)

Army Form C. 2118

Instructions regarding War Diaries and Intelligence Summaries are contained in F. S. Regs., Part II. and the Staff Manual respectively. Title Pages will be prepared in manuscript.

Place	Date	Hour	Summary of Events and Information	Remarks and references to Appendices
ESTREE (AUCHY)	July 19th (cont.)		7464743 Pte A. STEPHENSON. RAMC awarded 10 days Field Punishment No 2 - Offence (1) W.o.s complying with an order (2) Insolence to a N.C.O. - Visited Adv. Dressing Stn.	Fine
"	20th	-	Lieut. K. PRETTY. RAMC (T.C.) joined this unit for duty. Steben on his strength.	Fine
"	21st	-	Routine.	Showery
"	22nd	-	Routine.	Showery
"	23rd	-	Routine. Visited adv. Dressing Stn.	Rainy
"	24th	-	Routine.	Rainy
"	25th	-	No 2018 Pte C. WHISTLECRAFT. RAMC (T) 1st Cant Anglian Field Ambulance attd. to this unit granted the rate of Corps pay from date of proceeding overseas - Viz 6.11.14.	Fine
"	26th	-	Routine	Rainy

1875 Wt. W593/826 1,000,000 4/15 J.B.C. & A. A.D.S.S./Forms/C. 2118.

Army Form C. 2118

WAR DIARY
or
INTELLIGENCE SUMMARY
(Erase heading not required.)

Instructions regarding War Diaries and Intelligence Summaries are contained in F. S. Regs., Part II. and the Staff Manual respectively. Title Pages will be prepared in manuscript.

Place	Date	Hour	Summary of Events and Information	Remarks and references to Appendices
ESTREE CAUCHIE	July 27th	—	Acting Sergeant E. McCHRISTAL R.A.M.C. reverts to the permanent rank of Corporal — Offence: When on active Service, Drunkenness.	
		5.45pm.	D.M.S. 1st Army visited this Field Ambulance & inspected by attention & discharge books, order book etc. & visited some of the wounded.	
" "	28th	—	Routine. Killed adv. dressing Stn.	Routine
" "	29th	—	Routine.	Routine
" "	30th	—	Routine.	Routine

Morrison
Lt. Col. R.A.M.C.
O.C. 100 Fd. Ambulance

1875 Wt. W593/826 1,000,000 4/15 J.B.C. & A. A.D.S.S./Forms/C. 2118.

Army Form C. 2118

23rd Division
July
100 F Amb.

WAR DIARY
or
INTELLIGENCE SUMMARY
(Erase heading not required.)

Vol 9

CONFIDENTIAL

WAR DIARY
of
100 Field Ambulance
from July 1st to July 31st.
Volume 9.

COMMITTEE FOR THE
MEDICAL HISTORY OF THE WAR
Date 31 AUG 1915

Place	Date	Hour	Summary of Events and Information	Remarks and references to Appendices
	July 16			

Army Form C. 2118

WAR DIARY
INTELLIGENCE SUMMARY
(Erase heading not required.)

Instructions regarding War Diaries and Intelligence Summaries are contained in F. S. Regs., Part II. and the Staff Manual respectively. Title Pages will be prepared in manuscript.

Place	Date	Hour	Summary of Events and Information	Remarks and references to Appendices
ESTREE CAUCHIE	July 1st	—	Routine.	Shrubsole Lt.Col/R.A.M.C.
"	2nd	—	D.D.M.S. IV Corps visited No.6 Field Ambulance.	
"			The Yu.O.E.Y. Sergt. R.C. HOMES R.A.M.C. proceeded to Divisional Company en route to Base Depôt on account of ill health. Struck off strength of the unit. Visited Advanced Dressing Stn & found everything satisfactory.	Stormy
"	3rd	—	No. 66306 Pte H.W. HAWKE R.A.M.C. proceeded to LE HAVRE en route for England for instruction in fitters course. Struck off strength of the unit. Horses were inspected by the O.C. 2nd Divisional Train	Stormy
"	4th	—	The Horses & Horse Transport of this Unit were inspected by the O.C. 2nd Divisional Train Routine.	Stormy Stormy
"	5th	—	20 men sent under instruction from A.D.M.S. to advance Dressing Stn of No.6 Field Ambulance to help in reconstruction of the Dressing Stn. This party to proceed daily until further orders.	Stormy

Army Form C. 2118

WAR DIARY
INTELLIGENCE SUMMARY
(Erase heading not required.)

Instructions regarding War Diaries and Intelligence Summaries are contained in F. S. Regs., Part II. and the Staff Manual respectively. Title Pages will be prepared in manuscript.

Place	Date	Hour	Summary of Events and Information	Remarks and references to Appendices
ESTREE-CAUCHIE	July 5th	(cont)	I visited the Advanced Bearer Post. 100 7th - & found everything satisfactory. MO has been improving daily. He & his men been allowed to strengthen & in every way suitable for the reception of wounded.	Appendix
"	6th	—	Routine.	
"	7th	—	No. 94323 Pte O. BIRCH RAMC awarded 10 days No 1 Field Punishment for "absence without leave". No. 9460? Pte J. RODGERS. RAMC remanded for Trial by Court Martial (held June 9) for "Drunkenness"	Appendix
"	8th	—	Routine.	
"	9th	—	The new Bath house at the Rest Station - under construction during the last 14 days - is now completed with heating apparatus & shower bath. It has been decided to use this bath house for the troops in the vicinity as well as the Rest Station patients.	Appendix

1875 Wt. W593/826 1,000,000 4/15 J.B.C. & A. A.D.S.S./Forms/C. 2118.

Army Form C. 2118

WAR DIARY
INTELLIGENCE SUMMARY
(Erase heading not required.)

Instructions regarding War Diaries and Intelligence Summaries are contained in F. S. Regs., Part II. and the Staff Manual respectively. Title Pages will be prepared in manuscript.

Place	Date	Hour	Summary of Events and Information	Remarks and references to Appendices
ESSEX CAVALRY	July 10th	—	Routine. Visited Advanced Dressing Stn & found everything satisfactory	Appendix
"	11th	—	No 12006 Cpl. C. WARD R.A.M.C. } arrived for duty from Rouen & are No 4C17 Pte. A.D. SIME R.A.M.C. } taken on live strength as from 9 a.m.	Appendix
"	12th	—	No 26167 Cpl T MACKEY R.A.M.C. } departed for duty with 2nd Bn No 9843 Pte C W GRAY R.A.M.C. } S/Lancs Regt and are struck off the strength of Unit A.	Appendix
			No 9605 Pte J RODGERS R.A.M.C tried by H.Q Coy. marched at Caudelain l'Abbe.	Appendix
"	13th	—	Pte RODGERS sentenced to 90 days Field Punishment No 1 - confirmed by R.O.C 6 Brigade. Visited Advanced Dressing Station —	Appendix
"	14th	—	Sentence on Pte RODGERS (promulgated); Pte RODGERS sent to APM 2nd Division AD H.Q. 2nd Division visited – Telly in the road. Struck on 17th inst.	Appendix

Army Form C. 2118

WAR DIARY
INTELLIGENCE SUMMARY
(Erase heading not required.)

Instructions regarding War Diaries and Intelligence Summaries are contained in F.S. Regs., Part II. and the Staff Manual respectively. Title Pages will be prepared in manuscript.

Place	Date	Hour	Summary of Events and Information	Remarks and references to Appendices
ESTREE CAUCHIE	July 15th	—	Official Operation orders from A.D.M.S. 2nd Div. "100 F.A. to proceed to OURTON (I.34.b.6.6 map 36B) on 17th inst at 11.30 a.m. & take over "Hospital" premises to be vacated by 11 Field Ambulance Royal Naval Division. Advanced Dressing Station, 100 F.A. Bearer posts etc to be handed over to 1st London Field Ambulance on the night 15th to 16th inst. on relief the Personnel 100 F.A. to rejoin H.Q. Opn of the Unit.	[signature]
		3.30 pm	Orders received from A.D.M.S. for all cars to be disposed of from Rest Station by 12 noon 16th inst.	
		" "	Proceeded to OURTON to make arrangements with O.C. 1st F.A. R.N.D. for handing & taking over	[signature]
" "	16th	—	Advanced Dressing Sta, Bearer posts etc handed over to 1st London F.A. Personnel 100 F.A. returned to H.Q. Opn. Advance party sent to OURTON.	[signature]

Army Form C. 2118

WAR DIARY
INTELLIGENCE SUMMARY
(Erase heading not required.)

Instructions regarding War Diaries and Intelligence Summaries are contained in F. S. Regs., Part II. and the Staff Manual respectively. Title Pages will be prepared in manuscript.

Place	Date	Hour	Summary of Events and Information	Remarks and references to Appendices
ESTRÉE CAUCHIE	July 16th (cont)		Lieut. P.J. LANE. RAMC (T.C.) rejoined 100 F.A. from 2nd Divisional School Instruction PERNES.	Army
"	17th		No 14323 Pte. O. BIRCH RAMC reported sick for 10 days Field Punishment No 1.	Army
"	"		Buildings etc at ESTRÉE CAUCHIE and CAUCOURT handed over to 100 H.Q. Luton Field Ambulance.	
"	"	11.30am	100 F.A. marched from ESTRÉE CAUCHIE	
OURTON	"	3 pm	100 F.A. arrived at OURTON & took over Buildings etc vacated by 14th F.A. RMD. Men in accommodation for about 60 Cases in barn. Scabies cases treated in tent.	Army
"	18th	—	Lieut R. H. WILSON RAMC (T.C.) proceeded to 2nd D.H.Q. for Infirmary duty.	Army

1875 Wt. W593/826 1,000,000 4/15 J.B.C. & A. A.D.S.S./Forms/C. 2118.

Army Form C. 2118

WAR DIARY
INTELLIGENCE SUMMARY
(Erase heading not required.)

Instructions regarding War Diaries and Intelligence Summaries are contained in F.S. Regs., Part II. and the Staff Manual respectively. Title Pages will be prepared in manuscript.

Place	Date	Hour	Summary of Events and Information	Remarks and references to Appendices
OURTON	July 1916	—	Operation order from ADMS. "Field Ambulance to be at DIEVAL Station at 7 pm 20th inst. for entraining. Motor Ambulance Cars to proceed to CORBIE by road.	Appendix
"	20	6.30 p.m.	100 F.A. proceeded to DIEVAL Railway Station (O.13.b.22.) Map 36.B.	
DIEVAL	"	7.30	Horse transport loaded in train & men entrained. Train left 10 p.m.	Appendix
LONGUEAU	21st	5.30 a.m.	Arrived at LONGUEAU Railway Station (near AMIENS) Train unloaded. Ambulance marched via CORBIE (O.5.a.b. Map. 62.D.) to MORLAN COURT and billeted at H.q.a.8.6. (Map 62 D.) At CORBIE the following reinforcements joined for duty. No 737/4 Pte H.C. GARNER R.A.M.C. No 814/0 Pte W.G. RANNER R.A.M.C. } to have taken on the strength	Appendix

1875 W. W.593/826 1,000,000 4/15 J.B.C. & A. A.D.S.S./Forms/C. 2118.

Army Form C. 2118

WAR DIARY
INTELLIGENCE SUMMARY
(Erase heading not required.)

Instructions regarding War Diaries and Intelligence Summaries are contained in F. S. Regs., Part II. and the Staff Manual respectively. Title Pages will be prepared in manuscript.

Place	Date	Hour	Summary of Events and Information	Remarks and references to Appendices
MORLANCOURT	July 22nd	2 am	Orders received for 2nd Division to proceed at 12 noon to main Dressing Station, XIII Corps at DIVE COPSE. J.24.b (Map 62D) Bearer Division to remain at MORLANCOURT and to be attached to the 99th Infantry Brigade & to move with it on orders being received.	
"	"	12 noon	2nd Division marched to DIVE COPSE.	
DIVE COPSE			Reported arrival to O.C. Main Dressing Station XIII Corps. E hive of 4 Hospital Marquees (Small) taken over for treatment of wounded. There (were) four tents one for (1) Reception tent – (2) Waiting tent (3) Dressing Tent (4) Evacuation Tent. Motor Ambulance Cars handed over to O.C. M.D.S. for use of XIII Corps for collection wounded from Advanced Dressing Stations & transport to DIVE COPSE. Further instructions from A.D.M.S. Lieut. A. MACINTYRE and Lieut. K. PRETTY, R.A.M.C with 2 NCO's & 15 men proceeded for temporary duty to No 21 Casualty Clearing Station.	

1875 Wt. W593/826 1,000,000 4/15 J.B.C. & A. A.D.S.S./Forms/C. 2118.

WAR DIARY
INTELLIGENCE SUMMARY
(Erase heading not required.)

Army Form C. 2118

Instructions regarding War Diaries and Intelligence Summaries are contained in F.S. Regs., Part II. and the Staff Manual respectively. Title Pages will be prepared in manuscript.

Place	Date	Hour	Summary of Events and Information	Remarks and references to Appendices
DIVE COPSE	July 23rd	—	Bearer Division to be attached to 6th Infantry Brigade — not yet — Routine —	Army
"	24th	—	Orders received to send a motor Cart to "Walking Wounded Collecting Station" at BRONFAY FARM (F.29.6.5.1) (M.1:40,000 62.D) for duty until further orders. Bearer Division is still at MARICOURT. Ford Car No. A.D.17521 struck by shell, & put out of action, while conveying wounded at advanced dressing Station — No. Pte STUTHERIDGE. R.A.M.C. slightly wounded in the arm, but remained at duty. 19M.T./B24/86 Pte S. JONES. A.S.C. M.T. the driver of the Car suffering from shell shock.	Army
"	25th	—	No. 64426. Pte L.S. HAMMER. R.A.M.C. } moved to BRONFAY FARM for clerical No. 64050. Pte W.S. MARCHBANKS. R.A.M.C } work at the Walking Wounded Collecting Station in accordance with instruction from late D.D.M.S. XIII Corps.	Army

1875 Wt. W593/826 1,000,000 4/15 J.B.C. & A. A.D.S.S./Forms/C. 2118.

WAR DIARY
INTELLIGENCE SUMMARY

Army Form C. 2118

Instructions regarding War Diaries and Intelligence Summaries are contained in F.S. Regs., Part II. and the Staff Manual respectively. Title Pages will be prepared in manuscript.

(Erase heading not required.)

Place	Date	Hour	Summary of Events and Information	Remarks and references to Appendices
DIVE COPSE	July 25th	(cont)	Beaver Division proceed with 6th Infantry Brigade to a position South of MONTAUBAN about K.2.d. (map 62.C) & are in reserve. The Vehicles after unloading, & the Ambulance wagons to proceed to SAPPER CORNER E.9.d.9.1. (map 62 D.)	
"	26th	—	No T4/056017 Driver A. DYE A.S.C. M.T. reported unfit for "Hospital".	Casualty
"	27th	—	Casualties. No 64176 Pte (A/Lcpl) J.A. REDICK R.A.M.C. and No M/32173 Pte H. STAFFORD A.S.C. M.T. killed by shell while on duty in evacuating wounded from BERNAFAY WOOD on Ford Car No A.M.17521 which was severely damaged.	Casualty
"	28th	—	No 64635 Pte J WATSON R.A.M.C., Evacuated suffering from severe Shell Shock.	Casualty

WAR DIARY

INTELLIGENCE SUMMARY

Army Form C. 2118

Place	Date	Hour	Summary of Events and Information	Remarks and references to Appendices
DIVE (6 PSE)	July 28th	(cont)	Orders received from ADMS at 4:30pm to send men of this Division into 74th to BERNAFAY WOOD. (S.22.d.8.2. Map 57c) instructed to relieve some of the exhausted Bearers – H.Q. NCOs & men sent up at 5:30 pm.	
"	29th	1.0am	Bearer Division 100 Fd. moved out to BERNAFAY WOOD & took over the Bearer Post. All the 2nd Division Bearers are now under direct control of our ADMS & my own Bearers receive no nghn from me. Casualties: Pte 74322 Pte A.T. PRITCHARD, R.A.M.C. – wounded & evacuated. The Bearers from late Third Division who went up yesterday for a temporary relief – returned this evening & being reported as having done excellent work.	

WAR DIARY
INTELLIGENCE SUMMARY

Place	Date	Hour	Summary of Events and Information	Remarks and references to Appendices
DIVL COOSE	July 29th	Cont	Late Casualties	
			No 64713. Pte. W. GOLIGHTLY. RAMC — Since wounded & since died & bur.	
			No 38467. Pte. B.W. THORN. RAMC. wounded.	
			No 66915. Pte J.C. STURMEY. RAMC. wounded.	
			These men were evacuated.	
			Report from OC Bearer Division states that the NCOs & men are working splendidly & mentions Ptes. Gutsui, Cowes, Willis, Scribbery, Thomas, Callworth as showing patience, coolness, courage & fine example amongst their men.	Army
" "	30th	—	Lieut. R H WILSON. RAMC (Temp) rejoined this unit from temporary duty with 2nd DAC	
			No M/2 13248b. Pte. S. JONES, ASC M.T. proceeded to 2nd D.S.C. to be evacuated to the Base with No A.T. 17521 Ford Car. He is struck off the strength	Army

WAR DIARY or INTELLIGENCE SUMMARY

Army Form C. 2118

(Erase heading not required.)

Instructions regarding War Diaries and Intelligence Summaries are contained in F. S. Regs., Part II. and the Staff Manual respectively. Title Pages will be prepared in manuscript.

Place	Date	Hour	Summary of Events and Information	Remarks and references to Appendices
DIVE COPSE	July 30th		O.C. Bearers reports that the bearers failed to get through twice 15 hrs owing to heavy Rifle & m.g. fire & snipers. Their wounded orig letter is locality of the shelling. So Lieut P. J. LANE was sent with aspt squads to see what he could do. He managed to get three squads through safely & after waiting an opportunity three squads of N.S.F.A. were pushed through later to them arriving & all their bearers collected & evacuated. Lieut Lane's action was an extremely plucky one, & in connection with this Cpl Walton & Pte Rodgers of No 6 F.A. are mentioned as being very forward & helpful in their work & a fine example to the stretcher bearers. See report for No. 11 J Thwait in this place of their devotion to the exemplary coolness & cool behaviour under heavy fire. Pte Sutanie & Pte Sowell of No 7 F.A. there men were of great assistance in their fine example, volunteering to any dangerous errunias when numbers hp called for. When infantry men, RSM O & Sergt Men must had team retrieved stretcher-wounded & in team through the in ways of shelling, the heavy officers here stone up like a Beacon light."	Army

1875 SW. W593/826 1,000,000 4/15 J.B.C. & A. A.D.S.S./Forms/C. 2118.

WAR DIARY
INTELLIGENCE SUMMARY
(Erase heading not required.)

Army Form C. 2118

Place	Date	Hour	Summary of Events and Information	Remarks and references to Appendices
Dive Copse	July 31st	—	Casualties Lieut. P.J. Lane R.A.M.C. (temp) slightly wounded but still at duty. Lieut. S.J. Cowell R.A.M.C. (temp) wounded (not severely) & evacuated to Shrub Hill last night & this a.m. [signature] Lieut Colonel R.A.M.C. O.C. 100 Field Ambulance	

Army Form C. 2118

140/14/34

Vol 10

WAR DIARY
or
INTELLIGENCE SUMMARY

(Erase heading not required.)

CONFIDENTIAL

WAR DIARY
of
100 Field Ambulance
August 1st to August 31st
Volume 10.

33 ft 2 10½

COMMITTEE FOR THE
MEDICAL HISTORY OF THE WAR
Date 30 OCT. 1916

WAR DIARY or INTELLIGENCE SUMMARY

Army Form C. 2118

(Erase heading not required.)

Place	Date	Hour	Summary of Events and Information	Remarks and references to Appendices
DIVE COPSE J.24.6. Map (62J)	August 1st	—	One man evacuated sick & struck off her strength.	Wounded & Struck off over Fun
"	2nd	9 am	Bearer Divisn 100 F.A. relieved at BERNAFAY WOOD (S.28. map 57c) by Bearer Divisn of 6 F.A. & proceeded to BRONFAY FARM (F.29.6.5.1. map 62.D) to Reserve.	
"	"	—	Lieut R. H. WILSON R.A.M.C. & 8 other ranks proceeded to BRONFAY FARM for temporary duty with XIIIth Corps Walking Wounded Collecting Station	Spring
"	3rd	—	Three privates R.A.M.C. 100 F.A. wounded & evacuated & struck off the strength One " " " " " Six " " " sick Reinforcements reported for duty & were taken on Strength.	Spring Spring
"	4th	—	On Strength. Routine —	
"	5th	—	Received Ford Car No 145530 vice one put out of action by shellfire & sent to Base —	
			Two R.A.M.C & in A.D.O. Int. privates, reinforcements reported for duty, & were taken on the strength.	Army

Army Form C. 2118

WAR DIARY
INTELLIGENCE SUMMARY
(Erase heading not required.)

Instructions regarding War Diaries and Intelligence Summaries are contained in F. S. Regs., Part II. and the Staff Manual respectively. Title Pages will be prepared in manuscript.

Place	Date	Hour	Summary of Events and Information	Remarks and references to Appendices
DIVE COPSE	August 6th	—	Routine.	Sweeney
"	7th	—		
"	8th	—	Lieut. A.G. WINTER (from C (T.C.) joined this unit for duty & was taken on the strength.	Sweeney
"			4 Privates R.A.M.C reinforcements reported for duty & were taken on the strength.	
"	9th	—	Lieut. A.G WINTER D.A.C proceeded to Walking Wounded Collecting Sta at BROW FAR FARM Vice Lieut. R.H. WILSON who joined Bearer Division	Sweeney
"		9 to 4.A.		
"			One Private A.S.C. M.T. wounded & evacuated & struck off Strength.	
"	10th	—	Bearer Division too 7A proceeded to SAND PIT Area (E.16.d. in to G & D) with 99th Infantry Brigade.	Sweeney
"	11th	—	Bearer Division to 7A proceeded from SAND PIT Area to MERICOURT	Sweeney

1875 Wt. W593/826 1,000,000 4/15 J.B.C. & A. A.D.S.S./Forms/C. 2118.

Army Form C. 2118

Instructions regarding War Diaries and Intelligence Summaries are contained in F. S. Regs., Part II. and the Staff Manual respectively. Title Pages will be prepared in manuscript.

WAR DIARY
or
INTELLIGENCE SUMMARY
(Erase heading not required.)

Place	Date	Hour	Summary of Events and Information	Remarks and references to Appendices
DIVE COPSE	11th (cont)		Sending the Horses & Transport to a point on the BRAY–CORBIE ROAD to meet Transport of Tent Division.	
"	"	2 pm	Transport of Tent Division left DIVE COPSE – having picked up the Transport of the Bearer Division, the whole proceeded to DOURS to join 2nd Divisional Train & to march to ST SAUVEUR. (map France – AMIENS 1:100,000)	
"	"	5 pm	Tent Division left DIVE COPSE & marched to MERICOURT & joined the Bearer Division.	Appendix
MERICOURT	12th	–	Field Ambulance remained for the day awaiting further orders.	Appendix
"	13th	–	F.A. left unit at 10.30 a.m. leaving MERICOURT at 11 am Arrived at SALEUX (map AMIENS 1:100,000) at 2.30 pm & marched to ST SAUVEUR	Appendix
ST SAUVEUR	"	–		
"	14th	–	H.Q. open for reception & evacuation of Sick.	Appendix
"	15th	–	One Private R.A.M.C. reinforcement reported for duty & taken on Strength.	Appendix

Route

Army Form C. 2118

WAR DIARY
or
INTELLIGENCE SUMMARY
(Erase heading not required.)

Instructions regarding War Diaries and Intelligence Summaries are contained in F. S. Regs., Part II. and the Staff Manual respectively. Title Pages will be prepared in manuscript.

Place	Date	Hour	Summary of Events and Information	Remarks and references to Appendices
St SAUVEUR	August 16	—	Routine. Two men 100 F.A. evacuated sick to New Zealand Sr. F.P. at AMIENS & struck off strength.	
	"	2 pm	F.A. left ST SAUVEUR & marched to WARGNIES (Map. LENS. 1:100,000)	Fine
WARGNIES	"	5.30 pm	F.A. arrived at WARGNIES & billetted for the night.	
	" 17	9.30 a.m.	F.A. left WARGNIES & marched to MAIZIER. (Map. LENS. 1:100,000)	Fine
MAIZIER	"	2.30 pm	F.A. arrived at MAIZIER	
	" 18	5.30 a.m.	F.A. marched to VAUCHELLES-LES-AUTHIE (I 33.a. Map 57.D.)	
VAUCHELLES	"	12.45 pm	F.A. arrived at VAUCHELLES.	
	"	—	Instructions from A.D.M.S. 2nd Division Lieut. D.S. CASSIDY. R.A.M.C. & one Tent Subdivision (Personnel) proceed to the Corps Operating Station at AUTHIE (I.16.a. Map 57.D.) for temporary duty.	
	" 19	—	Orders received from A.D.M.S. for 100 F.A. to take over Main Dressing Station at COUIN (J.1.6) on 20th inst from No 4 Field Ambulance & to take over the advanced Dressing Station at HEBUTERNE (M.15.b.7.3)	Fine
				Map FRANCE 57.D

Army Form C. 2118

WAR DIARY
of
INTELLIGENCE SUMMARY
(Erase heading not required.)

Instructions regarding War Diaries and Intelligence Summaries are contained in F.S. Regs., Part II. and the Staff Manual respectively. Title Pages will be prepared in manuscript.

Place	Date	Hour	Summary of Events and Information	Remarks and references to Appendices
VAUCHELLES	August 19th	(cont)	and Field Ambulance billetings at COIGNEUX (S.9.b.1.3) from No 9 F.A. Went to look at Huts there also a dressing post at T.16.d.8.8. which had been used by No 9 F.O. as a medical dressing post	Surrey
COUIN	20th		100 F.A. Left VAUCHELLES at 12 noon and marched to COUIN & took over premises just vacated by No 4 F.A. (T.1.6.6.6.) Normal accommodation In huts - Officers 12. O.R. 120 Emergency accommodation In huts. Officers 20. O.R. 200	Map reference France Sheet 5.D. 1 in 40,000
		2.30 pm	Captain P.J. LANE RAMC proceeded with advance party to Advanced Dump Stn at HEBUTERNE (K.15.6.7.3) to take over from No 9 F.A. & learn his duties & route of evacuation	Surrey

1875 Wt. W593/826 1,000,000 4/15 J.B.C. & A. A.D.S.S./Forms/C. 2118.

6/

Army Form C. 2118

Instructions regarding War Diaries and Intelligence Summaries are contained in F.S. Regs., Part II. and the Staff Manual respectively. Title Pages will be prepared in manuscript.

WAR DIARY
or
INTELLIGENCE SUMMARY
(Erase heading not required.)

Place	Date	Hour	Summary of Events and Information	Remarks and references to Appendices
COVIN.	August 20th Cont.		No. 73703 Pte T.A. CARTER R.A.M.C. rejoined the Unit & again fallen in to strength. Captain T. BOURNE PRICE R.A.M.C. (Tp) departed for leave in lieu United Kingdom.	
"	21st	—	Main party under Captain R. H. Wilson proceeded to advanced dressing station. Remainder at T.9.6.1.3. & at J.16.d.S.E. were taken over from 9th Fd. A. holding party by 1 N.C.O. & 2 men were placed there on holding parties. Lieut. A.G. WINTER R.A.M.C.(T) under orders from A.D.M.S. proceeded to 23rd Royal Fusiliers as Regimental Medical Officer & struck off the strength of this Unit. Lieut V.M. COATES (R.A.M.C.(T.C.)) reported for duty with this Unit	

1375 Wt. W503/826 1,000,000 4/15 I.B.C. & A. A.D.S.S./Forms/C. 2118.

Army Form C. 2118

WAR DIARY
INTELLIGENCE SUMMARY
(Erase heading not required.)

Place	Date	Hour	Summary of Events and Information	Remarks and references to Appendices
COUIN	August 21st	Cont.	From 23rd Royal Fusiliers a taken on the strength of the unit.	
			To 66356 Pte F.G. SCRIBBENS R.A.M.C. evacuated to 2/1st South Midland C.C.S. suffering from Gastro Spinal Meningitis & struck off the strength of the unit.	
	22nd	—	Routine	
	23rd	—	Routine	
	24th	—	O.C. 2nd Division visited F.A. — Routine	
	25th	—	Routine —	
			To 74444 Pte E. HARRIS R.A.M.C. appointed acting Lance Corporal with pay whilst in charge of the Sanitary Squad. Two reinforcements, privates, joined for duty & taken on the strength.	
	26th	—	Routine —	

Army Form C. 2118

WAR DIARY
INTELLIGENCE SUMMARY
(Erase heading not required.)

Instructions regarding War Diaries and Intelligence Summaries are contained in F. S. Regs., Part II. and the Staff Manual respectively. Title Pages will be prepared in manuscript.

Place	Date	Hour	Summary of Events and Information	Remarks and references to Appendices
WIMN	August 27th	—	A.D.M.S. 2nd Division visited with reference to the hutting of this site for the hutment - Scheme Submitted. Buildings at POIGNEUX (J.9.C.4.3) handed over to No 67.A. with some equipment. The hutting party returned to H.Q.Ps.	Spring
"	28th	—	Routine. Captain T. BOURNE PRICE R.A.M.C (Tr.) returned from leave.	Spring
"	29th	—	Routine.	Spring
"	30th	—	Routine. Military Medal awarded to. No 38970 Sergeant J. McCALL R.A.M.C. No 66356 Private F.A. SCRIBBENS " 10 61651 " J. WILLIS " 10 64548 " M. GALLEWSKI "	
"	31st	—	Routine.	Spring

J.M.McC[signature]
O.C. No.7a.

1875 Wt. W593/826 1,000,000 4/15 J.B.C. & A. A.D.S.S./Forms/C. 2118.

2nd Div 2
Army Form C. 2118

2nd Div
SEPT 1916
140/1840
YM 11

WAR DIARY
INTELLIGENCE SUMMARY
(Erase heading not required.)

Instructions regarding War-Diaries and Intelligence Summaries are contained in F.S. Regs., Part II. and the Staff Manual respectively. Title Pages will be prepared in manuscript.

Place	Date	Hour	Summary of Events and Information	Remarks and references to Appendices

CONFIDENTIAL

War Diary
of
160 Field Ambulance
from September 1st to September 30th 1916.

Volume 11.

COMMITTEE FOR THE
MEDICAL HISTORY OF THE WAR
Date -3 JAN. 1917

1875 Wt. W593/826 1,000,000 4/15 J.B.C. & A. A.D.S.S./Forms/C. 2118.

WAR DIARY
or
INTELLIGENCE SUMMARY

(Erase heading not required.)

Army Form C. 2118

Place	Date	Hour	Summary of Events and Information	Remarks and references to Appendices
COUIN.	September 1st		Party of one NCO & 15 men sent to Advanced Dressing Stn to aug attack - As the carry was across the open, it was then decided to rig a trench from the Adv Dressing Stn (K.15.6.7.3. map 57D) to the Regimental Aid Post (K18a.u.5. map 57D) Lieut K. PRETTY R.A.M.C. proceeded for temporary duty with 252 Tunnelling Coy RE at BEAUSART. (P.11a map 57D) Sergeant (No 1048) W. MOORE. R.A.M.C. reported for duty with this Unit on Supernumary Diploma - from the Base - and is taken on the strength. No. 64062 Pte. C.W. MUIR. R.A.M.C. posted to 99th Machine Gun Coy for duty & is struck off the strength of this Unit.	

Signed
Lieut Col MacKenzie
O.C. 105 F.A.

WAR DIARY
INTELLIGENCE SUMMARY

Army Form C. 2118

Place	Date	Hour	Summary of Events and Information	Remarks and references to Appendices
ROUIN	September 2nd	—	Captain R.H. WILSON R.A.M.C proceeded to 23rd Royal Fusiliers for temporary duty with that Unit. Notice received of the promotion of No.66321 Quartermaster Sergeant F.W. JEFFRIES. R.A.M.C. to the rank of Sergeant Major. Orders received from A.D.M.S. for one Sergeant Major to proceed for duty to No.49 Casualty Clearing Station at CONTAY (U.26. map 57.D)	Spruce Bruce
	3rd	—	Routine.	
	4th	—	No.39251 Sergeant Major F. REASON R.A.M.C. proceeded to No.49 C.C.S. for duty & is struck off the strength of this Unit. In place of Sergt Major F.W. JEFFRIES R.A.M.C. Spruce	
	5th	—	A.D.M.S. 2nd Division having proceeded on leave & the wealth having proceeded to act as A.D.M.S. & handed over the charge of the Unit temporarily to Captain B.W. ARMSTRONG R.A.M.C. Spruce	

Army Form C. 2118

WAR DIARY
INTELLIGENCE SUMMARY
(Erase heading not required.)

Instructions regarding War Diaries and Intelligence Summaries are contained in F. S. Regs., Part II. and the Staff Manual respectively. Title Pages will be prepared in manuscript.

Place	Date	Hour	Summary of Events and Information	Remarks and references to Appendices
COUIN	September 5th		No 64640. Pte. A.S. STRADLING. R.A.M.C. proceeded as medical orderly to 2nd Divisional Train & to relieve Pte Shopter of this Unit.	Army Administration Copy received
			Took over temporary charge of Field Ambulance	
"	6th		No 83201 Pte A. ROBERTS } reported for duty & were taken on strength	B.W.A.
			No 72395 Pte B.E. RIPPON	
"	7th		Routine	P.W.A. 13W.A.
"	8th		"	
"	9th		Party of 15 men lent by No 55 F.A. proceeded to A.D.S. 100 F.H. to help in digging of new trench	B.W.A.
"	10th		Routine	13W.A.
"	11th		"	13W.A.
"	12th		Dental surgeon from No 29 C.C.S. replaced one from No 4 C.C.S.	B.W.A.

Army Form C. 2118.

WAR DIARY
INTELLIGENCE SUMMARY

(Erase heading not required.)

Instructions regarding War Diaries and Intelligence Summaries are contained in F.S. Regs., Part II. and the Staff Manual respectively. Title Pages will be prepared in manuscript.

Place	Date	Hour	Summary of Events and Information	Remarks and references to Appendices
COVIN	Sept. 13th	—	Returned to duty with the unit from a/Pltg 2nd Division.	Initial
"	14th	—	Lieut. R.H. Wilson R.A.M.C. (T.C.) returned from 23rd Royal Fusiliers for duty with the Unit.	Repng. Coving.
"	15th	—	Visited A.D.V. Dressing Stn. Trench work nearly finished. Routine.	Repng. Coving.
"	16th	—	No. 14190 Pte. H. Morrison R.A.M.C. posted to 1st King's Liverpool Regt. for water duties, & Shewell St. Lts strength of this unit. Capt. T. Bourne Price R.A.M.C. (T.C.) answered the Military Cross.	Repng.
"	17th	—	Trench work at A.D. Dressing Stn. being completed, the tents returned to H.Q. of Field Ambulance for duty.	Repng.
"	18th	—	Routine.	Repng.

1875. Wt. W593/826 1,000,000 4/15 J.B.C. & A. A.D.S.S./Forms/C. 2118.

Army Form C. 2118

WAR DIARY
INTELLIGENCE SUMMARY
(Erase heading not required.)

Instructions regarding War Diaries and Intelligence Summaries are contained in F.S. Regs., Part II. and the Staff Manual respectively. Title Pages will be prepared in manuscript.

Place	Date	Hour	Summary of Events and Information	Remarks and references to Appendices
COIGNEUX	Sept 19th	—	Appointments. No 663414. Corporal A.E. ROSE R.A.M.C. to be acting Sergeant. No 64641. Pte (a/L.Cpl.) J. FARTHING R.A.M.C. to be acting Corporal with Coy. Vacancy made by promotion of Q.M.S. JEFFRIES R.A.M.C. to Sergt. Major.	Appendix
"	20h	—	2nd Divisional Infantry being relieved by 39th Division, but under orders from A.D.M.S. 100 Fd. will keep the A.D.S. Dressing Stn. at HÉBUTERNE (K.15.b.7.3. huts STD) for collection of wounded & sick of 39th Division, who will be treated at Main Dressing Stn. 100 Fd.	
"	"	—	No. M2/140582. Corporal G.F. PIKE A.S.C. M.T. att to 100 Fd. evacuated to C.C.S. No. 131222. Pte. J. ROGERS " " " " evacuated to Base with Jaundice. Cor. No. 446. and struck off the strength. No M2/192635. Pte. G. SMILLIE A.S.C. M.T. reported for duty with MusDaimler Car. No 24957.	Appendix

1875 Wt. W593/826 1,000,000 4/15 J.B.C. & A. A.D.S.S./Forms/C. 2118.

Army Form C. 2118

WAR DIARY
or
INTELLIGENCE SUMMARY
(Erase heading not required.)

Instructions regarding War Diaries and Intelligence Summaries are contained in F. S. Regs., Part II. and the Staff Manual respectively. Title Pages will be prepared in manuscript.

Place	Date	Hour	Summary of Events and Information	Remarks and references to Appendices
GOUIN	Sept. 21st	—	No 3 Thos Sergeant J.W. EARNSHAW RAMC evacuated to C.C.S. Lieut. A MCINTYRE RAMC (T.C.) proceeded to 2/4th Royal Fusiliers for temporary duty.	[illeg]
"	22nd	—	Captain T. BOURNE PRICE RAMC proceeded for temporary duty as acting DADMS 2nd Division.	[illeg]
"	23rd	—	Lieut. V.M. COATES awarded the Military Cross.	[illeg]
"	24th	—	Routine	[illeg]
"	25th	—	Orders received from ADMS to detail a Medical Officer for permanent duty with 252 Tunnelling Company RE.	[illeg]
"	26th 11.30 a.m.		Orders received from ADMS for 100 Field Ambulance to be ready to move at no less than 1/4hr.	[illeg]

Army Form C. 2118.

WAR DIARY
or
INTELLIGENCE SUMMARY
(Erase heading not required.)

Instructions regarding War Diaries and Intelligence Summaries are contained in F. S. Regs., Part II. and the Staff Manual respectively. Title Pages will be prepared in manuscript.

Place	Date	Hour	Summary of Events and Information	Remarks and references to Appendices
COUIN	September 26th (cont)		Captain A. MACINTYRE. RAMC posted on M.O. to 252 Tunnelling Company RE	Army
"	27th		Captain A MACINTYRE RAMC proceeded to 252 Tn Coy RE for duty & struck off the strength of this Unit.	
			Lieut. K PRETTY RAMC proceeded to 24th Royal Fusiliers for temporary duty	
"	28th	-	Routine.	Army
"	29th	-	Orders received cancelling the order to be ready to move at 2 hours notice	Army
"	30th	-	Routine -	

J.A.W.Moore.
Lt. Col. RAMC
OC 100 Field Ambulance

146/349

2nd [ ]

100th Field Ambulance

Oct 1916

S/

COMMITTEE FOR THE
MEDICAL HISTORY OF THE WAR
Date −3 JAN. 1917

2nd Div.

Army Form C. 2118

Vol 12

WAR DIARY
or
INTELLIGENCE SUMMARY

(Erase heading not required.)

CONFIDENTIAL

WAR DIARY
of
100 Field Ambulance

October 1st to October 31st 1916.

Volume 12

WAR DIARY or INTELLIGENCE SUMMARY

Army Form C. 2118

(Erase heading not required.)

Instructions regarding War Diaries and Intelligence Summaries are contained in F.S. Regs., Part II. and the Staff Manual respectively. Title Pages will be prepared in manuscript.

Place	Date	Hour	Summary of Events and Information	Remarks and references to Appendices
COUIN	Oct 7 / 15	4 pm	Orders received from A.D.M.S. "100 Field Ambulance will take over Corps Collecting Station and Field Ambulance at ACHEUX in relief of a Field Ambulance of his 39th Division. On arrival the left at COUIN to deal with sick & wounded & continue evacuation of HEBUTERNE sector till relieved."	
"	"	—	2, 6, 4, 7 & 6 Pte. Q.A Coy R.T. R.A.M.C. evacuated sick to 27 C.C. & Struck off the Strength of this unit.	T. Guilford Lt Col R.A.M.C.
"	2nd	9 am	A Section we F.A marched from COUIN.	
ACHEUX	"	11 am	A Section 100 F.A. arrived. V.K. Coy R. Meeting station & Field Ambulance premises taken over from 134 th Field Ambulance. The accommodation in the Field Ambulance premises is poor & only sufficient for about 30 patients in different small rooms of portion of the "Maison de Retraite". There is a scheme on hand for the building of some huts in one house lean.	

Army Form C. 2118

WAR DIARY
or
INTELLIGENCE SUMMARY
(Erase heading not required.)

Instructions regarding War Diaries and Intelligence Summaries are contained in F. S. Regs., Part II. and the Staff Manual respectively. Title Pages will be prepared in manuscript.

Place	Date	Hour	Summary of Events and Information	Remarks and references to Appendices
ACHEUX	Feb. 2nd (continued)		The Corps Collecting Station is composed of 50 Marquee Tents, but all are not available for the housing of patients; some being used for store, operating tents etc, but lie remain du can shelter about 1200 patients including the marquees at the entraining point. "Walking" cases only an half with these being evacuated to No 29 Casualty Clearing Station by ambulance train. Map reference of Field Ambulance premises & Corps Collecting Station map of France No 57D. P. 13. a. 5. 4.	Appendix
"	3rd		Orders received from A.D.M.S. to hand over Divisional station at COIGNEUX, advanced Dressing station at HEROUTERNE, & Medical Inspector Post at THIEVRES on the 9/1st Highland field ambulance, 51st Division. Relief to be completed by 12 noon 4th inst. A Section to "A" & B section Bearer subdivision to join A Section at ACHEUX in the afternoon of the 4th inst.	Appendix

Army Form C. 2118

WAR DIARY
INTELLIGENCE SUMMARY
(Erase heading not required.)

Instructions regarding War Diaries and Intelligence Summaries are contained in F. S. Regs., Part II. and the Staff Manual respectively. Title Pages will be prepared in manuscript.

Place	Date	Hour	Summary of Events and Information	Remarks and references to Appendices
ACHEUX	Oct 4th	—	Field Ambulance premises at COVIN & advanced dressing station at HEBUTERNE handed over to O.C. 2/1st Highland Field Ambulance.	
	5th	11.30 am	C Section & Bearer SubDivision of B Section joined Head Quarters of the Field Ambulance. Tent SubDivision of B Section still remained at the Corps Operating Station at AUTHIE.	
	6th	—	Lieut. A.C.B. BIGGS, R.A.M.C. (T.C.) Lieut. L. KILROE, R.A.M.C. (T.C.) joined for duty with the Unit & taken on its strength.	Appendix Appendix
	7th	—	Routine.	
	8th	—	Recruits of the Military Cross, vice Capt T. BOURNE PRICE R.A.M.C. & Lieut V.A. PEATES R.A.M.C. presented with moral ribbons by M.G.C. 2nd Division on parade.	
		—	No. M.S/3699 Corporal W LARDNER A.S.C. M.T reported for duty & taken on the strength of the Unit.	Appendix

Army Form C. 2118

WAR DIARY
INTELLIGENCE SUMMARY
(Erase heading not required.)

Instructions regarding War Diaries and Intelligence Summaries are contained in F.S. Regs., Part II. and the Staff Manual respectively. Title Pages will be prepared in manuscript.

Place	Date	Hour	Summary of Events and Information	Remarks and references to Appendices
AMIENS	8/4	4.30 pm	In accordance with instructions from A.D.M.S. 60 men of this Unit proceeded as a working party to No 5. F.A. Advanced Dressing Station.	January
"	"		D.M.S. Reserve Army & D.D.M.S. 4th Corps visited with reference to formation of Corps Collecting Station. Do now P.P. Marquees are the accell, then making room for about 1500 patients.	
"	9th		The 6 P.M. having received orders to send our Stores advanced dressing station to A.D.M.S. 2nd Australian Division, the working party from the F.A. returned to duty. Captain T. Bourne Price R.A.M.C. reported this Unit for duty from H.S. On 2nd Division. Lieut A.C.B. Biggs R.A.M.C. under instructions from A.D.M.S. proceeded to No. 56 Field Ambulance for duty a struck off the strength of this Unit.	January

Army Form C. 2118

WAR DIARY
or
INTELLIGENCE SUMMARY
(Erase heading not required.)

Instructions regarding War Diaries and Intelligence Summaries are contained in F. S. Regs., Part II. and the Staff Manual respectively. Title Pages will be prepared in manuscript.

Place	Date	Hour	Summary of Events and Information	Remarks and references to Appendices
ACHIEX	Aug 9th	—	Lieut K. PRETTY R.A.M.C. (T.F.) having been posted permanently for duty with 2/4th Roy al Fusiliers, is struck off the strength of this Unit. 70 Recruits have arrived & the work of treating them is proceeding.	Army
	10	—	Captain A. MACINTYRE R.A.M.C. rejoined this Unit from Temporary duty with 350th Tunneling Coy. R.E. Appointments No 44369 Corporal W. DUNDER (D) & L & A.Cpl. M.C. to be acting Lance Sergeant with pay. No 66529 Pte. C. BOYD, 64500 Pte W. QUINN (?) & 6304 Pte. J.V. THOMAS to be acting Lance Corporals with no pay.	Army

1875 Wt. W593/826 1,000,000 4/15 J.B.C. & A. A.D.S.S./Forms/C. 2118.

Army Form C. 2118

WAR DIARY
or
INTELLIGENCE SUMMARY
(Erase heading not required.)

Instructions regarding War Diaries and Intelligence Summaries are contained in F. S. Regs., Part II. and the Staff Manual respectively. Title Pages will be prepared in manuscript.

Place	Date	Hour	Summary of Events and Information	Remarks and references to Appendices
ACHEUX	Nov 11th	—	Instructions received from A.D.M.S. for Officers & N.C.O.s of the Bearer Division to proceed to advanced dressing stns to get field ambulance which will be the A.D.S. of the Division to learn the duty. These Officers & NCOs will be sent in turn & return when learner has been complete.	Army
"	12th	—	No. 49762 Pte J.S. Williamson R.A.M.C. proceeded to 2nd Div H.Qrs for temporary duty	Army
"	13th	—	Captain J.S. Cassidy R.A.M.C. with the 77th Sub-division S.B. Section returned to H.Q. of this unit from Corps Operating Station at AUTHIE. During the last 9 days, work for the improvement & expansion of the 8th Corps Collecting Station has been progressing satisfactorily each day — the "Buffer bar" for the men has been built up & a Mullin Scott & tent erected for the men's Buffet	

1875 Wt. W593/826 1,000,000 4/15 J.B.C. & A. A.D.S.S./Forms/C. 2118.

WAR DIARY
INTELLIGENCE SUMMARY

(Erase heading not required.)

Army Form C. 2118

Instructions regarding War Diaries and Intelligence Summaries are contained in F. S. Regs., Part II. and the Staff Manual respectively. Title Pages will be prepared in manuscript.

Place	Date	Hour	Summary of Events and Information	Remarks and references to Appendices
POPERINGHE	Feb 13 (continued)		& fitted with seats to accommodate 50 patients at a time — an officers Buffet tent has been fitted with table & seats — also Shelter erected NC — the additional P. Maguire tents have been erected & equipped with partitions, blankets etc — these tents have been laced together and torn? roses to make large halls where the patients can lie down & rest until the train is in readiness to evacuate them — such "hall" comfortably holds 100 patients lying down & each could take 130 to 140 if necessary — rings, chains, walking sticks & other comforts for the wounded have been obtained from the Red Cross stores & everything is ready for the reception of large numbers of "walking wounded" cases	January
"	"		Section of new ablution hut for the girls' ambulance is now complete. Section of new Cook House, oven etc is being erected	January

Army Form C. 2118

WAR DIARY
or
INTELLIGENCE SUMMARY
(Erase heading not required.)

Instructions regarding War Diaries and Intelligence Summaries are contained in F. S. Regs., Part II. and the Staff Manual respectively. Title Pages will be prepared in manuscript.

Place	Date	Hour	Summary of Events and Information	Remarks and references to Appendices
ACHEUX	Feb 15th		2nd Lt & Pte. J.J. WILLIAMSON R.A.M.C. rejoined unit from temporary duty with 2nd Div. H.Q. Ops.	Appendix Appendix
"	16th	—	Routine.	
"	18th		Rec'd instructions from D.D.M.S. 5th Corps. in connection with the reduction of establishment of officers in a field ambulance. Lieut. L. HOLROS R.A.M.C proceeding for duty into No 5 Field Ambulance & is struck off the strength of this unit	Appendix
"	19th	—	Routine.	Appendix
"	"	Rtn. -	Capt. A. MCINTYRE R.A.M.C again proceeded to 252 Tunnelling Coy R.E. for temporary duty.	
"	19.15	—	Routine	Appendix
"	20th	—	Routine	Appendix

WAR DIARY
INTELLIGENCE SUMMARY
(Erase heading not required.)

Army Form C. 2118

Instructions regarding War Diaries and Intelligence Summaries are contained in F. S. Regs., Part II. and the Staff Manual respectively. Title Pages will be prepared in manuscript.

Place	Date	Hour	Summary of Events and Information	Remarks and references to Appendices
ACHEUX	Oct 21st	—	D.D.M.S. & Corps visited into reference to requirements of personnel for Corps collecting the during forthcoming operations. In addition to the Bearer Division of this field Ambulance party up, me that sub-division will presently be required. In this case it will be replaced by a sub division of another Div. Field Ambulance to keep carry on the works. Building operation at the field ambulance is now complete & the Cookhouse with Oven the has been heated — an old building which was in the course of repair is taking over is now completed — the other story being able to accommodate 20 patients if necessary — the forward floor is to be used as a men's dining room —	[signature] [signature]
"	22nd	—	Ribeaco.	

Army Form C. 2118

WAR DIARY
or
INTELLIGENCE SUMMARY
(Erase heading not required.)

Instructions regarding War Diaries and Intelligence Summaries are contained in F. S. Regs., Part II. and the Staff Manual respectively. Title Pages will be prepared in manuscript.

Place	Date	Hour	Summary of Events and Information	Remarks and references to Appendices
ACHEUX	Oct. 23rd	—	One Officer & tent Subdivision of 50 to Field Ambulance - 37th Division arrived for duty at two Corps. Checking station in accordance with orders from D.M.S. 4th Corps.	
"	"	—	Reference approaching active operations - Instructions issued that the day of attack were to be designated "Z" day & the day preceding it be called "Y" day. Z day now fixed for 26th inst.	Appendix
"	24	—	Orders received from ADMS to detail one Bearer Division Officer & one Field Ambulance to proceed to MAILLY MAILLET (Q.7.a.8.0 map 57D.) on "Y" day & arrive there by 5 p.m. Z day is now postponed 48 hours.	Appendix
			70016/33676 Pte. J. MacDONALD RAMC M.T. evacuated sick of the Strength.	Appendix

Army Form C. 2118.

WAR DIARY
INTELLIGENCE SUMMARY
(Erase heading not required.)

Instructions regarding War Diaries and Intelligence Summaries are contained in F.S. Regs., Part II. and the Staff Manual respectively. Title Pages will be prepared in manuscript.

Place	Date	Hour	Summary of Events and Information	Remarks and references to Appendices
ACHEUX	Oct 24 (cont)	—	No 33343 Sergeant. A. W. HAMLINGTON R.A.M.C. evacuated & struck off the strength.	Army
"	25th	—	One tent subdivision (B section) 1/1th. Field Ambulance proceeded to No 4 Casualty Clearing Station for temporary duty in accordance with instructions from A.D.M.S.	Army
"	26th	—	Routine.	Army
"	27th	—	"Z" day postponed till 30th inst.	Army
"	"	—	Captain D. S. CASSIDY R.A.M.C. (T.C.) proceeded for duty temporarily with 2nd Ox. & Bucks. Regt.	Army
"	28th	—	No 94732 Pte. A. ABRAHAM R.A.M.C. proceeded to No 2 water column for duty & struck off the strength.	Army
"	"	—	"Z" day postponed. A.D.M.S. for 48 hours.	Army

Army Form C. 2118.

WAR DIARY
or
INTELLIGENCE SUMMARY

(Erase heading not required.)

Instructions regarding War Diaries and Intelligence Summaries are contained in F. S. Regs., Part II. and the Staff Manual respectively. Title Pages will be prepared in manuscript.

Place	Date	Hour	Summary of Events and Information	Remarks and references to Appendices
ACHEUX	Feb 28th	—	A.D.M.S. 2nd Division visited Field Ambulance & Corps Collecting Station.	Appency
"	30th	—	Routine - Capt. D.S. CASSIDY & Capt. A. MACINTYRE reported unit for temporary duty. Instructions for the A.D.M.S. 37th Division, the tent sub-division of the 30th Field Ambulance was withdrawn to again be known as 7th/4th F.A. "Z" day postponed till Nov 5th.	Appency
"	31st	—	No 69662 Pte H. ROLPH R.A.M.C. proceeded to H.Q. 2nd Division for temporary duty of ordinaries	Appency

Signed
B. LovelRANE
Lt Colonel
A.D.M.S. 2nd F.A.

1875   Wt. W593/826   1,000,000   4/15   J.B.C. & A.   A.D.S.S./Forms/C. 2118.

140/1249

2nd 100

100th Field Ambulance

Nov 1916

COMMITTEE FOR THE
MEDICAL HISTORY OF THE WAR
Date -3 JAN. 1917

Army Form C. 2118

WAR DIARY
or
INTELLIGENCE SUMMARY
(Erase heading not required.)

Vol 13

CONFIDENTIAL

WAR DIARY
of
100 Field Ambulance.

November 1st to November 30th 1916.

Volume 13.

Army Form C. 2118.

WAR DIARY
or
INTELLIGENCE SUMMARY
(Erase heading not required.)

Instructions regarding War Diaries and Intelligence Summaries are contained in F. S. Regs., Part II. and the Staff Manual respectively. Title Pages will be prepared in manuscript.

Place	Date	Hour	Summary of Events and Information	Remarks and references to Appendices
ACHEUX	November 1st	—	Routine	Staunton Lt. Col. RAMC
"	2nd	—	Routine. "Z" day is now fixed for 5th inst.	Appx
"	3rd	—	Routine.	Appx
"	4th	—	Routine. D.M.S. Fifth Army visited 51st Corps Collecting Station.	Appx
"	5th	—	Routine. "Z" day postponed indefinitely. Waiting to be wired in "W" day	Appx
"	6th	—	The following awards for gallantry in the field have been granted to the undermentioned officer & men of this Field Ambulance. Captain P.J. LANE R.A.M.C. (T.C.) Military Cross No. 66539 Private C. GOULD No. 64650 Private W. GUTHRIE } Military Medal	Appx
"	7th	—	Routine. "Z" day is now fixed for the 10th inst.	Appx
"	8th	—	Routine. "Z" day again postponed.	Appx
"	9th	—	Routine.	Appx

Army Form C. 2118.

WAR DIARY
INTELLIGENCE SUMMARY
(Erase heading not required.)

Place	Date	Hour	Summary of Events and Information	Remarks and references to Appendices
ACHEUX	Nov 10th	—	Routine. 1 day pass to 13th inst.	Journey Journey
"	11th	—	Routine	
"	12th	—	"Y" day. Three Officers & 100 O.R. proceeded to No 6 Field Ambulance en route to the Divisional advanced dressing station (The Red House) "Bus Iverence" Q.1.a.33. & K.33.c.2.6. for duty with the Divisional R.A.M.C. Stretcher Bearers.	Map Ref. Fonver 57.D
			5 Ambulance Cars sent to O.C. 6" Field Ambulance for duty in connection with the evacuation of wounded.	
			3 Ambulance Wagons sent to O.C. Divisional Collecting Station BEAUSSART (P.5.a.3.3. (Map 57.D)) for duty.	
			2 Ambulance Cars from 30 th M.A.C. arrived for duty as the Corps Collecting Station.	
			The Officers & Rest detachment of No 50 Field Ambulance 37 to Division arrived for duty at Corps Collecting Station	Journey

Army Form C. 2118.

WAR DIARY
INTELLIGENCE SUMMARY
(Erase heading not required.)

Place	Date	Hour	Summary of Events and Information	Remarks and references to Appendices
ACHEUX	Nov 13th	—	Captains D.S. CASSIDY & A. MACINTYRE R.A.M.C. proceeded to 6 Field Ambulance for duty with 2nd Divisional Medical Units.	
"	"	10 am	"Walking wounded" from Division at Collecting Station, & Field Ambulances & L't Corps began to arrive at Corps Collecting Station.	
"	"	—	The Director General A.M.S. & the D.M.S. Fifth Army visited the Corps Collecting Station.	
"	"	—	Captain G.W. WOOD R.A.M.C. (TR) reported for temporary duty at the Corps Collecting Station.	Source
"	14th	—	The Reserve Division 100 F.A. proceeded to advanced dressing station. The Advancing Ambulance Cars 109 TR sent to A.D.S. TR for duty. The following are numbers of admissions & evacuations from Corps Collecting Station from 10 am 13th to 10 am 14th (24 hours): Admissions Officers 38 O.R. 1650 Remaining 158 Total 2046 Evacuations 1644	Source

Army Form C. 2118.

WAR DIARY
INTELLIGENCE SUMMARY
(Erase heading not required.)

Instructions regarding War Diaries and Intelligence Summaries are contained in F. S. Regs., Part II. and the Staff Manual respectively. Title Pages will be prepared in manuscript.

Place	Date	Hour	Summary of Events and Information	Remarks and references to Appendices
ACHEUX	Nov 14th (Contd)		Inspector Medical Services (Surgn General MacPherson), D.M.S. Army & D.D.M.S 1st Corps visited Corps Collecting Station. Casualties. Three privates R.A.M.C. 100 F.A. wounded & evacuated.	Appency
"	15th	—	Admissions & Evacuations Corps Collecting Station from 10 a.m 14th till 6.10 a.m today. Admissions Officers 16 O.R. 750 Prisoners 195 Total 961 Evacuations 1197 Casualties 100 F.A. No 44782 Private T.J. Wilkinson R.A.M.C. killed in action. Two privates wounded & evacuated. Five privates lightly wounded but remained at duty.	Appency Appency Appency

Army Form C. 2118.

WAR DIARY
or
INTELLIGENCE SUMMARY

(Erase heading not required.)

Place	Date	Hour	Summary of Events and Information	Remarks and references to Appendices
ACMFUX.	Nov 16th	—	Admission & Evacuation Corps Collecting Station 10 am 15th inst. to 10 am today.	
			Admission	
			Officers . 9	
			O.R. 500.	
			French soldiers . 8.	
			Prisoners . 38	
			Total . 555	
			Evacuation	
			390.	
			Orders received from D.D.M.S. 4 Corps "100 Field Ambulance will be relieved by a Field Ambulance of 32nd Division on 17th inst. O.C. 100 F.A. & Guard have however to remain at Corps Collecting Station until further orders from D.D.M.S. O.C. 100 F.A. to remain in command of Corps Collecting Station for present."	Appny

Army Form C. 2118.

WAR DIARY
INTELLIGENCE SUMMARY
(Erase heading not required.)

Instructions regarding War Diaries and Intelligence Summaries are contained in F. S. Regs., Part II. and the Staff Manual respectively. Title Pages will be prepared in manuscript.

Place	Date	Hour	Summary of Events and Information	Remarks and references to Appendices
ACHEUX	Nov. 17th	—	Admissions at Meredith Corps Clearing Station 10 am 16 Evg Total today. Admissions Officers 1. O.R. 176. Prisoners 48. Total 225. Evacuations 388. Major R.G. MEREDITH R.A.M.C. & Captain H.A. CUTLER R.A.M.C. (T.C.) arrived for temporary duty at Corps Clearing Station. 91st Field Ambulance arrived for duty in relief of 100 (Field) Ambulance. Beaver Division 91st Fd proceeded to 32nd Divisional Beaver Division in for duty while Fd. Division Unwounded at ACHEUX for duty at Corps Clearing Station	appeny

2449 Wt. W14957/M90 750,000 1/16 J.B.C. & A. Forms/C.2118/12.

WAR DIARY
INTELLIGENCE SUMMARY

Army Form C. 2118.

Place	Date	Hour	Summary of Events and Information	Remarks and references to Appendices
ACHEUX	Nov 17th	(cont)	Instrs orders from D.D.M.S. Vth Corps that one officer and two SubDivisions 50th Field Ambulance (37th Div.) proceeded to Vth Corps Rest Station for duty. Captain. A. MACINTYRE. R.AM.C. (T.C.) returned to the Field Ambulance from 2nd Divisional Medical Unit, & proceeded to 1st Kings Liverpool Regiment for temporary duty.	
		2.30pm	Lieut. Atherton A.D.M.S 2nd Division, Captain CASSIDY & Captain COATES with me took Lieut.Chisholm 100 feet proceeded to Cinema Theatre SARTON. to open for the reception given. The Beaver Division 100 ft. returned to No 6 Field Ambulance at BERTRANCOURT, from his attendance Evening Station	Appendix

Army Form C. 2118.

WAR DIARY
or
INTELLIGENCE SUMMARY

(Erase heading not required.)

Place	Date	Hour	Summary of Events and Information	Remarks and references to Appendices
ACHEUX	Nov 18th	—	Administration & Evacuation. Corps Collecting Station. 10 a.m. 17th inst to 10 a.m. today. Admission Officers 4 O.R. 171 T.O.T. 175 Evacuation 142 Lieut. G W BERESFORD. R.A.M.C. (T.C.) arrived for temporary duty at Corps Collecting Station. Handing over of Corps Collecting Station & Field Ambulance premises at ACHEUX proceeding. D.M.S. Fifth Army visited Corps Collecting Station.	heavy

WAR DIARY or INTELLIGENCE SUMMARY

Army Form C. 2118.

(Erase heading not required.)

Place	Date	Hour	Summary of Events and Information	Remarks and references to Appendices
ACHEUX	May 18th (cont)		Reach Division 100 Field Ambulance returned to ACHEUX from BEAUMONT.	
"	"	6 p.m.	Under orders from A.D.M.S. 2nd Division the Field Ambulance Hors., O.C. & Headquarters & the no Tent Subdivisions (already at JARTON) proceeded to BARTON.	
"	19th	—	Admissions & Evacuations. Corps Collecting Station – 10 a.m. 18th up to 10 a.m. today	

Admissions
Officers   28.
O.R.   988.
Prisoners   92
Total   1108

Evacuations
          1016.

Captain BRYSON & Captain STEWART. R.A.M.C. (T.C.) arrived for temporary duty with V Corps Collecting Station.

(Signed) ?

Army Form C. 2118.

WAR DIARY
INTELLIGENCE SUMMARY
(Erase heading not required.)

Place	Date	Hour	Summary of Events and Information	Remarks and references to Appendices
ACHEUX	November 19th & 20th	—	1/0 Field Ambulance marched from BERTON to BEAUVAL.	Annex
"	20th		Handed over 1/1 Corps Collecting Station & Field Ambulance premises to O.C. 91st Field Ambulance.	
			Admission & evacuation 1/1 Corps Collecting Station. 10 a.m. 19th to 10 a.m. today.	
			Admission Officers 12. O.R. 340. Prisoners 13. Total 365.	Evacuation 238.
			Total admission 10 a.m. 13th to 10 a.m. 20th (7 days). 5435. Total Evacuation " " " " " " 5015. Remaining. 420.	Annex

WAR DIARY
INTELLIGENCE SUMMARY
(Erase heading not required.)

Army Form C. 2118.

Place	Date	Hour	Summary of Events and Information	Remarks and references to Appendices
BEAUVAL	November 20th (cont)		Instrs. rolws from D.D.M.S. & to Capn. Y proceeded from HETEUX to join my unit at BEAUVAL.	Steven
GORGES	21st	—	Field Ambulance moved from BEAUVAL to GORGES	Steven
			Two O.R. of this unit invented to C.C.S. & these off the strength.	Steven
"	22nd	—	Field Ambulance remained at GORGES.	Steven
½ BEAUVAL	23rd	—	Field Ambulance marched from GORGES to RIBEAUCOURT.	Map reference FRANCE LENS. 11. 1/100,000
			Captain. V.M. COATES, M.C. R.A.M.C. (T.C.) proceeded to 1st. Roy al Berkshire Regt. for temporary duty.	
			5 reinforcements (in ranks) reported for duty & have taken on the Strength of this unit.	Steven

Army Form C. 2118.

WAR DIARY
INTELLIGENCE SUMMARY
(Erase heading not required.)

Instructions regarding War Diaries and Intelligence Summaries are contained in F. S. Regs., Part II. and the Staff Manual respectively. Title Pages will be prepared in manuscript.

Place	Date	Hour	Summary of Events and Information	Remarks and references to Appendices
GAPENNES	Nov. 24th	—	Field Ambulance marched from RIBEAUCOURT to GAPENNES. (Map ref. France ABBEVILLE. 14. 1/80000) I.O.R. seconded to C.C.S. & three officers.	Army
CAOURS	25th	—	Field Ambulance marched from GAPENNES to CAOURS —	Army
"	26th	—	F.A. remained at CAOURS.	
CONTEVILLE	27th	—	F.A. marched from CAOURS to CONTEVILLE. (map ref Lens. 11. 1/10000). Billets at L'ABBAYE D'AMONT FARM.	Army
"	28th	—	Orders from A.D.M.S. 2nd Division to open a Divisional Rest Station. There is no suitable accommodation for them present — awaiting further instructions.	Army
"	29th	—	Proceeded on leave to U.K. handed over temporary command of Field Ambulance to Captain B.W. ARMSTRONG, R.A.M.C. (TC)	Army

2449 Wt. W14957/M90 750,000 1/16 J.B.C. & A. Forms/C.2118/12.

Army Form C. 2118.

WAR DIARY
or
INTELLIGENCE SUMMARY

(Erase heading not required.)

Instructions regarding War Diaries and Intelligence Summaries are contained in F. S. Regs., Part II. and the Staff Manual respectively. Title Pages will be prepared in manuscript.

Place	Date	Hour	Summary of Events and Information	Remarks and references to Appendices
BONTEVILLE	29th		Assumed temporary command of F.A. during absence of Lt. Col. E.H.W. MOORE R.A.M.C. Managed to secure from proprietors of farm one room of type January which on advice of A.D.M.S. who visited F.A. I transferred personnel every recommendation for a larger number of R.S. patients in the barn where own staff were sleeping — the floor of which barn is deep in old straw manure. Must in normal to move before the place is habitable of reinforcements (2 male R.A.M.C.) joined today known taken on to strength of F.A.	R.M. Murphy
	30th		A.D.M.S. with A.A. & Q.M.G. 2nd Div. visited F.A. His memo to can with me the possible recommendation. 7 Nissen huts promised for use as wards for sick — Huts arrived in afternoon 8 R.A.M.C. reinforcements (No 8645 Sgt R.J. COLEMAN & 7 privates) joined today known taken on strength of F.A.	R.M.

140/1900

2nd Div.

100th Field Ambulance

COMMITTEE FOR THE
MEDICAL HISTORY OF THE WAR

Date **31 JAN. 1917**

Army Form C. 2118.

Vol 14

WAR DIARY
or
INTELLIGENCE SUMMARY
(Erase heading not required.)

Instructions regarding War Diaries and Intelligence Summaries are contained in F. S. Regs., Part II. and the Staff Manual respectively. Title Pages will be prepared in manuscript.

Place	Date	Hour	Summary of Events and Information	Remarks and references to Appendices
			CONFIDENTIAL

WAR DIARY

of

100 Field Ambulance

December 1st —— December 31st 1916

Volume 14. | |

Army Form C. 2118.

WAR DIARY
or
INTELLIGENCE SUMMARY
(Erase heading not required.)

Instructions regarding War Diaries and Intelligence Summaries are contained in F. S. Regs., Part II. and the Staff Manual respectively. Title Pages will be prepared in manuscript.

Place	Date	Hour	Summary of Events and Information	Remarks and references to Appendices
FONTEVILLE	Dec 1	—	Capt D.S. CASSIDY RAMC (T.C.) granted leave to UK 1/12/15 - 15/12/15. Selected site for 7 Nissen Bow Huts which we have received to be used as homes for sick & commenced erecting them	Nothing of importance
"	Dec 2	—	A.D.M.S. and Dr. visited F.A. this morning. Work of clearing out large dump for Red Cross Cases proceeding.	RMA
"	Dec 3	—	1 Nissen hut nearly completed — work has been very difficult owing to advancement plans in connection of any kind.	MA
"	Dec 4		Routine. Lieut W. THOMSON RAMC (T.C.) reported for duty. was taken on the strength of 7 Ambulance accordingly	
"	Dec 5		Capt T. BOURNE-PRICE RAMC (T.C.) & Capt VAN COATES RAMC (T.C.) rejoined unit today from temporary duty as D.A.D.M.S. & M.O. 1/R Berks Regt respectively.	MA
"	Dec 6		Capt R.A. WILSON RAMC (T.C) departed on leave to U.K. (5/12/15 — 20/12/15) A.D.M.S visited F.A.	MA

WAR DIARY or INTELLIGENCE SUMMARY

Army Form C. 2118.

Place	Date	Hour	Summary of Events and Information	Remarks and references to Appendices
CONTEVILLE	Dec 7		Capt T. BOURNE PRICE MC RAMC(TC) departed on leave to U.K. D.D.M.S. II Corps & A.D.M.S. 2nd Div visited F.A. this morning. Considerable inconvenience is being caused by the excessive amount of accommodation occupied by the "Q" men belonging to R.T.O. (Contiville) — who take up central block of large barn when Rest Station (No 2) are being fitted in addition to a second large barn more than large enough for their needs. Equivalent accommodation offered b.R.T.O. if he could vacate former have what he proposes is to remain to do without authority from ADMINISTRATIVE COMMANDANT III ARMY. Matter represented to D.D.M.S. II Corps today. Letters of commendation from G.O.C. 2nd Div received for & distributed to be made to the following N.C.O.S., Sergt D. FOREMAN RAMC (bt/a/sgt) DUNDERDALE a/L/Cpl THOMAS a/Cpl DUTTON	

Army Form C. 2118.

WAR DIARY
or
INTELLIGENCE SUMMARY
(Erase heading not required.)

Place	Date	Hour	Summary of Events and Information	Remarks and references to Appendices
Contville	Dec 8		Lt. W. Thomson. R.A.M.C. (T.C.) detailed for temporary duty with 24th R.F. & departed thither today	D.M.S.
	Dec 9		D.M.S. V Army visited F.A. this morning	D.M.S.
			Lt. Col. E.H.M. Moore reported and from leave in U.K.	D.M.S.
	Dec 10		Major General Walker V.C. & A.D.M.S. 2nd Div. visited F.A. this morning	D.M.S.
	Dec 11		Routine	D.M.S.
	Dec 12		Lt. Col. E.H.M. Moore R.A.M.C. departed for temporary duty as A.D.M.S. 2nd Div.	
	Dec 13		Under instructions from A.D.M.S. 2nd Div. Capt. P.J. Lane Mc Ran. (T.C.) departed this day for temporary duty with 24th R.F. in relief of Lt. W. Thomson. R.A.M.C. (T.C.) who reported unit.	D.M.S.

Army Form C. 2118.

WAR DIARY
or
INTELLIGENCE SUMMARY
(Erase heading not required.)

Instructions regarding War Diaries and Intelligence Summaries are contained in F. S. Regs., Part II. and the Staff Manual respectively. Title Pages will be prepared in manuscript.

Place	Date	Hour	Summary of Events and Information	Remarks and references to Appendices
CONTEVILLE	Dec 14		R.T.Os men finally ejected from R.S. train	MA
"	15		Routine	
"	16		Routine – Capt D.S. CASSIDY R.A.M.C. (T.C.) reported return from leave	BMA
"	17		in U.K. Routine	BMA
"	18		Capt V.H.M. COATES M.C. R.A.M.C (T.C.) departed on 14 days leave to U.K.	BMA
"	19		Routine	BMA
"	20		D.A.D.M.S. III Corps visited F.A.	MA
"	21		Capt R.H. WILSON reported return from leave in U.K. (22.12.16 – 1.1.17) Lieut & Q.Mr E.B SNOWDEN departed on leave to U.K.	
"	22		Capt D.S. CASSIDY detailed for temporary duty with 10th D.C.L.I.	BMA

Army Form C. 2118.

WAR DIARY
or
INTELLIGENCE SUMMARY

(Erase heading not required.)

Instructions regarding War Diaries and Intelligence
Summaries are contained in F. S. Regs., Part II.
and the Staff Manual respectively. Title Pages
will be prepared in manuscript.

Place	Date	Hour	Summary of Events and Information	Remarks and references to Appendices
CONTEVILLE	Dec 23	—	Routine	AMA
"	24	—	Lt Col E.H.M. MOORE rejoined unit for duty	AMA
"	25	—	Captain P.J. LANE RAMC (Temp) rejoined unit for temporary duty with 266th Field Ambulance	Appendix attached Copy
"	26th	"	Captain S.A. KUNY RAMC (Temp) joined this unit for temporary duty. Copy	
			Captain P.J. LANE RAMC (Temp) proceeded on 14 days leave to U.K. Copy	
"	27th	"	Captain B.W. ARMSTRONG RAMC (Temp) proceeded on 14 days leave to U.K. Copy	Appendix
"	28th	"	Lieut. W. THOMPSON RAMC (Temp) evacuated to Base - sick.	
			Undermentioned NCOs awarded the Military Medal.	Appendix
			No. 39905 Sergeant D. FOREMAN RAMC	
			" 495-69 Corpl. (a/a Sergt) W. DUNSFORD RAMC.	
			" 66354 Private (a/a Corpl) H. W. DUTTON RAMC	

Army Form C. 2118.

WAR DIARY
or
INTELLIGENCE SUMMARY
(Erase heading not required.)

Place	Date	Hour	Summary of Events and Information	Remarks and references to Appendices
CONTEVILLE	December 30th	—	Routine.	
"	31st	—	Routine.	

2nd Division
War Diaries
100th Field Ambulance

January, To 31st December
1917

Army Form C. 2118.

WAR DIARY
INTELLIGENCE SUMMARY
(Erase heading not required.)

Vol 15

CONFIDENTIAL

WAR DIARY.
of
100 Field Ambulance

January 1st to January 31st 1917.

Volume 15.

Army Form C. 2118

WAR DIARY
or
INTELLIGENCE SUMMARY
(Erase heading not required.)

Instructions regarding War Diaries and Intelligence Summaries are contained in F. S. Regs., Part II. and the Staff Manual respectively. Title Pages will be prepared in manuscript.

Place	Date	Hour	Summary of Events and Information	Remarks and references to Appendices
CONTEVILLE	January 1st		Routine	January 1st CONTEVILLE
"	2nd		No 39908 Sgt. D. FOREMAN R.A.M.C. in charge of drunkenness. Lieut. & Q.M. E. BROWDEN R.A.M.C. rejoined unit today from leave in U.K.	Routine
"	3rd		Routine	Routine
"	4th		Col 2nd Div. Train inspected horses & transport of F.A.	Routine
"	5th		Lt.Col. E.A.H.M. MOORE R.A.M.C. proceeded to 2nd Div. H.Q. as acting A.D.M.S. vice Col. W.L. GRAY. A.M.S. evacuated sick. Command of F.A. handed over temporarily to Capt. R.M. WILSON R.A.M.C. (T.C.)	Routine

1875 Wt. W593/826 1,000,000 4/15 J.B.C. & A. A.D.S.S./Forms/C.2118.

Army Form C. 2118

WAR DIARY
or
INTELLIGENCE SUMMARY
(Erase heading not required.)

Instructions regarding War Diaries and Intelligence Summaries are contained in F. S. Regs., Part II. and the Staff Manual respectively. Title Pages will be prepared in manuscript.

Place	Date	Hour	Summary of Events and Information	Remarks and references to Appendices
(INTENSE)	January 6th		Capt. T. BOURNE-PRICE MC RAMC (T.C.) reported unit for duty from return in U.K. & assumed command of F.A.	JBP Nov/VBP
"	7th		Capt. D.S. CASSIDY RAMC (T.C.) reported unit from temporary duty with 10th D.L.I.	VBP
"	8th	3.25 pm	Ambulance left ABBAYE D'AIMONT FARM & proceeded to LE MEILLARD arriving 7.30 pm	JBP
				Map Reference LENS (II) FRANCE JBP/100,000 JBP
LE MEILLARD	10		Capt. S.A. KUNY RAMC (T.C.) proceeded to 23rd R.E. & Capt. R.H. WITSON RAMC (T.C.) to 1st ROYAL BERKS — both for temporary duty.	JBP
LE MEILLARD	11th	7.45 am	Ambulance left LE MEILLARD & proceeded to PUCHEVILLERS arriving at 3.30 pm. (Capt. P.J. LANE MC RAMC (T.C.) reported from leave in U.K.	VBP
PUCHEVILLERS	12th	9 am	Ambulance left PUCHEVILLERS & arrived at AVELUY chateau at 6 pm. Taking over premises from 1/3 Highland F.A. & opened for reception of sick & wounded.	JBP

Army Form C. 2118

WAR DIARY
or
INTELLIGENCE SUMMARY
(Erase heading not required.)

Instructions regarding War Diaries and Intelligence Summaries are contained in F.S. Regs., Part II. and the Staff Manual respectively. Title Pages will be prepared in manuscript.

Place	Date	Hour	Summary of Events and Information	Remarks and references to Appendices
AVELUY	January 13th		Capt. B.W. ARMSTRONG R.A.M.C. (T.C.) rejoined and today from leave - U.K. & assumed command of F.A. D.D.M.S. 4th Corps visited F.A. this morning & D.D.M.S. 2nd Div this afternoon. Lt. & Q.M. E.B. SNOWDEN R.A.M.C. departed on special leave to U.K. (14th - 21st Jan). There is accommodation here for about 30 patients in cellars both reception and tunnel (both above ground) - The Chateau & vicinity is shelled occasionally and may, if made & advisable keep patients longer than necessary. Personnel is billeted in any good shelter but underground passages — old trenches with the town - but what they can arrange in case of necessity. All horses in stables.	Multimoeth Capt RAMC
	14th		Capt P.J. LANE. M.C. R.A.M.C. (T.C.) departed for temporary duty with 13th ESSEX Regt. Wounded admitted 2 O.R. Evacuated 2 O.R. to C.C.S.	R.W.A.

Army Form C. 2118

WAR DIARY
or
INTELLIGENCE SUMMARY
(Erase heading not required.)

Instructions regarding War Diaries and Intelligence Summaries are contained in F. S. Regs., Part II. and the Staff Manual respectively. Title Pages will be prepared in manuscript.

Place	Date	Hour	Summary of Events and Information	Remarks and references to Appendices
AVELUY	Jan 15th		Enemy shelling round for the morning. One shell very near "Section hutch". No casualties. A.D.M.S. visited H.Q. this afternoon. Capt V.M. Coates M.C. R.A.M.C. T.C. (Wounded) admitted 4 O.R. reported sick from leave in U.K. Shelled again evening & no.	MHA
"	16th		Routine. Some shelling. Wounded Admitted 1 officer 20 O.R. Evacuated 1 officer 1 O.R. to C.C.S. 2 O.R. to D.R.S.	BMA
"	17th		Rev N. Cooney C.F. evacuated sick to No 29 C.C.S. (Wounded) Admitted 13 O.R. Evacuated 10 O.R. to C.C.S. 5 O.R. to D.R.S.	RMA
"	18th		Capt-S.A. Kenny R.A.M.C. (TC) 23rd R.F. reported route from temporary duty with Wounded Adm Admitted 7 O.R. Evacuated 10 O.R. to C.C.S. 2 O.R. to D.R.S.	MMA

Army Form C. 2118

WAR DIARY
or
INTELLIGENCE SUMMARY
(Erase heading not required.)

Instructions regarding War Diaries and Intelligence Summaries are contained in F. S. Regs., Part II. and the Staff Manual respectively. Title Pages will be prepared in manuscript.

Place	Date	Hour	Summary of Events and Information	Remarks and references to Appendices
AVELUY	Jan 19th		Capt D.S. CASSIDY RAMC (T) detailed for temporary duty with 34th Bde R.F.A. & proceeded there today. Wounded Admitted 1 officer 3 O.R. Evacuated 1 officer to C.C.S. 1 O.R. to D.R.S.	RMH
	20th		A.D.M.S. visited F.A. this afternoon (Capt A. MACINTYRE RAMC (TC) posted for duty with 1st KINGS (The Liverpool Regiment) from today. W.E. struck off the strength of F.A. accordingly. Wounded Admitted 8 O.R. Evacuated 5 O.R. to C.C.S. 5 O.R. to D.R.S.	RMH
"	21st		Routine. Wounded Admitted 10 O.R. Evacuated 10 O.R. to C.C.S.	RMH
"	22nd		Sgt D. FOREMAN found guilty of drunkenness by F.G.C.M. & Award 2 of— Sentence promulgated today. Wounded Admitted 1 officer 11 O.R. Evacuated 1 officer 2 O.R. to C.C.S.	RMH

Army Form C. 2118

WAR DIARY
or
INTELLIGENCE SUMMARY
(Erase heading not required.)

Place	Date	Hour	Summary of Events and Information	Remarks and references to Appendices
AVELUY	Jan 23		Routine. Wounded. Admitted 3 O.R. Evacuated 3 O.R. to C.C.S.	ADMS
"	24		Capt. A. GALLETLY. R.A.M.C. (T.C.) reported for duty and was taken on to the strength of the unit. Interpreter M. DELVAS departed for duty with 5th Infantry Bde. Wounded. Admitted 9 O.R. Evacuated 9 O.R. to C.C.S.	ADMS
	25		Capt. F.D. FISHER. R.A.M.C. (T.C.) reported for duty and was taken on strength of unit. Wounded. Admitted 15 O.R. Evacuated 11 O.R. to C.C.S. 1 O.R. to D.R.S.	ADMS
	26		Capt. R.H. WILSON. R.A.M.C. (T.C.) posted as M.O. i/c 34th Bde R.F.A., Capt D.S. Cassidy R.A.M.C. (T.C.) posted as M.O. i/c 1st R. Berks, both from today's date. Strength off the strength of the unit accordingly. Capt. V.H.M. COATES M.C. (R.A.M.C. T.C.) to 20th Notts & Derby Regt. on temporary medical charge. Wounded admitted 3 O.R. Evacuated 3 O.R. to C.C.S. 1 O.R. to D.R.S.	ADMS ADMS

Army Form C. 2118.

WAR DIARY
or
INTELLIGENCE SUMMARY
(Erase heading not required.)

Instructions regarding War Diaries and Intelligence Summaries are contained in F. S. Regs., Part II. and the Staff Manual respectively. Title Pages will be prepared in manuscript.

Place	Date	Hour	Summary of Events and Information	Remarks and references to Appendices
AVELUY	June 27		Routine. Wounded. Admitted 2 O.R. Evacuated 4 O.R. to C.C.S.	BMA
	28		Routine. Wounded Admitted 12 O.R. Evacuated 7 O.R. to C.C.S. 1 O.R. to D.R.S.	BMA
	29		Capt. S.A. KUNY R.A.M.C. (T.C.) evacuated to No. 49 C.C.S. suffering from P.U.O. Appd. L/ me M.O. arranged reinft from temporary duty with 13th Essex Regt. Wounded admitted 16 O.R. Evacuated 4 O.R. to C.C.S. 2 died.	BMA
	30		Routine. Wounded Admitted 11 O.R. Evac 10 O.R. to C.C.S. 3 O.R. to D.R.S.	BMA
	31		Lt. Col. E.H.M. MOORE resumed work from temporary duty as A.D.M.S. 2nd Div. Wounded Admitted 1 officer. Evacuated 1 officer 14 O.R. to O.R.	BMA

2449 Wt. W14957/M90 750,000 1/16 J.B.C. & A. Forms/C.2118/12.

Army Form C. 2118.

WAR DIARY

INTELLIGENCE SUMMARY

(Erase heading not required.)

Vol 19

CONFIDENTIAL.

WAR DIARY
of
1 oo Field Ambulance
February 1st to February 28th 1917

Volume 16.

Army Form C. 2118.

WAR DIARY
INTELLIGENCE SUMMARY
(Erase heading not required.)

Instructions regarding War Diaries and Intelligence Summaries are contained in F. S. Regs., Part II. and the Staff Manual respectively. Title Pages will be prepared in manuscript.

Place	Date	Hour	Summary of Events and Information	Remarks and references to Appendices
AVELUY	February 1st		Routine -	
		1.	attended Conference at DDMS II.nd Corps into ADMS 2nd Division	President Lt Col Tam C.
	2		ADMS. 2nd Division visited the Field Ambulance. I accompanied ADMS. to ho 54 Field Ambulance - 18th Division - with reference to my taking over site, buildings, huts etc at AVELUY POST, With A.D.S.'s an Aeroplane Dressing Station - This is to be taken by a Field Division of ho 54 Fd. & 18th Division & a later Division of ho 100 Fd Ambulance - 2nd Division. Arrangements made for Equipment to be procured, as for temporary hints to be done - Party of 36 men, 100 FA sent over for road making.	hut of 5th D. (Frames) Approved

Army Form C. 2118.

WAR DIARY
INTELLIGENCE SUMMARY
(Erase heading not required.)

Instructions regarding War Diaries and Intelligence Summaries are contained in F. S. Regs., Part II and the Staff Manual respectively. Title Pages will be prepared in manuscript.

Place	Date	Hour	Summary of Events and Information	Remarks and references to Appendices
AVELUY	Sept 3rd		Orders received to send a party of 30 men for Tucker's cutting & hauling to AVELUY WOOD. Party went. AVELUY heavily shelled from 9.30 am till past midday. Casualties in the Field Ambulance. 1 N.C.O. wounded slightly by fragment of shell, but he remained at duty. The stall for 6 direct hits on one of the stables, killing 6 horses & wounding 2.	Stormy
	4th		Visited British Red Cross Stores at HEM, with reference to equipment for Corps Main Dressing Station. 2nd Lieut. D. FOREMAN. R.A.M.C. evacuated to Base, & struck off the strength of the F.A.	Stormy

Army Form C. 2118.

WAR DIARY
INTELLIGENCE SUMMARY
(Erase heading not required.)

Instructions regarding War Diaries and Intelligence Summaries are contained in F. S. Regs., Part II. and the Staff Manual respectively. Title Pages will be prepared in manuscript.

Place	Date	Hour	Summary of Events and Information	Remarks and references to Appendices
AVELUY	Feb. 5th	—	Work at AVELUY POST progressing slowly. Owing to heavy frost it is impossible to put on with the building of huts, or the erection of tents	Army
"	6th	—	Visited D.D.M.S. II'd Corps with reference to equipment for M.Bs. have frequent Station.	However
"	7th	—	1 OR R.A.M.C. returned from duty at Div. H.Q. Gr. & taken on strength of Mun. Field Ambulance. 1 horse had to be destroyed on account of a broken leg.	However
"	8th	—	No. 66304 Pte. J. V. THOMAS R.A.M.C. awarded the Medaille Militaire for Gallantry in the Field.	Army
"	9th	—	Routine	Appendix
"	10th	—	Routine	Appendix

Army Form C. 2118.

WAR DIARY
or
INTELLIGENCE SUMMARY
(Erase heading not required.)

Instructions regarding War Diaries and Intelligence Summaries are contained in F. S. Regs., Part II. and the Staff Manual respectively. Title Pages will be prepared in manuscript.

Place	Date	Hour	Summary of Events and Information	Remarks and references to Appendices
AVELUY	February 11th	-	No 303169. Staff Sergeant R. H. HENDERSON R.A.M.C. proceeded to England for a Temporary Commission in the Infantry & struck off the strength after noon.	Appendix
"	12th	-	Captain S.A. KUNK R.A.M.C. (T) proceeded to Base from No 49 Casualty Clearing Station & reinforcement applied for.	Appendix
"	13th	-	Bearer Officers & M.O. field Ambulance, having reconnoitred routes of Evacuation from 2nd Division's new front, attended a conference at A.D.M.S. 2nd Division in view of opening of active operations.	Appendix
"	14th	-	Routine.	Appendix
"	15th	-	Work sufficient for reception & treatment of 200 wounded at AVELUY POST completed.	Appendix

Army Form C. 2118.

WAR DIARY
INTELLIGENCE SUMMARY
(Erase heading not required.)

Place	Date	Hour	Summary of Events and Information	Remarks and references to Appendices
AVELUY	February 16th	7	Captain P.J. KANE. M.C. R.A.M.C (T) & Captain A. GALLETLY. with the Brown Division Main Fd A Ambulance proceeded to OVILLERS (X.8 central). They are to be in reserve. Captain T. BOURNE PRICE M.C. R.A.M.C (T) proceeded to POZIERES (X.4. central) as O.C. "Po in 5 Post". J 10th on AVELUY POST from O.C. 54 Fd (A) Ambulance. AVELUY shelled for 2 hours at nipur. & been been hit is in the Village.	Appuy
"	17th		The two Coys made an attack towards MIRAUMONT at 5.45 am. Wounded began coming to their Dressing Station about 6.30 am From 9 am onwards they were brought in very rapidly. All the Cases were by up cases, & a large percentage were turning wounded owing to which evacuation to the Casualty Clearing Station were sometimes slow, been relatively	Appuy

Army Form C. 2118.

WAR DIARY
INTELLIGENCE SUMMARY
(Erase heading not required.)

Instructions regarding War Diaries and Intelligence Summaries are contained in F. S. Regs., Part II. and the Staff Manual respectively. Title Pages will be prepared in manuscript.

Place	Date	Hour	Summary of Events and Information	Remarks and references to Appendices

MAILLY	February 17th (cont)		Admissions & Evacuations. 6 a.m. to 5 p.m.
			
			 2nd Division 18th Division
			 Officers. 4. 5.
			 O.R. 46. 67.
			 German 2 4
			       Total <u>55</u> <u>76</u>
			
			              Total two Divisions <u>121</u>
			
			 O.C. 2nd Div. Bearers having been evacuated sick, Captain T. BOURNE PRICE, M.C. R.A.M.C (T) proceeded from "POZIERES" Post" to COURCELETTE to take over charge of Bearer Division.	

Army Form C. 2118.

WAR DIARY
or
INTELLIGENCE SUMMARY
(Erase heading not required.)

Place	Date	Hour	Summary of Events and Information	Remarks and references to Appendices
NEUVE	February 18th		Admission & evacuations (wounded) 5 pm 17th inst to 6 am 18th inst.	
			2nd Division. 18th Division	
			Officers: 3. 11.	
			O.R. 69. 113.	
			Germans: 6. —	
			Total 78 124	Total both Divisions 202
			6 am to 6 pm	
			Officers: — 32.	
			O.R. 19. 4	
			Germans — —	
			Total 19 36	Total both Divisions 575
			Artillery again shelled from 4 pm to 6 pm.	

WAR DIARY
INTELLIGENCE SUMMARY
(Erase heading not required.)

Army Form C. 2118.

Place	Date	Hour	Summary of Events and Information	Remarks and references to Appendices
ALBERT	February 19	—	Casualties among personnel of 100 field ambulances – 2 Privates R.A.M.C. Killed 18th inst. 3 " " wounded " 1 N.C.O. R.A.M.C. died of wounds 19th inst. (admitted 18th) 1 Private " " " " " (admitted 17th) Admissions & Evacuations (wounded) 5pm 18th inst to 6 am 19th inst. 3rd Division 18th Division Officers 1 — O.R. 30 36 Germans 1 4 Total 32 40 Total both Divisions 72	Army

Army Form C. 2118.

WAR DIARY
or
INTELLIGENCE SUMMARY
(Erase heading not required.)

Place	Date	Hour	Summary of Events and Information	Remarks and references to Appendices
ANZAC	February 19th (cont)		Admissions & Evacuations (contd.) 6 am to 5 pm	
			2nd Division 19th Division	
			Officers. 1 —	
			O.R. 20 12	
			Servants. 1 —	
			Total 22 12 Total both Divisions 34	
"	20/16		5 pm 19th inst to 6 am 20th inst	
			Officers. — 2	
			O.R. 9 5	
			Servants. — 2	
			Total 9 9 Total both Divisions 18	

WAR DIARY
INTELLIGENCE SUMMARY

Army Form C. 2118.

Place	Date	Hour	Summary of Events and Information	Remarks and references to Appendices
AVELUY	January 26th (at)		Division & Evacuations (wounded) 6 a.m. to 5 p.m.	
			2nd Division 15th Division 11th Div.	
			Officers. 1. 6. Division	
			O.R. 4. 1.	
			Germans. — —	
			Total 6 7 15	
			Total from 6 a.m. 17th inst. to 5 p.m. 26th inst. 517	
			of whom died in main Dressing Station	
			2nd Division 18th Division	
			Officers. 1. 8.	
			O.R. 2. 1.	
			Germans —	
			Total 3 9 Total 12	

Army Form C. 2118.

WAR DIARY
INTELLIGENCE SUMMARY
(Erase heading not required.)

Place	Date	Hour	Summary of Events and Information	Remarks and references to Appendices
NELLY	February 20th (Cont)		No. 46292. Sergeant B. GOOCH RAMC joined for duty & is taken on the strength of this Field Ambulance.	Appendix
"	21st		Lieutenant H.R. MARSH RAMC (T) joined for duty & taken on strength of this Field Ambulance.	Appendix
"	22nd		D.D.M.S. 1st Corps visited here Dressing Station. To No 46 Sergeant W. MOORE RAMC proceeded to No 3 Casualty Clearing Station for duty & struck off the strength of this Field Ambulance.	
				Appendix
"	23rd		Artillery again shelled during the night.	Appendix

Army Form C. 2118.

WAR DIARY
or
INTELLIGENCE SUMMARY

(Erase heading not required.)

Instructions regarding War Diaries and Intelligence Summaries are contained in F. S. Regs., Part II. and the Staff Manual respectively. Title Pages will be prepared in manuscript.

Place	Date	Hour	Summary of Events and Information	Remarks and references to Appendices
AVELUY	February 23rd	—	The following appointments have been authorized to date from 13th inst. To acting Sergeant with pay. No 49569 Corporal W. DUNDERDALE. R.A.M.C. No 64419 Corporal C.H. ANDERSON. R.A.M.C. To acting Corporal with pay. No 84068 Pte. G. SINCLAIR R.A.M.C. No 66304 Pte. J. V. THOMAS R.A.M.C.	February
"	24th	—	Five R.A.M.C. (Privates) reinforcements reported for duty.	
"	25th	—	No 66457 Pte. W.G.E. TAYLOR R.A.M.C. proceeded to England for a Temporary Commission in the Infantry	February

2449 Wt. W14957/M90 750,000 1/16 J.B.C. & A. Forms/C.2118/12.

WAR DIARY

INTELLIGENCE SUMMARY

Army Form C. 2118.

Place	Date	Hour	Summary of Events and Information	Remarks and references to Appendices
AVELUY	February 26th	—	One (Private) reinforcement, reported for duty on deference. Vice Sgt W. MOORE.	Army
"	27th	—	Captain F.P. FISHER, R.A.M.C. (T) appointed as Medical Officer to the 1st K.R.R.C. & is struck off the strength of this unit.	
			Orders received from A.D.M.S to form a Divisional heavy Dressing Station at POZIERES on site at X.9.b.2.2.	Maps France 57.D
"	28th	—	Two Officers & 30 O.R. proceeded to POZIERES to begin work on the site of the new heavy Dressing Station.	January
			The Corps heavy Dressing Station having been dissolved, I handed over AVELUY Post to O.C. No 54 Field Ambulance & interviews personnel of 100 F.A.	

J. Littlewood
Lieut Col RAMC
O.C. 100 F.A.

Army Form C. 2118.

WAR DIARY
or
INTELLIGENCE SUMMARY
(Erase heading not required.)

Vol 20

Confidential

WAR DIARY OF 100 Field Ambulance

March 1917

Vol. 17.

[Stamp: OFFICER COMMANDING, 100TH FIELD AMBULANCE R.A.M.C., -2 APR 1917, No. 20.92/11]

Army Form C. 2118.

WAR DIARY
INTELLIGENCE SUMMARY
(Erase heading not required.)

Instructions regarding War Diaries and Intelligence Summaries are contained in F. S. Regs., Part II. and the Staff Manual respectively. Title Pages will be prepared in manuscript.

Place	Date	Hour	Summary of Events and Information	Remarks and references to Appendices
AVELUY.	March 1st	—	Visited site for new Main dressing Station near POZIERES at X.9.c.3.2. (Map of France. 57D.) with D.D.M.S. 2nd Division.	[initials]
"	2nd	—	Work begun on the ground at the site of new M.D.S. which is to be completed by the evening of the 4th inst.	[initials]
"	3rd & 4th	—	Work progressing — A.D.M.S. Anzac Corps arrived & said as the site of the M.D.S. was not of the 1st Corps Area, I should have gone back. This was reported to A/D.M.S. 2nd Division.	[initials]

2449 Wt. W14957/M90 750,000 1/16 J.B.C. & A. Forms/C.2118/12.

Army Form C. 2118.

WAR DIARY
or
INTELLIGENCE SUMMARY

(Erase heading not required.)

Instructions regarding War Diaries and Intelligence Summaries are contained in F.S. Regs., Part II. and the Staff Manual respectively. Title Pages will be prepared in manuscript.

Place	Date	Hour	Summary of Events and Information	Remarks and references to Appendices
AVELUY.	March 5th	11 a.m.	Orders received from 2/U.S. 2nd Corps to Strike Camp immediately & register it at X.9.a.8.9. (map 57.D.) Work began at once.	Appendix
"	6th	—	Erection of new Camp postponing.	Appendix
"	7th	—	Lieutenant H.R. MARSH. R.A.M.C. (T.C.) received orders from A.D.M.S. to proceed to 49 Casualty Clearing Station for duty.	
"	8th	—	Lieutenant Munir Ahmin Khan (hospenning) Satisfactory. Captain J. VALLANCE R.A.M.C. (S.R.) reported for duty with 100 Field Ambulance & is taken on the strength.	Appendix

2449 Wt. W14957/M90 750,000 1/16 J.B.C. & A. Forms/C.2118/12.

Army Form C. 2118.

WAR DIARY
or
INTELLIGENCE SUMMARY
(Erase heading not required.)

Instructions regarding War Diaries and Intelligence Summaries are contained in F. S. Regs., Part II. and the Staff Manual respectively. Title Pages will be prepared in manuscript.

Place	Date	Hour	Summary of Events and Information	Remarks and references to Appendices
HEAVY.	March 9th	—	Main dining Station now ready for the reception of cases. Accommodation sufficient for 130 lying cases. Lieutenant H. R. MARSH. R.A.M.C. (T.C.) proceeded to 49 Casualty Clearing Station for duty & is struck off the strength of 100 FA.	Shorney
POZIERES	10th	—	"L" day. Zero hour 6.15 a.m. 2nd Division take Grevillers Trench, without much opposition.	
"	11th	—	Wounded Admission & evacuations. 6 a.m. 9th inst to 6 a.m. today. Officers 7 Others 4 O.R. 75 Total 86 — 2 O.R. died 7 4 73 84	Shorney

2449 Wt. W14957/M90 750,000 1/16 J.B.C. & A. Forms/C.2118/12.

Army Form C. 2118.

WAR DIARY
INTELLIGENCE SUMMARY
(Erase heading not required.)

Instructions regarding War Diaries and Intelligence Summaries are contained in F. S. Regs., Part II. and the Staff Manual respectively. Title Pages will be prepared in manuscript.

Place	Date	Hour	Summary of Events and Information	Remarks and references to Appendices
POZIERES	March 11th (cont)		Captain. R.W. ARMSTRONG. RAMC (TC) evacuated sick to 44 Casualty Clearing Station.	Appny
"	12	—	D.D.M.S. II Corps visited Main Dressing Stn. — He wishes preparation made for the reception of 250 lying Cases.	
			Admissions & evacuations (wounded) for 24 hours ending 6 a.m.	
			admitted evacuated	
			Officers. — —	
			O.R. 13 13	
			Total. 13. 13.	
			Captain. P.J. LANE. M.C. RAMC (TC.) awarded a bar to the Military Cross.	Appny

Army Form C. 2118.

WAR DIARY
INTELLIGENCE SUMMARY
(Erase heading not required.)

Instructions regarding War Diaries and Intelligence Summaries are contained in F. S. Regs., Part II. and the Staff Manual respectively. Title Pages will be prepared in manuscript.

Place	Date	Hour	Summary of Events and Information	Remarks and references to Appendices
POZIERES	March 12th	-	1 Nissen hut & 2 more marquees erected to increase accommodation at M.D. Stn.	
"			Captain. D.F.A. NEILSON. RAMC (T.C.) } joined 100 Field Captain. L. HORSLEY. RAMC (T.C.) } Ambulance for duty & were taken on the strength. Wounded admitted O.R. 11	January
"	14th	-	Major R.G. MEREDITH. RAMC. joined 100 F.A. for duty & taken on the strength. 2 O.R. wounded (enemy) to C.C.S. Wounded admitted O.R. 13 Evacuated 13	January

2449 Wt. W14957/M90 750,000 1/16 J.B.C. & A. Forms/C.2118/12.

Army Form C. 2118.

WAR DIARY
or
INTELLIGENCE SUMMARY
(Erase heading not required.)

Place	Date	Hour	Summary of Events and Information	Remarks and references to Appendices
POZIERES	November 15th	-	Made orders for ADS/MDS, 100 Field Ambulance are to take on the evacuation of the wounded from the line.	
			3 Officers & 74 O.R. proceeded to Advanced Dressing Station at the "QUARRY" (Map ref. 57D.c. M15 d.4.8.)	
			Wounded O.R. 15 admitted 16 evacuated died	
			Gassed O.R. 2	
	16th	-	Relief. I visited advanced Dressing Stn.	Appendix
			Wounded Officers 2, admitted 2	Appendix
	17th	-	Ratios	Appendix
	18th	-	One Officer & 50 O.R. proceeded to "RED CHATEAU" COURCELETTE	
			(Map ref. 57D.C M 25 t 0.9.) to form a collecting station	
			for walking sick	Appendix

Army Form C. 2118.

WAR DIARY
or
INTELLIGENCE SUMMARY

(Erase heading not required.)

Place	Date	Hour	Summary of Events and Information	Remarks and references to Appendices
POZIERES	March RA (Cont)		Visited Advanced Dressing Station - from there with D.A.D.M.S. and Division I proceeded to AVESNE (57c A26.6.) near BAPAUME to reconnoitre ground for new advanced dressing station. Decided to put it at BIEFVILLERS (57.c H.19 central) but on standing at AVESNE - orders later affect back to the Bearer Division.	appendix
"	19th		Advanced Dressing Station moved to BIEFVILLERS (57.c H.19 central) with an advanced post at SAPIGNIES (57c H.8.a.)	
"		5 pm	Orders received from A.D.M.S. for Bearer Division to return to M.D.S. Further A.D.S. to be handed over to F.A. of 18th Division.	appendix

WAR DIARY

INTELLIGENCE SUMMARY

Army Form C. 2118.

Place	Date	Hour	Summary of Events and Information	Remarks and references to Appendices
POZIERES	March 20th	—	2 Officers with majority of Bearer Division returned to M.D.S.	Appx
"	21st	—	1 Officer & remainder of Bearers returned to M.D.S. after keeping on advanced dressing station to F.A. of 18th Division	Appx
"	22nd	2pm	Rcvd. orders from A.D.M.S. 100 Field Ambulance to M.D. at Pozieres to Avenly.	
"	"	—	Lt Colonel. E.H.H. MOORE. R.A.M.C. wounded (mine) to 147th South Midland Casualty Clearing St.	
"	"	—	Captain. B.W. ARMSTRONG. R.A.M.C. (OC) rejoined 100 F.A. for duty	Appx

Army Form C. 2118.

WAR DIARY
or
INTELLIGENCE SUMMARY

(Erase heading not required.)

Instructions regarding War Diaries and Intelligence Summaries are contained in F. S. Regs., Part II. and the Staff Manual respectively. Title Pages will be prepared in manuscript.

Place	Date	Hour	Summary of Events and Information	Remarks and references to Appendices
AVELUY	March 23rd		Routine	
"	24th		Field Ambulance left AVELUY (Cromwell Huts) at 10 a.m. & marching with 3rd Div. Group proceeded to VADENCOURT Chateau (Lens II 1/100,000). 9 miles march	
VADENCOURT	25th		Routine	
VADENCOURT	26th		F.A. left VADENCOURT at 7.30 am & reached GEZAINCOURT (LENS II 1/100,000) at 3 pm after a 15 mile march	
GEZAINCOURT	27th		F.A. left GEZAINCOURT at 10 a.m. & arrived & billets at SERICOURT & SIBIVILLE (LENS II 1/100,000) at 4 pm — about 15 miles	

Rev. N. COONEY C.F. left Ambulance to proceed to U.K. on completion of contract & was struck off strength of unit.

Army Form C. 2118.

WAR DIARY
-or-
INTELLIGENCE SUMMARY
(Erase heading not required.)

Instructions regarding War Diaries and Intelligence Summaries are contained in F.S. Regs., Part II. and the Staff Manual respectively. Title Pages will be prepared in manuscript.

Place	Date	Hour	Summary of Events and Information	Remarks and references to Appendices
SERICOURT	March 28th		T.A. left SERICOURT at 9.45 a.m. arriving 3.30 p.m. — 10 mile march.	18 M.A.
SIRACOURT	29th		Routine	19 M.A.
SIRACOURT	30th		Left SIRACOURT at 10 a.m. arriving at PERNES (LENS II 1/100000) at 3 p.m. — 12½ miles. Fair excellently billeted in convent which also serves as hospital. Learned the enemy from A.D.M.S. that we should be reorganised practically the whole with of the Division also to find for scabies patients soon to inspection the D.R.S. & Scabies patients by A.D.M.S.	M.A.
PERNES	31st		Considerable work done in clearing respiratory wounds. Lt. Col. F.H.M. MOORE R.A.M.C. rejoined unit this evening for duty from hospital.	20 M.A.

2449 Wt. W14957/M90 750,000 1/16 J.B.C. & A. Forms/C.2118/12.

B.E.F.

SUMMARY OF MEDICAL WAR DIARIES FOR 100th F.A., 2nd Divn., 13th Corps.
1st Army.
17th Corps, 3rd Army from 10/4/17.
13th Corps from 13/4/17.

WESTERN FRONT April- May· '17.

O.C. Lt· Col. E.H.W.I. Moore.

SUMMARISED UNDER THE FOLLOWING HEADINGS.

Phase "B" Battle of Arras- April- May· 1917.

1st Period Attack on Vimy Ridge April.

2nd Period Capture of Siegfried Line May·

B.E.F.

100th F.A., 2nd Divn. 13th Corps, 1st Army.   WESTERN FRONT
O.C. Lt. Col. E.H.W.I. Moore.   April. '17.
<u>1st Army.</u>
17th Corps, 3rd Army from 10/4/17.

<u>Phase "B" Battle of Arras- April- May. 1917.</u>
<u>1st Period Attack on Vimy Ridge April.</u>

1917.	<u>Headquarters.</u> at Pernes.
April 1st-8th.	Nothing of note.
9th.	<u>Moves:</u> To Bajus.
10th.	" To Maroeuil.
	<u>Transfers.</u> 17th Corps 3rd Army.

B.E.F.

100th F.A., 2nd Divn. 17th Corps, 3rd Army.   WESTERN FRONT
O.C. Lt. Col. E.H.W.I. Moore.   April.'17.
13th Corps from 13/4/17.

Phase "B" Battle of Arras- April- May. 1917.
1st Period Attack on Vimy Ridge April.

1917.
April. 10th.   Transfers. 17th Corps 3rd Army.

12th.   Moves Detachment: 3 and Br. Division to Lille Post
A.28.c.20.30. (51 B.) and relieved Brs. 1/2nd High.
Field Ambulance, also took over Fish Post A.29.a.60.20
and Adv. Post. behind 99th Bde. in Right Sector of
Divisional line.

T.D. relieved T.D. of 1/2nd High. Field Ambulance at
Advanced Dressing Station Anzin G.7.b.7.8. (51.B.) with
accommodation for nearly 100.

Moves: Headquarters. to Anzin.

13th.   Transport. 6 M.A.C. for evacuation.
Transfer. 13th Corps.

B.E.F. 3.

100th F.A., 2nd Divn. 13th Corps.   WESTERN FRONT
O.C. Lt. Col. E.H.W.I. Moure.   April. '17
3rd Army.

Phase "B" Battle of Arras- April- May. 1917.
1st Period Attack on Vimy Ridge April.

1917.

April
13th.   Transfer. 13th Corps.

14th.   Medical Arrangements: A.D.S. Anzin changed to Divisional
         M.D.S.

19th.   Lille Post. handed over to 5th Field Ambulance as
         evacuation control post.

27th.   Accommodation: "Y" Day with tents and re-arrangement,
         accommodation increased for upwards of 200.

28th.   Operations. "Z" Day 2nd Division attacked on Oppy line
         at dawn.

         Casualties. From 7 a.m. until evening a steady stream
         of wounded, great predominence of L.D.W. over walking
         wounded.

         Total   27th- 28th:-

         11 and 140 L.D.W.)
) British.
         2 and 10 sitting   )

         6 and 24 German

         Assistance. Officers attached for temp. duty at M.D.S..
         1 of 5th Field Ambulance
         1 "   2nd Divn. Train.
         1 "   2nd D.A.C.

         Transport. 20 M.A.C. cars attached to M.D.S. for
         evacuation of wounded.

29th,   Operations. Division attacked in a.m.

B.E.F. 4.

<u>100th F.A., 2nd Divn. 13th Corps.</u>   <u>WESTERN FRONT.</u>
<u>O.C. Lt. Col. E.H.W.I. Moure.</u>   <u>April. '17.</u>
<u>3rd Army.</u>

<u>Phase "B" Battle of Arras- April- May. 1917.</u>
<u>1st Period Attack on Vimy Ridge April.</u>

1917.

May. 29th cont.   <u>Casualties:</u>

11 and 122 L.D.W.)
) British.
2 and 1 Sitting   )

27   German.

<u>Casualties R.A.M.C.</u> 0 and 1 killed.

0 and 1 wounded (Gas.)

<u>Casualties.</u> Total for month Attached Appendix "A" (Put back in Diary)

B.E.F.

100th F.A., 2nd Divn. 13th Corps, 1st Army.   WESTERN FRONT
O.C. Lt. Col. E.H.W.I. Moore.   April. '17.
   1st Army.
   17th Corps, 3rd Army from 10/4/17.

   Phase "B" Battle of Arras- April- May. 1917.
   1st Period Attack on Vimy Ridge April.

1917.	Headquarters. at Pernes.
April 1st-8th.	Nothing of note.
9th.	Moves: To Bajus.
10th.	" To Maroeuil.
	Transfers. 17th Corps 3rd Army.

B.E.F.

100th F.A., 2nd Divn. 17th Corps, 3rd Army.　WESTERN FRONT
O.C. Lt. Col. E.H.W.I. Moore.　　　　　　　　April.'17.
13th Corps from 13/4/17.

Phase "B" Battle of Arras- April- May. 1917.
1st Period Attack on Vimy Ridge April.

1917.
April. 10th.　Transfers. 17th Corps 3rd Army.

12th.　Moves Detachment: 3 and Br. Division to Lille Post
A.28.c.20.30. (51 B.) and relieved Brs. 1/2nd High.
Field Ambulance, also took over Fish Post A.29.a.60.20
and Adv. Post. behind 99th Bde. in Right Sector of
Divisional line.

T.D. relieved T.D. of 1/2nd High. Field Ambulance at
Advanced Dressing Station Anzin B.7.b.7.8. (51.B.) with
accommodation for nearly 100.

Moves: Headquarters. to Anzin.

13th.　Transport. 6 M.A.C. for evacuation.

Transfer. 13th Corps.

B.E.F.   3.

<u>100th F.A., 2nd Divn. 13th Corps.</u>   <u>WESTERN FRONT</u>
<u>O.C. Lt. Col. E.H.W.I. Moure.</u>   <u>April. '17</u>
<u>3rd Army.</u>

<u>Phase "B" Battle of Arras- April- May. 1917.</u>
<u>1st Period Attack on Vimy Ridge April.</u>

1917.

April
13th.   <u>Transfer.</u> 13th Corps.

14th.   <u>Medical Arrangements:</u> A.D.S. Anzin changed to Divisional M.D.S.

19th.   Lille Post. handed over to 5th Field Ambulance as evacuation control post.

27th.   <u>Accommodation:</u> "Y" Day with tents and re-arrangement, accommodation increased for upwards of 200.

28th.   <u>Operations.</u> "Z" Day 2nd Division attacked on Oppy line at dawn.

<u>Casualties.</u> From 7 a.m. until evening a steady stream of wounded, great predominence of L.D.W. over walking wounded.

Total   27th- 28th:-

11 and 140 L.D.W.)
) British.
2 and 10 sitting   )

6 and 24 German

<u>Assistance.</u> Officers attached for temp. duty at M.D.S..

1 of 5th Field Ambulance

1 " 2nd Divn. Train.

1 " 2nd D.A.C.

<u>Transport.</u> 20 M.A.C. cars attached to M.D.S. for evacuation of wounded.

29th,   <u>Operations.</u> Division attacked in a.m.

B.E.F.

100th F.A., 2nd Divn. 13th Corps.   WESTERN FRONT.
O.C. Lt. Col. E.H.W.E. Moure.   April. '17.
3rd Army.

Phase "B" Battle of Arras- April- May. 1917.
1st Period Attack on Vimy Ridge April.

1917.

May. 29th cont.   Casualties:

11 and 122 L.D.W.   )
) British.
2 and 1 Sitting   )

27h German.

Casualties R.A.M.C. 0 and 1 killed.

0 and 1 wounded (Gas.)

Casualties. Total for month Attached Appendix "A"

Appendix "A" attached to first copy.

Army Form C. 2118.

WAR DIARY
INTELLIGENCE SUMMARY
(Erase heading not required.)

Vol 21

Confidential

WAR DIARY of 100 Field Ambulance

April 1917

Vol 18

Stamp: OFFICER COMMANDING 100TH FIELD AMBULANCE R.A.M.C. — 1 MAY 1917 — No. 2098/13

WAR DIARY
or
INTELLIGENCE SUMMARY

(Erase heading not required.)

Army Form C. 2118.

Place	Date	Hour	Summary of Events and Information	Remarks and references to Appendices
PERNES	April 1		Routine. Capt. D. F. A. NEILSON. RAMC(T.C.) detailed for temporary duty with Divisional R.E. under instructions from A.D.M.S. 2nd Div.	Attenuators Capt. Blake
	2		Lt. Colonel. E.H.M. MOORE RAMC departed this morning on special leave to U.K. (2nd – 13th April) 1 wounded man (S.I.) admitted & sent to paid Hospital BUSNES.	13/M4 /M4
	3		Routine	
	4		6321 Sgt. F. S. WEBB RAMC reported unit for duty from Hospital taken on the strength.	12/M4
	5		Routine	13/M4
	6		Capt. L. HORSLEY. RAMC (T.C.) to 1st K.R.R.C. for temporary duty	/M4

Army Form C. 2118.

WAR DIARY
or
INTELLIGENCE SUMMARY

(Erase heading not required.)

Instructions regarding War Diaries and Intelligence Summaries are contained in F. S. Regs., Part II. and the Staff Manual respectively. Title Pages will be prepared in manuscript.

Place	Date	Hour	Summary of Events and Information	Remarks and references to Appendices
PERNES	April 2		Routine	
	7		Field Ambulance left PERNES at 3 pm & marched	MA
	8		to BAJUS (map of FRANCE – LENS 11.)	BJA
BAJUS	9		Orders today received from D.D.M.S. XIII Corps that 'A.D.M.S.2 Div' Major R.G. MEREDITH R.A.M.C. was today detailed to proceed to leave for temporary duty at XIII Corps Depôt. Major (D/pot) ROGERS (N.a. Res. HAZEBROUCK 3ʳᵈ A) under A.D.M.S. instructions Capt R.W. ARMSTRONG R.A.M.C. (T.C.) assumed temporary command of F.A. A/temp A.D.M.S. & officers this afternoon to company hdqts (R. & Nos 5 & 6) F.A. & received certain information re impending operations.	BJA

2449 Wt. W14957/M90 750,000 1/16 J.B.C. & A. Forms/C.2118/12.

Army Form C. 2118.

WAR DIARY
or
INTELLIGENCE SUMMARY
(Erase heading not required.)

Place	Date	Hour	Summary of Events and Information	Remarks and references to Appendices
BAJUS (LENS 11) 1/100000	April 10th	9.30 am	Ambulance left BAJUS at 9.30am & marched to MAREUIL. Very bad weather. Billets in 8 Nissen Huts in ANZIN Rd.	(FRANCE 51c 1/20.000 sheet 2) L.4.R.2.38.
MAREUIL			Bearer Officers went with D.A.D.M.S. 2nd Div. to reconnoitre line for evacuation of wounded.	
"	12		Bearer Division under Capt. P.J. LANE M.C. R.A.M.C. with Capt. J. WALLANCE R.A.M.C. & Capt A. GHEETLY R.A.M.C. relieved bearers of 1/3rd Highland F.A. at Lille Post (A28 c.20.20), Fish Post (A29 a 60.20) & advance posts held by 99th Bgde. in Rt. Sector of Divisional Line at 6.30 am.	
"		9 am	Tent division relieved T.D. of 1/2nd Highland F.A. at A.D.S. ANZIN (G.7.F.7.8) where there is accommodation for nearly 100 patients. R.E.M.S. 2nd Div. visited A.D.S. ANZIN this afternoon.	

Army Form C. 2118.

WAR DIARY
or
INTELLIGENCE SUMMARY
(Erase heading not required.)

Instructions regarding War Diaries and Intelligence Summaries are contained in F.S. Regs., Part II. and the Staff Manual respectively. Title Pages will be prepared in manuscript.

Place	Date	Hour	Summary of Events and Information	Remarks and references to Appendices
ANZIN	April 13.		Routine. Back work done in clearing & ...... Visited Line Post & Fish Post Ma afternoon. 6 M.A.C. car reported here tonight for evacuation of cases. 1 large car (Napier) & 1 Ford received from D.S.C. to replace two DAIMLERS vacuated to base.	BMA BMA
	14.		Under instructions of A.D.M.S., A.D.S. ANZIN becomes Headqrs of Div. M.D.S. Capt RUMWOOD R.A.M.C. & Capt R.J. ROGERS R.A.M.C. No 5 F.A. reported here for temporary duty under instructions of A.D.M.S.	
"	15		P/C A.W. BARKER R.A.M.C. proceeded to England for temporary commission. Capt L. A.M. SILEY returned two F.A. for duty from F/R/P.C.	BMA

2449 Wt. W14957/M90 750,000 1/16 J.B.C. & A. Forms/C.2118/12.

Army Form C. 2118.

WAR DIARY
or
INTELLIGENCE SUMMARY
(Erase heading not required.)

Instructions regarding War Diaries and Intelligence Summaries are contained in F. S. Regs., Part II. and the Staff Manual respectively. Title Pages will be prepared in manuscript.

Place	Date	Hour	Summary of Events and Information	Remarks and references to Appendices
ANZAC	April 16th		Lt. J. McCabe & Pte. A.P. Cooper. R.A.M.C. to XIII Cas: Draft. Many Repts for duty & struck off strength of F.A.	MMA
	17		2 Hospital Marquees (small) drawn & erected	MMA
	18		Pte. R. Park. R.A.M.C. T.F. (and for temporary commn.) Reinstate. Under instructions of KPMS. Capt. D.F.A. Neilson R.A.M.C. (T.C.) transferred from C.R.E. 2nd Div. to 2nd D.A.C. for temporary duty.	MMA
	19		Lth Post landed on it. O.C. No 5 F.A. withdrawn & returned to his control post. Capt. R.J. Rogers R.A.M.C. (No 5 F.A.)	MMA

Army Form C. 2118.

WAR DIARY
or
INTELLIGENCE SUMMARY
(Erase heading not required.)

Instructions regarding War Diaries and Intelligence Summaries are contained in F. S. Regs., Part II. and the Staff Manual respectively. Title Pages will be prepared in manuscript.

Place	Date	Hour	Summary of Events and Information	Remarks and references to Appendices
	April			
AUBIN	20		Capt. J. VALLANCE. RAMC (S.R.) evacuated sick to No 42 C.C.S.	
			no 90678 Pte COLES F. proceeded to XIII Corps Dropt. Tramy Depot vis	
			no 64682 Pte BELL J. who returned to the unit from temporary duty there	
			Pte COLES struck off strength.	
			Notified today that Lt. Col. E.M.M. MOORE RAMC. had been	
	21		granted extension of leave in U.K. until May 8th (War office AM.D.1. d/11/4/17)	BMA
			Visited A.D.S. at Fish Post	BMA
	22		Routine. Capt J. VALLANCE RAMC (S.R.) evacuated sick to	BMA
			base from no 42 C.C.S.	
	23		Routine	BMA
	24		Routine	BMA
	25		Routine	BMA

Army Form C. 2118.

WAR DIARY
or
INTELLIGENCE SUMMARY
(Erase heading not required.)

Instructions regarding War Diaries and Intelligence Summaries are contained in F. S. Regs., Part II. and the Staff Manual respectively. Title Pages will be prepared in manuscript.

Place	Date	Hour	Summary of Events and Information	Remarks and references to Appendices
ANZIN	April 26th		Two Douglas Motor Cycles drawn today from D.S.C. to replace Caradhis	B.M.A
	27th		"Y" Day. Hoisted A.D.S. in morning — everything ready. All preparations at M.D.S. complete. With tents & marquees, etc. & additions to existing accommodation, there is room here for upwards of 200 cases now.	M.O
	28th		"Z" day. 2nd Div. attack on Oppy line at dawn. Casualties commenced to arrive in a steady stream at about 7 am & came down steadily during the day until evening when things quietened down somewhat. Great performance of flying on sitting cases. Total from 12 midnight 27th — 12 midnight 28th Officers 11 bsy 1 sity 2 sety Gunmen 6 10 Gas 140 24	B.M.A

2449 Wt. W14957/M90 750,000 1/16 J.B.C. & A. Forms/C.2118/12.

WAR DIARY or INTELLIGENCE SUMMARY

Army Form C. 2118.

Place	Date	Hour	Summary of Events and Information	Remarks and references to Appendices
ANZIN	April 28		In addition to 3 officers of 100 F.A. & Capt G.W. WOOD 17 to 5 F.A. The following were attached for temporary duty at MDS. & gave great assistance during 2 subsequent days:— Capt. KEITCH WILSON R.A.M.C. 2nd Div Train & Capt. D.F.A. NEILSON R.A.M.C. 2nd DAC. An additional 14 M.A.C. cars (making 20 in all) were attached to MDS. for evacuation of wounded. Four Cable wires in use for always lying near during most of the day & evacuations throughout kept pace with admissions. 20 O.R. from 1st R. Berks. Regt. were attached as Convoy.	JBWH
	29th		Diversion attacks began this morning & the day here was a repetition of yesterday. Total (from midnight 26th – midnight 29th) — Officers 11 Dgrl 2 sitting O.R. 122 lying 1 sitting 27. Germans	MMH

Army Form C. 2118.

WAR DIARY
or
INTELLIGENCE SUMMARY

(Erase heading not required.)

Instructions regarding War Diaries and Intelligence Summaries are contained in F. S. Regs., Part II. and the Staff Manual respectively. Title Pages will be prepared in manuscript.

Place	Date	Hour	Summary of Events and Information	Remarks and references to Appendices
ANZIN	April 30		64639 Pte. THOMPSON: J. Killed in action last night. 64593 Pte. COLLIER T.W. Slightly gassed (B) W. (enemy) activity	W Armstrong Capt. R.W.R.

2449 Wt. W14957/M90 750,000 1/16 J.B.C. & A. Forms/C.2118/12.

Army Form C. 2118.

WAR DIARY
or
INTELLIGENCE SUMMARY
(Erase heading not required.)

Summary of Events and Information

Monthly strength return of other ranks

April 30th   165
March 31st   172

Decrease in
strength   7

Drafts received   1

Casualties   2 sgts
              5 ptes

              2 sgts.
              1 cpl.
              11 ptes —

Place	Date	Hour

Wounded Admissions & Evacuations thro'out APRIL. daily for 24 hours end 9 a.m.

April	Admissions			Evacuations			Deaths
	Officers	O.R.	Germans	Officers	O.R.	Germans	
1st to 14th	—	NIL					
15	2	26	—	2	25	—	1 O.R.
16	—	16	—	—	15	—	1 O.R.
17	2	49	—	2	48	—	1 O.R.
18	4	44	—	4	38	—	
19	—	17	—	—	13	—	2 O.R
20	—	15	—	—	15	—	
21	1	11	—	1	11	—	
22	2	28	—	2	22	—	
23	2	46	1	2	46	1	
24	4	49	21	4	48	21	1 O.R.
25	1	39	—	1	37	—	1 O.R.
26	1	25	—	1	25	—	
27	1	18	—	1	18	—	
28	5	34	—	5	33	—	
29	14	144	33	14	142	33	2 O.R.
30	12	132	26	12	127	26	5 O.R.
May 1st	6	80	3	5	78	3	1 Off.

B.E.F.

SUMMARY OF MEDICAL WAR DIARIES FOR 100th F.A., 2nd Divn., 13th Corps.

1st Army.

17th Corps, 3rd Army from 10/4/17.

13th Corps from 13/4/17.

WESTERN FRONT April- May '17.

O.C. Lt. Col. E.H.W.I. Moore.

SUMMARISED UNDER THE FOLLOWING HEADINGS.

Phase "B" Battle of Arras- April- May. 1917.

1st Period Attack on Vimy Ridge April.

2nd Period Capture of Siegfried Line May.

B.E.F.

100th F.A., 2nd Divn. 13th Corps. WESTERN FRONT.
O.C Lt. Col. E.H.W..I. Moure. May. '17.
3rd Army.

Phase "B" Battle of Arras- April- May. 1917.
2nd Period Capture of Siegfried Line May.

1917.

May. 3rd. Operations. 2nd Divn. attacked on a one Bde. front on Left of Oppy.

Casualties. First arrived about 8 a.m. and came in steadily throughout day.

4th. Large numbers of wounded received early a.m. chiefly wounded rescued from forward positions by Br. parties after dark.

Moves Detachment: Br. relieved by Br. 13th Field Ambulance and returned to Anzin.

Medical Arrangements: T.D. at Anzin relieved by 15th Field Ambulance.

Moves: To Ecoivres X Huts.

5th. Casualties. Attached Appendix "A".

6th. Moves. To Rocourt En L'Eau O.34.a.3½.5½ (36 B)

Operations R.A.M.C. Tents erected for sick of 99th Bde.

7th-22nd. Nothing of note.

23rd. Moves Detachment: 1 and 70 Brs. to Roclincourt to relieve Brs. of 13th Field Ambulance at Advanced Dressing Station. " Brown Line " B.14.c.9.5. (51 B. N.W. 1/20,000)

Moves: To Maroeuil.

24th. " To Roclincourt, and took over M.D.S. from 13th Field Ambulance.

B.E.F.

100th F.A. 2nd Divn. 13th Corps.   WESTERN FRONT.
bO.C. Lt. Col. E.H.W.I. Moure.   May. '17.
3rd Army.

Phase "B" cont.
2nd Period cont.

1917.
May. 24th. cont.

Accommodation: 8 small hospital marquees.

Evacuation: Medical Arrangements: R.A.Ps. of the 2 front Btlns. of R. Bde. at Sucrerie B.16.a.1.7. whence wounded walk - or are carried via Rly. embankment B.15.c.5.5. to Advanced Dressing Station. " Brown Line " B.14.c.9.5. and thence by 2 alternative routes:-

(1). Cross country to Commandant's House where trolley line ran to Main Dressing Station 5th Field Ambulance Nine Elms.

(2). Through Ouse Tommy trenches to Trolley railhead B.19.b.6.3. then by trucks drawn by light engine to Main Dressing Station Roclincourt.

This light Rly. had extension up to Rly. embankment Approx.B.15.c.3.0. where hand-pushed trucks could be used at night.

30th.

Medical Arrangements. Evacuation: 100th Field Ambulance took over evacuation of whole of Divisional line R.A.Ps L. Bde. T.29.d.1.8. (36.c. S.W. 1/20,000)
            -B.5.d.4.5.

1 Br. squad at each R.A.P.

Wounded carried by hand from these R.A.Ps. via sunken road between Arleux and Bailleul to A.D.S. B.14.c.7.7. Br. Relay Ps. at B.5.a.7.8. B.10.d.5.6. and B.15.c.4.5.

R.A.Ps R. Bde- Sugar Factory B.16.a.3.8. where there

B.E.F.

100th F.A. 2nd Divn. 13th Corps.　　WESTERN FRONT.
O.C. Lt. Col. E.H.W.I. Moure.　　May. '17.
3rd Army.

Phase "B" cont.

2nd Period cont.

1917 May 30th.　Medical Arrangements. Evacuation: cont,
cont.
are 2 squads of Brs. wounded carried via Rly Tunnel
B. 15.c.4.5. to Advanced Dressing Station B.14.c.7.7.
From Advanced Dressing Station wounded hand carried
via trenches to B.19.b.5.2. (No carrying across open
permitted) and loaded on to specially constructed
trucks on light rly. to Main Dressing Station A.29.c.7.6.
(51.b. N.W.)

B.E.F.

100th F.A., 2nd Divn. 13th Corps.   WESTERN FRONT.
O.C Lt. Col. E.H.W..I. Moure.   May. 1 '17.
3rd Army.

Phase "B" Battle of Arras- April- May. 1917.
2nd Period Capture of Siegfried Line May.

1917.

May. 3rd.   Operations. 2nd Divn. attacked on a one Bde. front on Left of Oppy.

Casualties. Front arrived about 8 a.m. and came in steadily throughout day.

4th.   Large numbers of wounded received early a.m. chiefly wounded rescued from forward positions by Br. parties after dark.

Moves Detachment: Br. relieved by Br. 13th Field Ambulance and returned to Anzin.

Medical Arrangements: T.D. at Anzin relieved by 15th Field Ambulance.

Moves: To Ecoivres X Huts.

5th.   Casualties. Attached Appendix "A".

6th.   Moves. To Rocourt En L'Eau O.34.a.3½.5½ (36 B) Operations R.A.M.C. Tents erected for sick of 99th Bde.

7th-22nd.   Nothing of note.

23rd.   Moves Detachment: 1 and 70 Brs. to Roclincourt to relieve Brs. of 13th Field Ambulance at Advanced Dressing Station. " Brown Line " B.14.c.9.5. (51 B. N.W. 1/20,000)

Moves: To Maroeuil.

24th.   "   To Roclincourt, and took over M.D.S. from 13th Field Ambulance.

B.E.F. 2.

100th F.A. 2nd Divn. 13th Corps.   WESTERN FRONT.
bO.C. Lt. Col. E.H.W.I. Moure.   April, '17.
3rd Army.

Phase "B" cont.

2nd Period cont.

1917.
May. 24th. cont.

Accommodation: 8 small hospital marquees.

Evacuation: Medical Arrangements: R.A.Ps. of the 2 front Btlns. of R. Bde. at Sucrerie B.16.a.1.7. whence wounded walk - or are carried via Rly. embankment B.15.c.5.5. to Advanced Dressing Station. " Brown Line " B.14.c.9.5. and thence by 2 alternative routes:-

(1). Cross country to Commandant's House where trolling line ran to Main Dressing Station 5th Field Ambulance Nine Elms.

(2). Through Ouse Tommy trenches to Trolley railhead B.19.b.6.3. then by trucks drawn by light engine to Main Dressing Station Roclincourt.

This light Rly. had extension up to Rly. embankment Approx. B.15.c.3.0. where hand-pushed trucks could be used at night.

30th. Medical Arrangements. Evacuation: 100th Field Ambulance took over evacuation of whole of Divisional line R.A.Ps L. Bde. T.29.d.1.8. (36.c. S.W. 1/20,000)
                  -B.5.d.4.5.

1 Br. squad at each R.A.P.

Wounded carried by hand from these R.A.Ps. via sunken road between Arleux and Bailleul to A.D.S. B.14.c.7.7. Br. Relay Ps. at B.5.a.7.8. B.10.d.5.6. and B.15.c.4.5.

R.A.Ps R. Bde- Sugar Factory B.16.a.3.8. where there

B.E.F.

100th F.A. 2nd Divn. 13th Corps.   WESTERN FRONT.
O.C. Lt. Col. E.H.W.I. Moure.   May. '17.
3rd Army.

Phase "B" cont.

2nd Period cont.

1917 May 30th. cont.   Medical Arrangements. Evacuation: cont, are 2 squads of Brs. wounded carried via Rly Tunnel B. 15.c.4.5. to Advanced Dressing Station B.14.c.7.7. From Advanced Dressing Station wounded hand carried via trenches to B.19.b.5.2. (No carrying across open permitted) and loaded on to specially constructed trucks on light rly. to Main Dressing Station A.29.c.7.6. (51.b. N.W.)

Appendix "A" attached to first copy.

Army Form C. 2118.

WAR DIARY
INTELLIGENCE SUMMARY
(Erase heading not required.)

WO 95/22

Confidential

War Diary of 100 Field Ambulance

May 1st to 31st 1917.

Vol. 19

WAR DIARY / INTELLIGENCE SUMMARY

Army Form C. 2118.

Place	Date	Hour	Summary of Events and Information	Remarks and references to Appendices
ANZIN - ST. AUBIN (51 Division H.Q.)	May 1.		Visited A.D.S. at ROCKINCOURT this morning. Brazing out of the front area since evening of 29th. Trench mortar activity. Quiet day at ANZIN.	A.Moriarty Capt RAMC
	2.		Routine.	AMcM
	3.		2nd Division attacked on a one Brigade front at 6.10 a.m. OPPY. Casualties commenced to arrive at ANZIN relatively slowly & came in steady throughout the day until the evening when they slackened off until the early hours of the following morning during which large numbers came in chiefly men rescued from forward positions of large craters which went out after dark. All walking wounded at ANZIN were the same as am. 28th+29th April. Throughout worked very smoothly.	AMcM

Army Form C. 2118.

WAR DIARY
or
INTELLIGENCE SUMMARY
(Erase heading not required.)

Place	Date	Hour	Summary of Events and Information	Remarks and references to Appendices
ANZIN	10/7		Bivouac relieved at 7.30 am. by those of No 13 F.A. returned to ANZIN in the early afternoon. Tent division at ANZIN relieved by No 15" F.A. who arrived there at midday.	
			Ambulance moved off from ANZIN to ELOIRES ("x"- h.R) at 4.30 p.m. & arrived about 6.30 p.m. Capt T. BOURNE-PRICE MC RAMC proceeded today to H.Q. 1st Div. & per temporary duty as D.A.D.M.S.	
ELOIRES	6		Rested at LICOURES. Field Ambulance moved to ROCOURT EN L'EAU (Ref reference 36.b.4. 0.3.4 a 38.38) French into Billets.	

2449 Wt. W14957/M90 750,000 1/16 J.B.C. & A. Forms/C.2118/12.

Army Form C. 2118.

WAR DIARY
or
INTELLIGENCE SUMMARY
(Erase heading not required.)

Place	Date	Hour	Summary of Events and Information	Remarks and references to Appendices
ROCLINCOURT	May 6 (continued)		Truck searched for week who are being collected from 99th Bde. same.	
			66168 Pte HALL G.H. Invacuated to No 6 C.C.S. BARLIN nt tonsillitis (since) returned off Strength. No. 90785 Pte DOW J.A. RAMC & No. 90679 Pte CROCKER G.A. RAMC posted for duty to 2/1st Lab. Coy. DID. & 2nd Lab.Coy Northants. respectively. Lieut. Col. J. VALLANCE RAMC (S.R.) reported unit from hospital.	B.W.H.
	7		Major ——MEREDITH RAMC. Struck off strength of Armutieres RBSM 9.4.17 (ADMS 2nd. 1/552 alp - 3/5/17) R——	B.W.H.
	8		Under instructions received from A.D.M.S., Capt. R.M.WOOD RAMC. (S.R.) 2/O C.F.A. (attached No 18 D F.A) was posted to C.R.E. 2nd Div for duty in place of Capt. D.F.A. NELSON RAMC. (T.C.) No. 64788 Pte. R. FRIEKEN reported unit from Base depot	B.W.H.

Army Form C. 2118.

WAR DIARY
or
INTELLIGENCE SUMMARY

(Erase heading not required.)

Instructions regarding War Diaries and Intelligence Summaries are contained in F. S. Regs., Part II. and the Staff Manual respectively. Title Pages will be prepared in manuscript.

Place	Date	Hour	Summary of Events and Information	Remarks and references to Appendices
ROUEN	Aug 10		M2/148952 Pte PEFFERS J. ASC (MT) granted special leave to UK	B/M/A
	11.		Capt A. RAZELEY RAMC. granted leave to UK.	p/M/A
	12		Lt Colonel E.H.M. MOORE RAMC signed unit for duty from sick leave in UK.	
	13.		No 36047 Pte ASHTON E. RAMC, K/M/S, attached for duty. Struck off strength of R.A.	B/M/A
	14.		No 16283 Pte (acting Cpl a/paid) CO E. C.E. RAMC posted to 2/2 N. Train Att to 53CO a/Lt Hunn A. RAMC. the former taken on strength of unit for duty, the latter on strength accordingly.	
			No 90946 Cpl (a/S/Sgt) COOK E. W.A. RAMC transferred sick furlough	B/M/A

2449 Wt. W14957/M90 750,000 1/16 J.B.C. & A. Forms/C.2118/12.

Army Form C. 2118.

WAR DIARY
or
INTELLIGENCE SUMMARY
(Erase heading not required.)

Place	Date	Hour	Summary of Events and Information	Remarks and references to Appendices
ROCOURT	Feb 14		T4/210 561 Dvr. E.E. DAY ASC (H.T.) ⎱ Joined F.A. for duty to-day ⎰ from base on strength accordingly	MM4
			T/SR/716 Dvr. W. JONES	
			T/SR/019425 Dvr. V. SAUNDERS " "	
	16		Lt Col. E.M.N. MOORE RAMC delegated for temporary duty as a/ADMS 2nd Div	MM4
			80349 Pte A.W. CREEK R.A.M.C. ⎱ transferred sick to No 58 C.C.S. returned 17th ⎰	BM4
			80326 Pte V. FLINT R.A.M.C. ⎰	
	17		Routine	
	18		No 1 Ambulance Skoda held this afternoon	
			Gateway bath 2nd Div Band	
			(Capt. V. FLORENCE R.A.M.C. (SR.) to 1st Royals (7th Lancashire Regt.) from F.A. Duty	BM4
	19		Capt. T. BEATRICE PRICE M.C. RAMC rejoined F.A. from temporary duty as a/DADMS 2nd Div	

Army Form C. 2118.

WAR DIARY
or
INTELLIGENCE SUMMARY

(Erase heading not required.)

Instructions regarding War Diaries and Intelligence Summaries are contained in F. S. Regs., Part II. and the Staff Manual respectively. Title Pages will be prepared in manuscript.

Place	Date	Hour	Summary of Events and Information	Remarks and references to Appendices
ROCLINCOURT	May 19		Pte T. BROWN R.A.M.C. Special leave to U.K. (19/5 – 29/5)	R.M.J.
	20		75468 Pte PATKINSON R.A.M.C. proceeded to H. Stats of Hosp. returned off strength	P.M.P.
	21		(Capt P.J. LANE M.C. R.A.M.(T.C.) proceeded leave to U.K. 22/5 – 3/5)	P.M.P.
	22		(Capt S. HORSLEY R.A.M.C.(T.C.) to 2nd S. STAFFS for temporary duty. Notified from O. of 143 M.S. that the Ambulance would be relieving No 12 F.A. (5th Div) in the S.A.F. at ROCLINCOURT. Proceeded to Rother H.Q./ordered with Capt T. Browne Price M.C. + Sarw O.C. 13th to arrange details of relief of the two.	R.M.J.

2449 Wt. W14957/Mp0 750,000 1/16 J.B.C. & A. Forms/C.2118/12.

Place	Date	Hour	Summary of Events and Information	Remarks and references to Appendices
ROCOURT	May 23		Burying party of 70 under Capt. Brown, Price M.L. left ROCOURT with horses at 9 a.m. & proceeded to ROCKINCOURT, where they tied up to relieve the horses of No. 13 F.A. at the M.D.S. on the "Brown Line" (51.B.N.W. /5000 B.14.C.9.5) during the night of 23-24 May. The remainder of 7th Ambulance with the transport left ROCOURT 2.20 a.m. for a point at MARQUVIK (same sheet F.21.a.2.9) where they arrived at 4.20 p.m. Lieut. J. SKIFFIN RAMC. funeral leave to U.K. (24.5-3.6) with 2 men transport left MARQUVIK at 10 a.m. en route to ROCKINCOURT (51.B.N.W. /5000 A.29.C.7.6) arriving at midday of	

Army Form C. 2118.

Instructions regarding War Diaries and Intelligence Summaries are contained in F. S. Regs., Part II. and the Staff Manual respectively. Title Pages will be prepared in manuscript.

WAR DIARY
or
INTELLIGENCE SUMMARY

(Erase heading not required.)

Place	Date	Hour	Summary of Events and Information	Remarks and references to Appendices
ROCLIN-COURT	May 24		Taking over M.D.S. & Walking Wounded Post from 13th. The events of present of 8 small hospital marquees. The personnel are in tents themselves. The lorry whip has safely completed by 6 am this morning & the route of evacuation at present is as follows:— The Regimental A.P.s of the two front battalions of the Right Brigade to the Source (B.16.a.1.7) (three cross trails or on cars) via the Railway Embankment (B.15-C.5.5) to A.D.S. at Bronstins (B.16.C.9.5). Thence by 2 ambulance cars to M.D.S. at no 5 F.A. at "North End" (A.17.a.1.7) or 2 two hour by tramcar tracks (a totally railway at B.19.6.63. Place by tramcars by tracks thence by light railway again to	

2449 Wt. W14957/M90 750,000 1/16 J.B.C. & A. Forms/C.2118/12.

Army Form C. 2118.

WAR DIARY
or
INTELLIGENCE SUMMARY
(Erase heading not required.)

Instructions regarding War Diaries and Intelligence Summaries are contained in F. S. Regs., Part II. and the Staff Manual respectively. Title Pages will be prepared in manuscript.

Place	Date	Hour	Summary of Events and Information	Remarks and references to Appendices
ROCKINCOURT	May 24.		M.D.S. at ROCKINCOURT. This light railway has an extension up to Railway Embankment (about B.15.c.5.0) which can be used by night (trucks pushed by hand only) Capt. D.F.A. NEILSON R.A.M.C. whom Capt. T. BURNS R.N.C. at A.D.S. this morning is the latter proceeding on leave to U.K. (25/5 - 4/6) Capt. A. GAFFNEY R.A.M.C. returned today from leave in U.K. Capt. A. GAFFNEY proceeded to A.D.S. this afternoon & took over charge of same. Capt. R.J. ROGERS R.A.M.C. No 5 F.A. joined for temporary duty at M.D.S. ROCKINCOURT today. The Rev. J.A. PATTEN, C.F. departed today for 1st Army H.Q. en route to A.P.C. if Army gazette officer brigade of the	

Army Form C. 2118.

WAR DIARY
or
INTELLIGENCE SUMMARY
(Erase heading not required.)

Instructions regarding War Diaries and Intelligence Summaries are contained in F. S. Regs., Part II. and the Staff Manual respectively. Title Pages will be prepared in manuscript.

Place	Date	Hour	Summary of Events and Information	Remarks and references to Appendices
ROCLINCOURT	May 26	—	Reinforcements. The Rev. J.C. RENDALL C.F. posted to F.A. & taken on strength	MW
"	27	—	Lt. Col. E.A.M. MOORE R.A.M.C. rejoined F.A. from duty as a/ADMS & resumed command of F.A.	A.M.A.
"	28th	—	Routine.	
"	29th	—	5 O.R. reinforcements joined 100 F.A. for duty	Routine
"	30th	—	2 OR 8/15/98 Pte I.W. COLLINS R.A.M.C. evacuated to 2/1 D.C. & thence to strength. Captain R.J. ROGERS returned to the 5th F.A. from temporary duty with this F.A. Transport of this Unit was inspected by O.C. 2nd Div. Train.	Routine

Army Form C. 2118.

WAR DIARY
INTELLIGENCE SUMMARY
(Erase heading not required.)

Instructions regarding War Diaries and Intelligence Summaries are contained in F. S. Regs., Part II. and the Staff Manual respectively. Title Pages will be prepared in manuscript.

Place	Date	Hour	Summary of Events and Information	Remarks and references to Appendices
ROCLINCOURT	May 30th (cont)		Under orders from A.D.M.S. 2nd Division, 10.0 p.m. took over the evacuation of the whole Division at Line. The Regimental Aid Posts of the left Brigade are at T.29.d.1.8. (map France 36c S.W. 1/20,000) & at B.5.d.4.5. (map France 51b N.W. 1/20,000) Wounded leave squad at each R.A.P. Wounded are carried by hand from these posts via the sunken road between ARLEUX & BAILLEUL to the Advanced Dressing Station at B.4.c.7.7. Bearer relay posts are at B.5.a.7.8., B.10.d.5.6., & B.15.c.4.5. The Regimental Aid posts of the right Brigade are at the Sugar factory B.16.a.3.8., where there are two squads of 4a bearers, & Wounded are carried via the Railway Tunnel at B.15.c.4.5. to the Advanced Dressing Stn at B.14.c.7.7. From the	Map ref. France 51b N.W. 1/20,000

Army Form C. 2118.

WAR DIARY
INTELLIGENCE SUMMARY
(Erase heading not required.)

Instructions regarding War Diaries and Intelligence Summaries are contained in F. S. Regs., Part II. and the Staff Manual respectively. Title Pages will be prepared in manuscript.

Place	Date	Hour	Summary of Events and Information	Remarks and references to Appendices
RECIPIENT				
	May 30th/31st		Attacked Jenin Station. Six wounded on hand carried via the trenches to B.19.c.5.2. (no carrying is allowed by day) where they are loaded on to specially constructed trucks & run on a light railway into the main Jenin Station at A.29.c.7.6. (ref. 51 6 N.W.)	Army
"	31st	-	1 O.R. A. & C. M.T. reported for duty with new Jadhla Car - is taken on the strength.	Attached is Appendix showing admission & evacuations, number of wounded during action Jenin Station. Army

W. Wilmore
Lieut R.A.M.C.

Appendix 1.

WAR DIARY or INTELLIGENCE SUMMARY

Army Form C. 2118.

Table of wounded admitted & evacuated during active operations of May from M.D.S. ANZIN in Apr A.
(Each day to previous 24 hrs ending 9 a.m.)

Date	Admissions			Evacuations			Deaths	
	Officers	O.R.	Germans	Off.	O.R.	Germans		
May 1	6	50	3	5	78	3	1 Officer	
2	2	51	—	2	50	—	1 O.R.	
3	1	11	—	1	11	—		
4	8	159	23	8	157	23		
5	—	14	—	—	13	—		

Maitland
Lt Col R.A.M.C.

Army Form C. 2118.

WAR DIARY
INTELLIGENCE SUMMARY

(Erase heading not required.)

CONFIDENTIAL

War Diary of 100 Field Ambulance
June 1st to June 30th 1917

Vol. 20.

Army Form C. 2118.

WAR DIARY
INTELLIGENCE SUMMARY
(Erase heading not required.)

Place	Date	Hour	Summary of Events and Information	Remarks and references to Appendices
ROCLINCOURT	July 1st	-	No. 86045 Sergeant A.J. COLEMAN R.A.M.C. evacuated sick to 7.S.V.C. 2 O.R. men S.T.A. to strength	Appendix one 2nd Lt R.A.M.C.
"	2nd	-	No. 66539 a/ee Cpl C. COOKS appointed a/ee Cpl/ unto pay. The military Medal has been awarded to the u/m:- No 66304 Pte (a/Corpl) J.V. THOMAS " 66177 Pte J. STICKLAND } R.A.M.C. " 64707 Pte M.L. MOORE.	Appendix Appendix
"	3rd	-	Routine	
"	4th	-	1 O.R. R.A.M.C. & 1 O.R. A.S.C. H.T. evacuated sick to H.S/C. 1 O.R. men S.T.A. to his strength. The Regimental aid posts at B.16.a.3.8. have been moved (map 51bN.W. 1/20,000)	

Army Form C. 2118.

WAR DIARY
or
INTELLIGENCE SUMMARY

(Erase heading not required.)

Instructions regarding War Diaries and Intelligence Summaries are contained in F. S. Regs., Part II. and the Staff Manual respectively. Title Pages will be prepared in manuscript.

Place	Date	Hour	Summary of Events and Information	Remarks and references to Appendices
ROCLINCOURT	June 4th (cont)		to dug out at B.10.c.3.3 & B.10.c.7.7. The 100 Ft. Beaver Spouts have been moved from B.16.a.3.8. on ground being posted at B.W.C.3.3. & B.10.c.3.3. on ground being posted at B.10.d.5.6. (map 51.b.N.W. 1 in 20,000) & the Men at a new relay post at B.10.d.5.6.	Army
"			A trench was dropped from a German aeroplane about 10 p.m. only a few yards from the Frankfort line - no damage was done	Army
"	5		T/Captain J. PATON RAMC (No 5 Field Ambulance) reported for temporary duty with the 2nd Field Ambulance.	
"			No. n.2/049654 Pte D.S. CAMPBELL A.S.C. M.T. joined for duty with 2nd Ambulance Car No 14166.	Army
"	6		General TWINING 1st Army & D.I.M.S. XIII Corps visited the Field Ambulance.	Army

Army Form C. 2118.

WAR DIARY
INTELLIGENCE SUMMARY
(Erase heading not required.)

Instructions regarding War Diaries and Intelligence Summaries are contained in F. S. Regs., Part II. and the Staff Manual respectively. Title Pages will be prepared in manuscript.

Place	Date	Hour	Summary of Events and Information	Remarks and references to Appendices
ROCLINCOURT	July 7th	—	Advanced Dressing Station (B.14.c.9.5 - map 51.b.N.W. 1:20,000 -) & bearer posts handed over to O.C. 2/5 Field Ambulance who will for tonight be responsible for the evacuation of patients from the front line. 100 F.A. still provide bearer party at the Dressing Station at the light railway head at B.19.b.6.3. (map 51.b.N.W. 1:20,000) to evacuate patients by rail to the main Dressing Station.	
"		—	T/Captain. A.GILLIETH. R.A.M.C. proceeded to 2/1 North Staff Regt. for temporary duty in relief of T/Captain. I. HORSLEY. R.A.M.C. who proceeds on leave to U.K. Tomorrow -	January
"		—	T/Captain. J. PATON. R.A.M.C. returned to his 5th Field Ambulance	

Army Form C. 2118.

WAR DIARY
or
INTELLIGENCE SUMMARY
(Erase heading not required.)

Instructions regarding War Diaries and Intelligence Summaries are contained in F. S. Regs., Part II. and the Staff Manual respectively. Title Pages will be prepared in manuscript.

Place	Date	Hour	Summary of Events and Information	Remarks and references to Appendices
RECINCOURT	June & the end		Captain J. VALLANCE R.A.M.C (S.R) proceeded to 1st Army H.Qrs for duty & is struck off the strength of No 7 F.A.	
			No 26276 Sergeant F H FLOWER R.A.M.C proceeded to D of A.P. & S.S to take a temporary Commission - & is struck off the strength of No 7 F.A	
			T/Captain L. HORSLEY R.A.M.C. proceeded on leave to U.K.	January
"	9.	—	T/Captain P. J. LANE M.C. R.A.M.C. rejoined from leave to U.K. T/Captain K. GALLETLY R.A.M.C. rejoined from temporary duty with 2nd South Staff. Regt.	
			One O.R. A.S.C. H.T. rein proceeded joined for duty from 2nd Div. Train	January

2449 Wt. W14957/M90 750,000 1/16 J.B.C. & A. Forms/C.2118/12.

Army Form C. 2118.

WAR DIARY
INTELLIGENCE SUMMARY
(Erase heading not required.)

Place	Date	Hour	Summary of Events and Information	Remarks and references to Appendices
ROCLINCOURT	June 10th	—	T/Captain T. BOURNE PRICE M.C. (RAMC) rejoined from leave U.K.	Bourne
"	11th	—	T/Captain D.F.A. NEILSON RAMC proceeded to 24th Royal Fusiliers for temporary duty. One A.R. RAMC joined for duty. O.C. 16th Field Ambulance visited with reference to taking over at an early date.	Bourne Neilson
"	12th	—	Routine.	
"	13th	—	Orders received from A.D.M.S. to hand over F.A. premises at ROCLINCOURT to the 15 Field Ambulance tomorrow. 100 F.A. to move to CAMBLIGNEUL (W.15.C.3.6. Map 26G. 1 = 40000) a/c relief.	Bourne
"	14th	—	Having handed over to 15th F.A. 100 F.A. proceeded from ROCLINCOURT at 10.30 a.m. + arrived at CAMBLIGNEUL at 4 p.m.	Bourne

Army Form C. 2118.

WAR DIARY
INTELLIGENCE SUMMARY
(Erase heading not required.)

Place	Date	Hour	Summary of Events and Information	Remarks and references to Appendices
CAMBRIGNEUL	June 15th	—	Lieut & Q. Mr. E.B. SNOWDEN R.A.M.C. proceeded on leave to U.K.	Appendix
"	16.6	—	No 55156. Pte. J. ALEXANDER proceeded to 62nd Sanitary Section to learn to work Green in Director in Sanitation.	Appendix
"	16.6	—	T/Captain. A. GALLETLY. R.A.M.C awarded the Military Cross	Appendix
"	17.6	—	T/Captain. B.W. ARMSTRONG R.A.M.C returned from leave to U.K.	Appendix
"	18.6	—	T/Captain. H. GALLETLY. R.A.M.C. proceeded to 13th Force Reft for Kidney dis't. R.A.M.C. Operation orders received from A/D.M.S. that 2nd Division were being to XI Corps in relief of 66th Division. An advance party of 1 Officer & 3 O.R.s proceeded to MESPLAUX FARM near LOCON (X.14.a.9.6) for the purpose of reconnoitring the line. (Map Bethune Trench Sheet 1 = 40,000)	

Army Form C. 2118.

WAR DIARY
or
INTELLIGENCE SUMMARY
(Erase heading not required.)

Instructions regarding War Diaries and Intelligence Summaries are contained in F. S. Regs., Part II. and the Staff Manual respectively. Title Pages will be prepared in manuscript.

Place	Date	Hour	Summary of Events and Information	Remarks and references to Appendices
CAMBRIN	June 19th	—	Another advance party N° 1 h c o & 6 o r s proceeded to MESPLAUX for the purpose of leaving the portion of his A.D.Stn & Bearer posts & reconnoitring the line.	
"	"	—	No 66321 Sergt Major F. W. JEFFRIES R.A.M.C proceeded on leave to U.K.	
"	"	—	1 OR RAMC reinforcement arrived for duty	
BETHUNE	20th	—	No field Ambulance left CAMBIGNEUL at 7.30 a.m. & marched to MONT ST ELOY (map LENS 1:100,000, from where they proceeded 2.1.20.15 by transport to MUIZIEL Ambulance proceeded BETHUNE The personnel were billeted in & around at 6 a.m. by road — Les ECOLE CATO RIVE — (E.S.C - Map Bethune Central Sheet 1:10,000) for the night	

2449 Wt. W14957/M90 750,000 1/16 J.B.C. & A. Forms/C.2118/12.

Army Form C. 2118.

WAR DIARY
INTELLIGENCE SUMMARY
(Erase heading not required.)

Instructions regarding War Diaries and Intelligence Summaries are contained in F. S. Regs., Part II. and the Staff Manual respectively. Title Pages will be prepared in manuscript.

Place	Date	Hour	Summary of Events and Information	Remarks and references to Appendices
BETHUNE	June 20th (Cont)		Visited 2/1st East Lancs Field Ambulance with reference to taking over tomorrow. Captain P.J. HAVE R.A.M.C. with 15 O.Rs. proceeded to F.12.C.7.1 & took over his advanced Dressing Stn "LONE FARM" at 9.30 p.m. from O.C. A.D.S. 2/1st East Lancs F.A.	
LOCON	21st	—	Captain T. BOURNE PRICE M.C. R.A.M.C. with 15 O.Rs proceeded to F.5.a.6.0 & took over the Advanced Dressing Stn "TUNING FORK" from O.C. A.D.S. 2/1st East Lancs F.A. The remainder of the 100 R.R. marched from BETHUNE at 11 a.m. to MESPLAUX FARM near LOCON - X.14.a.9.6. Main Dressing Station taken over from O.C. 2/1st East Lancs F.E. Captain (late) S. MURRAY R.A.M.C. reported for duty & in taken on the strength of the unit.	Moving up. BETHUNE to LOCON 1:

2449 Wt. W14957/M90 750,000 1/16 J.B.C. & A. Forms/C.2118/12.

Army Form C. 2118.

WAR DIARY
or
INTELLIGENCE SUMMARY
(Erase heading not required.)

Instructions regarding War Diaries and Intelligence Summaries are contained in F. S. Regs., Part II. and the Staff Manual respectively. Title Pages will be prepared in manuscript.

Place	Date	Hour	Summary of Events and Information	Remarks and references to Appendices
LOCON	June 21st (cont)		16 ORs RAMC reinforcements reported for duty & were taken on war strength of this unit. Appointments: No 66354 a/Lce Sergeant H.W. DUTTON RAMC to be a/Sergeant. No 66910 a/Lce Cpl T.W. LEE RAMC to be a/Cpl. No 1337 a/Cpl H. FARROW RAMC to be a/Cpl. No 64650 a/Lce Cpl W. GUTHRIE RAMC to be a/Cpl.	Penury army
"	22nd	—	Visited advanced Dressing Stations at "LONG" FARM & "TUNING FORK"	army
"	23rd	—	No 90506 Pte. J.R. CREWE RAMC posted to 41st Brigade R.F.A. for water duties, & struck off the strength of this Unit.	Penury army
	28th 29th		Routine	army

2449 Wt. W14957/M90 750,000 1/16 J.B.C. & A. Forms/C.2118/12.

Army Form C. 2118.

WAR DIARY
of
INTELLIGENCE SUMMARY
(Erase heading not required.)

Instructions regarding War Diaries and Intelligence Summaries are contained in F. S. Regs., Part II. and the Staff Manual respectively. Title Pages will be prepared in manuscript.

Place	Date	Hour	Summary of Events and Information	Remarks and references to Appendices
LOCON.	June 25th	-	Routine -	Spruce
"	26th	-	41 Wounded Casualties admitted during last night - Interred in a German Raid -	
			1 OR A.V.C. M.T evacuated this Base into Danish Con In M.999 a stranger off the strength of this unit.	Spruce
"	27th	-	Temp Captain L. HORSLEY R.A.M.C proceeded for temporary duty with 22nd Royal Fusiliers. Lieut & Qr Mr E. B. SNOWDEN returned from leave 6.00 P.M.	Spruce
"	28th		Temp Captain T. BOURNE PRICE M.C R.A.M.C proceeded 6-2 P.M. Div H.Q On on temporary D.A.D.M.S	Spruce

2449 Wt. W14957/M90 750,000 1/16 J.B.C. & A. Forms/C.2118/M6.

Army Form C. 2118.

WAR DIARY
or
INTELLIGENCE SUMMARY
(Erase heading not required.)

Place	Date	Hour	Summary of Events and Information	Remarks and references to Appendices
Locon.	June 29th	—	8 ORs RAMC reinforcements arrived for duty & taken on his strength. The Btn. is now up to strength in WO, Officers & ORs Strong	
"	30th	—	Routine.	Morning

J. A. Hudson.
Lieut Colonel O.R. Payne.
O.C. 1/5 7-a

Army Form C. 2118.

WAR DIARY
or
INTELLIGENCE SUMMARY

(Erase heading not required.)

100TH FIELD AMBULANCE.
No. 2098/16.
Date. 1.8.17.

CONFIDENTIAL

War Diary of 100 Field Ambulance
July 1st to July 31st 1917

Vol. 21.

Army Form C. 2118.

WAR DIARY
or
INTELLIGENCE SUMMARY
(Erase heading not required.)

Place	Date	Hour	Summary of Events and Information	Remarks and references to Appendices
LOCON	JULY 1st	—	T/Captain A. GALLETLY. R.A.M.C. rejoined from Temporary duty with 13th Essex Regt. T/Captain D.F.A. NEILSON. R.A.M.C. rejoined from temporary duty with 24th Royal Fusiliers & proceeded on leave to the U.K. <u>Appointments</u> No 1327 a/Cpl. H. FARROW R.A.M.C. to be acting Serjeant with pay. No 64650 a/Lce Cpl W. GUTHRIE R.A.M.C. to be acting Corporal with pay - Posh appointments to date from 23.6.17. One Private a.s.c. m.T. proceeded for duty with 2nd Div. Supply Column & struck off strength of this Unit.	

L. Moore
Lieut Col. R.A.M.C.

WAR DIARY
INTELLIGENCE SUMMARY
(Erase heading not required.)

Army Form C. 2118.

Place	Date	Hour	Summary of Events and Information	Remarks and references to Appendices
LOCON	July 2nd	—	Routine.	Appendices
"	3rd	—	One Private A.S.C. M.T. joined for duty, with new Sunbeam Ambulance Car, & is taken on the strength of this Unit.	Appendices
			No 73193. a/Lce Cpl J.T. SMITH R.A.M.C. (without pay) to be acting Lance Corpl with pay.	
"	4th	—	a/D.M.S. First Army visited the field Ambulance & inspected the wards & previous.	Appendices
"	5th	—	Thirteen Cases of Shell Gas poisoning admitted & evacuated. Ye result of a Gas bomb Raid by the Germans on 17th Royal Fusiliers. The Officer & 2 men belonging to working parties behind the line were gassed. All were slight cases into two Reception of three.	Appendices

Army Form C. 2118.

WAR DIARY
INTELLIGENCE SUMMARY.
(Erase heading not required.)

Instructions regarding War Diaries and Intelligence Summaries are contained in F.S. Regs., Part II. and the Staff Manual respectively. Title pages will be prepared in manuscript.

Place	Date	Hour	Summary of Events and Information	Remarks and references to Appendices
LOCON.	July 6th	—	3 private R.A.M.C. struck off ht strength of this unit - on wounded sick, two men transferred to 205th Employment Coy.	Appendix
"	7th	—	Major General Commanding 2nd Division visited h/s Field Ambulance & inspected h/s wards & personnel.	Appendix
"	8th	—	10 wounded cases admitted during the night - h/s went by a raid upon the Portugese troops.	Appendix
"	9th	—	D.D.M.S. XIth Corps visited the Field Ambulance & inspected h/s wards & premises.	Appendix
"	—	—	Captain T. BOURNE-PRICE. M.C. R.A.M.C. & T/Capt T. BOURNE-PRICE M.C. R.A.M.C. rejoined the unit for duty from temporary duty as a/D.A.D.M.S.	Appendix
"	10th	—	Lt.Col. E.A.M. MOORE R.A.M.C. & T/Capt T. BOURNE-PRICE M.C. R.A.M.C. Lieut President. were members of a Medical Board at BETHUNE on "P.B" & "U" men - Col. H. HERRICK. D.S.O. A.M.S. Lieut President. One O.R. R.A.M.C. taken on h/s strength of this unit.	Appendix

Army Form C. 2118.

WAR DIARY

INTELLIGENCE SUMMARY.

(Erase heading not required.)

Instructions regarding War Diaries and Intelligence Summaries are contained in F. S. Regs., Part II. and the Staff Manual respectively. Title pages will be prepared in manuscript.

Place	Date	Hour	Summary of Events and Information	Remarks and references to Appendices
LOCON	July 11th	—	Routine	Routine
"	12th	—	Lt. Col. E.H.M. MOORE. R.A.M.C. proceeded on leave to the U.K. Temporary Command of the Unit handed over to T/Captain B.W. ARMSTRONG. R.A.M.C.	Routine Armstrong Capt RAMC
"	13th	—	Routine	
"	14th	—	2nd Div. R.O. 267 of. 13/7 cancels Transfer of No.64652 Pte J. HOOD R.A.M.C. to 205th Employment Company & he is accordingly taken back on to Strength	MH
"	15th	—	Capt. D.F.A. NEILSON R.A.M.C. (T.C.) rejoined Unit today from leave in U.K. 1 Sgt. & 1 O.R. R.A.M.C. sent today to 2nd Div. Draft Training Depot for temporary duty	MH

A7092 Wt. W28 9/M1293 750,000. 1/17. D. D. & I. Ltd. Forms/C2118/14.

Army Form C. 2118.

WAR DIARY
~~INTELLIGENCE~~ SUMMARY.
(Erase heading not required.)

Instructions regarding War Diaries and Intelligence Summaries are contained in F. S. Regs., Part II. and the Staff Manual respectively. Title pages will be prepared in manuscript.

Place	Date	Hour	Summary of Events and Information	Remarks and references to Appendices
LOCON	July 16th		Capt. L. HORSLEY R.A.M.C. (T.C.) rejoined unit today from Temporary duty with 22nd Fd Amb. A.D.M.S. 2nd Div. visited F.A. today.	
"	17th		M2 106200 Pte A.W. PEGRAM A.S.C. (M.T.) & Dunham Ambulance joined unit for duty today.	
"	18th		17821 Capt. S. MURRAY R.A.M.C. (T.C.) departed today on leave to UK Routine. Attended lecture with S.Sgt-Major Pinches & Sgt Matson A.S.C. (H.T.) by Corps A.D.V.S. in horsemastership & horse lines	18MA
"	19th		Routine	13MA
"	20th		G.O.C. XI Corps visited F.A. this morning in company with the G.O.C. 2nd Div., A.D.M.S., A.A. & Q.M.G. 2nd Div. O.C. & inspected Hospital Premises & horse lines	17MA

A7092 Wt. W125 9/M1295 750,000. 1/17. D/D & L. Ltd. Forms/C2118/14.

Army Form C. 2118.

WAR DIARY
INTELLIGENCE SUMMARY.
(Erase heading not required.)

Instructions regarding War Diaries and Intelligence Summaries are contained in F. S. Regs., Part II. and the Staff Manual respectively. Title pages will be prepared in manuscript.

Place	Date	Hour	Summary of Events and Information	Remarks and references to Appendices
LOCON	July 21/17		Under instructions of A.D.M.S. 2nd Div., Capt. L. HORSLEY R.A.M.C. (T.C.) left the unit to-day to proceed to England on relinquishing his temporary commission being struck off the strength of the unit accordingly	
"	22nd		Routine	
"	23rd		The Rev. J.C. RENDALL C.F. (Non C. of E.) left the unit to-day on re-posting to 99th M.G.C. struck off the strength of the unit.	
"	24th		Routine	
"	25th		Wire received by A.D.M.S. from Lieut: Colonel E.H.M. MOORE R.A.M.C. stating that he had a sudden attack of Appendicitis & was being operated on. Under orders of A.D.M.S. 2nd Div. Capt. R.F.A. NEILSON R.A.M.C. (TC) departed this morning for temporary duty under D.M.S. II Army	

Army Form C. 2118.

WAR DIARY
or
INTELLIGENCE SUMMARY.
(Erase heading not required.)

7.

Instructions regarding War Diaries and Intelligence Summaries are contained in F. S. Regs., Part II. and the Staff Manual respectively. Title pages will be prepared in manuscript.

Place	Date	Hour	Summary of Events and Information	Remarks and references to Appendices
LOCONDA	July 26		Routine	BWA.
"	27		T3/023537 Dr. PARKIN. T. ASC(H.T.) proceed to 65 ASC. Base Depot for release for mining duties struck off the strength	BWA
"	28		Routine	BWA
"	29		Cpl. S. MURRAY rejoined unit from leave in U.K.	BWA
"	30		Routine	BWA
"	31		Routine	B.McAnerty. Capt. RAMC O.C. 100 F.A.

Army Form C. 2118.

WAR DIARY
INTELLIGENCE SUMMARY.
(Erase heading not required.)

Vol 25

CONFIDENTIAL

War Diary of 100 Field Ambulance
August 1st to August 31st 1917

Vol. 22.

Army Form C. 2118.

WAR DIARY
or
INTELLIGENCE SUMMARY.
(Erase heading not required.)

Instructions regarding War Diaries and Intelligence Summaries are contained in F. S. Regs., Part II. and the Staff Manual respectively. Title pages will be prepared in manuscript.

Place	Date	Hour	Summary of Events and Information	Remarks and references to Appendices
LOCON	August 1st		Routine	Withdrawing Corp-CRHQ
HOSPLAUX FARM X.14.b.9.6 Ref. map BETHUNE (Contoured Sheet) Scale 1/6	2nd		Capt T. BOURNE PRICE. M.C. RAMC(T.C.) proceeded to A.D.M.S. 2nd Div for temporary duty as a/D.A.D.M.S. T2/5796 Dr. R. SHARKEY A.S.C.(H.T.) joined unit for duty was taken on to the strength.	BWA BWA
	3rd		Routine	BWA
	4th		Routine. First Army Instructor in Catering visited F.A. + inspected Kitchens	BWA
	5th		Routine	BWA
	6th		Lieut Colonel. E.A.M. MOORE. R.A.M.C. struck off the strength of the unit from 24th July (Authority War office no. 56782/8(A.M.D.1) of 31 July) Capt J. LEITCH WILSON R.A.M.C.(T.C.) joined the unit from 2nd Div Train on the strength accordingly. Under instructions of A.D.M.S. he is to remain in medical + sanitary charge of the Train.	BWA
	7th		S86045 Sgt A.J. COLEMAN R.A.M.C. joined the unit for duty + was taken on strength according [to] following report received from 1st Army Instructor in Catering — 100 Field Ambulance "I formed the opinion that this is the best catered for unit in the Division"	BWA
	8th			BWA
	9th		1st Lieut. E.F. SCHMITZ. U.S.M.C. joined for duty with this unit + was taken on the strength accordingly	BWA
	10th		Sgt F.S. WEBB. R.A.M.C. departed for duty with O.C. Transportation of Troops Depot; under authority of D.M.S. L. of C. no M14/97/17 of 3/6/17 was struck off the strength	BWA

Army Form C. 2118.

WAR DIARY
or
INTELLIGENCE SUMMARY.
(Erase heading not required.)

No. 100 Field Amb.

Instructions regarding War Diaries and Intelligence Summaries are contained in F.S. Regs, Part II. and the Staff Manual respectively. Title pages will be prepared in manuscript.

Place	Date	Hour	Summary of Events and Information	Remarks and references to Appendices
LOCON	10th	4 pm	Has S.P. Army inspected unit at 3 pm. Accompanied by A/DMS XI Corps & A/DMS Division.	
NESPLAUX FARM X.14.6.9.6. Ref. Map. 36⁵ S.E.			Capt. R.E.V. NEWMAN, RAMC assumed command of unit in afternoon vice Lt Col. E.H.R. MOORE, struck off strength of B.E.F. "sick". Capt. S. MURRAY RAMC (T.C.) went to 23rd R. Fuseliers for temp. duty as M.O. K.	[sig] Capt. Army
	11th	8.45 pm	Routine: AD MS visited unit at 5 pm to see two men proposed to transfer to another depot.	[sig]
	12th	7.15 pm	17 wounded in during night + during day. One French Civilian (Boy 4 yrs) admitted multiple — multiple shrapnel wound (Christmas Eve — noted) Seen me by Intelligence Section (Colligne Coy HQ Staff). Eye J and died 1 hour after admission. Visited LONE FARM A.D.S. and R.A.P.s of Light Beta during morning.	[sig]
	13th	7.30 pm	Routine: Visited TUNING FORK A.D.S. & R.A.P. in "Barnton Rd".	[sig]
	14th	7 pm	Routine:	[sig]
	15th		Capt. R.E.V. NEWMAN R.A.M.C. departed on leave to U.K. (15.8.17 – 26.8.17) handing over command of the unit to Capt. B.W. ARMSTRONG R.A.M.C. (T.C.) Capt. J. LEITCH WILSON R.A.M.C. (T.C.) proceeded to 13th ESSEX Regt. for Temporary duty. Capt. T. BOURNE PRICE M.C. R.A.M.C.(T.C.) reported return from temporary duty as a/D.A.D.M.S. 2nd Div.	[sig] Capt. RAMC
	16th		1st Lieut. E.J. SCHMITZ U.S.M.C. proceeded to P. of W. Camp (HOOGRAES for Temporary duty under orders of D.M.S. 1st ARMY.	[sig]

Army Form C. 2118.

WAR DIARY
or
INTELLIGENCE SUMMARY.
(Erase heading not required.)

Instructions regarding War Diaries and Intelligence Summaries are contained in F.S. Regs., Part II. and the Staff Manual respectively. Title pages will be prepared in manuscript.

Place	Date	Hour	Summary of Events and Information	Remarks and references to Appendices
LOCON (MESPLAUX farm)	Aug 17th		Three Ambulance Commanders from the 57th Division rented two F.A. + were shown M.D.S. MESPLAUX FARM + A.D.S. LONE FARM	AMA
	18th		Ten riding horses arrived today handed in to No 3 M.V.S. + struck off strength on reduction of number of riding horses of F.A. by Six. No 64667 Pte D.S. GRANT R.A.M.C. transferred to R.E. under A.O.204/15 struck off strength of unit from 12/8/17 Authority O/c R.A.M.C. Section Base No 1696 af-16/7/17.	AMA
	19th		Routine. Notified by O/c R.A.M.C. Section Base that No 64768 Pte G. FRISKEN R.A.M.C. was then admitted to hospital in the U.K. but was to be retained on the strength.	AMA
	20th		Routine. Vis. Fed A.D.S. Tommy Fork Road.	AMA
	21st		Routine. 1 L.D. man died of "Dag" colic	AMA
	22nd		Routine.	AMA

Army Form C. 2118.

WAR DIARY
or
INTELLIGENCE SUMMARY.
(Erase heading not required.)

Instructions regarding War Diaries and Intelligence Summaries are contained in F. S. Regs., Part II. and the Staff Manual respectively. Title pages will be prepared in manuscript.

Place	Date	Hour	Summary of Events and Information	Remarks and references to Appendices
LOCON (MESPLAUX Farm)	Aug 23		Routine	BHA.
"	" 24		Routine	BHA.
"	" 25		Routine. Visited A.D.S. Turning Post Road. The work of building a new entrance to one of the elephant shelters is progressing	MA.
"	" 26		1st Lieut. E. F. SCHMITZ U.S.M.C. reporting unit from temporary duty at P. of W. Camp CHOCQUES	MMA.

Army Form C. 2118.

WAR DIARY
or
INTELLIGENCE SUMMARY.
(Erase heading not required.)

Instructions regarding War Diaries and Intelligence Summaries are contained in F. S. Regs., Part II. and the Staff Manual respectively. Title pages will be prepared in manuscript.

Place	Date	Hour	Summary of Events and Information	Remarks and references to Appendices
LOCON (MESPLAUX F21)	July 27th	7/rn	Routine: Lt.Col. Kell-Newman returned from leave from U.K. Capt. S. MURRAY Reims rejoined tr unit from temp. duty at H.Q. 2 2/3rd Fusiliers. R.S. Officer inspected Horse Standings with two Veterinary 3 Officers + 1 man of Portuguese Corps. evacuated to No.51 C.C.S. 2 day (local sick).	Heavy Rain.
"	28th	7 Am.	Routine: Visited "Tuning Fork" A.D.S. 1st Lieut. E. F. SCHMITZ (U.S.A.M.O.R.C.) to "Rose Farm" A.D.S. for temporary duty (Instruction). Capt. J. LEITCH WILSON Reims rejoined unit from leave.	Fine
"	"	7 Pm.	Capt J LEITCH WILSON for temp duty at H.Q. 2 13th Essex Regt.	
"	29th	7 Pm.	Routine: Transport inspected by O.C. Divisional Train. - A few stragglers fallen out.	Rain
"	30th	"	Routine: Held "Marching Order" Parade of all available men. Capt. J. Murray to Bethune for temp. duty as Sanitary Advisor to Town troops.	Fine
"	31st	4/rn	Routine: Capt T. BOURNE - PRICE to Divl. H.Q. for temp. duty as a/g/S.O.S.; Visited "Rose Farm" A.D.S. + Reme Post, Queen St. 2 Shell Gas cases in during past 48 hours.	Fine

Alys r Newman
Lt.Col. Reime
O.C. No100 Field Ambulance

Return of Sick & Wounded Admissions, Evacuations etc during Month of August. 1917.

Date Augt	Admiss		Evac'ns		Duty		Died		Remarks	
	Off	OR	Off	OR	Off	OR	Off	OR		
1	3	15	1	12	-	5	-	-		
2	-	9	2	9	-	3	-	-		
3	-	10	-	10	-	2	-	-		
4	-	20	-	9	-	2	-	-		
5	4	10	1	11	-	-	-	-		
6	-	9	3	9	-	1	-	-		
7	1	20	-	11	-	3	-	-		
8	1	24	2	15	-	4	-	-		
9	1	10	1	15	-	5	-	-		
10	-	14	-	7	-	-	-	-		
11	1	31	-	21	-	3	-	1		
12	-	18	1	23	-	5	-	-		
13	1	17	1	17	-	2	-	1		
14	-	19	-	18	-	2	-	-		
15	-	11	-	18	-	1	-	-		
16	-	15	-	7	-	-	-	-		
17	-	14	-	8	-	1	-	1		
18	1	15	1	14	-	1	-	-		
19	2	11	-	14	-	2	-	-		
20	-	15	1	11	-	1	-	-		
21	-	14	-	10	-	1	-	-		
22	1	12	-	15	-	6	-	-		
23	-	10	1	11	-	-	-	-		
24	-	12	-	9	-	2	-	-		
25	1	13	-	14	-	2	-	-		
26	2	8	2	9	1	1	-	-		
27	3⊛	17⊕	3⊛	9	-	-	-	-	⊛ 3 Portuguese	⊕ 1 Portuguese
28	1	15	-	11⊕	-	-	-	-	⊕ 1 - do -	
29	-	16⊕	1	10⊕	-	2	-	-	⊕ 2 do.	
30	2	11	1	8	1	2	-	-		
31	-	8⊕	1	11⊕	-	3	-	-	⊕ 2 do.	
	25	443	23	376	2	62	-	3		

100TH FIELD AMBULANCE.

Notes on 2nd Division Diet Records.
by Instructor in Catering, First Army.

Copy.

Unit.	Standard attained.	Remarks.
5th Field Amb'ce.	Fairly Good.	Not a good enough standard for a Fd. Amb'ce, which has all the advantages.
6th Field Amb'ce.	Good.	Capable of much improvement, however.
100th Field Amb'ce.	Very good indeed.	Easily the best record.

Although this was not known when diet sheets were asked for, on four days in succession there was practically no fresh meat. The test may therefore be regarded as a fairly severe one. The Instructor in Catering can only conjecture which Infantry Battalions were in trenches in most cases by the quality of the diets given although about two units furnished the information.

The Artillery are disappointingly poor in some cases and should certainly do better than the Infantry.

In judging the standard, due regard is paid to the circumstances as far as known in each case.

(Sd) W. H. Fowler, Capt.
Instructor in Catering,
First Army.

Report by Instructor in Catering, First Army.

Copy.

Headquarters
   2nd. Division.

The following notes apply to Field Ambulances of the 2nd Division visited today, 4th August:—

100th Field Ambulance.

I formed the opinion that this is the best catered for unit in the Division.

6th. Field Ambulance.

A very clean, well arranged and equipped cookhouse. The diet was good and well varied but hardly up to the excellent standard of 100th. Field Ambulance.

* * * * * * * * * * *

General Remarks.

The cult of the stockpot is not studied sufficiently by some of the units.

Tea-bags — made from the muslin bacon wrappers were not being used everywhere.

Economy & under indenting of rations was being practised to some extent.

Cleanliness was good in all cases.

4. 8. 17.

(Signed) W. H. Fowler,
Captain,
Instructor in Catering,
First Army.

100TH
FIELD AMBULANCE.

No ....
Date ....

Army Form C. 2118

WAR DIARY
or
INTELLIGENCE SUMMARY
(Erase heading not required.)

100TH FIELD AMBULANCE.

No ....
Date ....

WO 26

140/2438

Confidential
War Diary No 100 F^d A^{mb}
Volume 23

COMMITTEE FOR THE
MEDICAL HISTORY OF THE WAR
Date -5 NOV 1917

Army Form C. 2118.

WAR DIARY
or
~~INTELLIGENCE SUMMARY.~~
(Erase heading not required.)

Instructions regarding War Diaries and Intelligence Summaries are contained in F. S. Regs., Part II. and the Staff Manual respectively. Title pages will be prepared in manuscript.

Place	Date	Hour	Summary of Events and Information	Remarks and references to Appendices
LOCON (MESPLAUX Fm) X.14.B.9.6.	Sept 1st		Ref. Map. BETHUNE (Combined Sheets) 1/40,000 Routine: 10 P.B. men joined from Base for duty as Officers Batmen in replacement of 10 A.S.C. Batmen Category "A" who will later proceed to the Base for general duty.	WM/testament that sent
"	2nd	7 am	Routine: Capt A. GALLETLY M.C. R.Army went on leave to U.K. being relieved at "Tuning Fork" A.D.S. by 1st Lieut SCHMITZ, U.S.A. – M.O.R.C.	MWZ
"	3rd	5.30 pm	Routine: Capt J. LEITCH WILSON R.Army who proceeds for temp. duty as M.O. 17th R. Fusiliers from over from 1st Lieut. SCHMITZ this afternoon preparatory to taking work of extending & improving horse standings proceeding	MWZ
"	4th	5.15 pm	Routine: 9 A.S.C. Batmen (Category "A") struck off strength on departure to report to A.S.C. (H.T.) Depot, HAVRE.	MWZ
"	5th	7 pm	Routine: 3 officers 1/13th Essex Regt + 1 Portuguese Officer, all wounded by same shell, passed through Dressing Station in evening.	MWZ
"	6th	5.30	Routine:	MWZ
"	7th	3.6 am	Routine: Capt. S. MURRAY R.Army reported unit on relief as San. Advisor to Town Major, BETHUNE, by Capt. T. BOURNE - Price M.C. R.Army from a L.84 O.M.S. 2nd Division. Held Kit Authorities of Whole unit. Name A.S.C. (H.T. +M.T.)	MWZ

A7092 Wt. W.125 y/M.1293 750,000. 1/17. D. D & L Ltd Forms/C.2118/14.

Army Form C. 2118.

WAR DIARY
or
~~INTELLIGENCE SUMMARY~~
(Erase heading not required.)

Instructions regarding War Diaries and Intelligence Summaries are contained in F. S. Regs., Part II. and the Staff Manual respectively. Title pages will be prepared in manuscript.

Place	Date	Hour	Summary of Events and Information	Remarks and references to Appendices
LOCON	8/2		Routine: visited A.D.S. at "Tuning Fork" and "Lone Farm"	
	9/2		Routine: Capt. LESTER WILSON Allison granted 48 hrs leave to go to BOULOGNE	
	10/2	7/n	Routine: I.O.C. Simson inspected F.A. Hqs in afternoon	
	11/2	7/n	Allison (T.F.) Officer from England & 5md L.E. Brigade Portuguese Corps visited units to see work of a Field Ambulance. Visited A.D.Ss. Field inspection of all Sn. Bn. Reservists & P.A.Helmets. Capt Lester Wilson returned from 48 hrs leave. Capt. T Bourne-Price M.C. reported back from temp. duty with Town Major BETHUNE	
	12/2		Routine: Medical B.P. DORAN U.S.A. M.O.R.C. joined to unit for instruction and a/c	
	13/2	7/n	Visited Lone Farm A.D.S. & R.A.P. in front sector in forenoon. Lieut P.J LANE RAMC passed on leave to U.K. - Replaced at Lone FARM A.D.S. by Capt S. MURRAY RAMC, who later in the day was ordered to join 2nd Oxfd & Bucks L.I. in consequence duty and was relieved at LONE FARM A.D.S. by Capt. T. BOURNE - PRICE M.C. RAMC. No.5 Field Amb. visited MESPLAUX FARM preparatory to taking over the men Corps Rest Station, Skin Sept. & officers Rest Home. This unit will be billeted & take over Corps Rest Station, Skin sept. etc at MERVILLE from No.5 F.A.	

Army Form C. 2118.

WAR DIARY
or
INTELLIGENCE SUMMARY.
(Erase heading not required.)

Instructions regarding War Diaries and Intelligence Summaries are contained in F. S. Regs., Part II. and the Staff Manual respectively. Title pages will be prepared in manuscript.

Place	Date	Hour	Summary of Events and Information	Remarks and references to Appendices
LOCON (MESPLAUX FARM)	14th		Routine: Visited Corps Rest Station, Officers Rest Station and Corps Skin Depot at MERVILLE preparatory to taking over charge on 18th inst.	Nil
"	15th	7 hrs	Routine. Captain A GARRETY M.C. Reime reported unit on leave from U.K.	Nil
	16th		Routine: Visited A.D.S. Lavrange re handing over on 17th inst. I.N.C.D. 84 men went to Corps Rest Station, MERVILLE for instruction.	Nil
	17	7:30	Capt. A GARRETY M.C. Reime and 39 O.R. left at 9 pm to take over charge of Corps Rest Station MERVILLE from No. 5 F.A. Handed over charge of A.D.S. at LONE FARM & TUNING FORK MERVILLE from No.5 F.A. at 6 pm. Advance Parties from No.5 F.A.	
MERVILLE {XI Corps Rest Station}	18	9 am 1 pm	Unit left MESPLAUX Farm & marched to MERVILLE. Took over charge of XI Corps Rest Station, Corps head Skin Depot, and Corps Officers Rest Station from No.5 Field Ambulance, leaving over A.D.S. at MESPLAUX Farm to same Unit. Capt. T. BOURKE-PRICE the Reime posted to Medical charge of 2nd Div R.E. & struck off strength of the Unit. Capt. G. MURRAY Reime defastated for England, under orders ex India, and struck off strength Sirint 1st Lieut. E.F. Schmitz USA-MORE posted for temp. duty as N.O.K. 2nd Div. & Brooks I.O.	Nil

A7092 Wt. W128 9/M1293 750,000. 1/17. D. D & I. Ltd. Forms/C2118/14.

Army Form C. 2118.

WAR DIARY
or
INTELLIGENCE SUMMARY.
(Erase heading not required.)

Instructions regarding War Diaries and Intelligence Summaries are contained in F. S. Regs., Part II. and the Staff Manual respectively. Title pages will be prepared in manuscript.

Place	Date	Hour	Summary of Events and Information	Remarks and references to Appendices
MERVILLE (Corps Rest Station)	19th	10am	Routine: Inspection of C.R.S. Officers Rest Station	
		3pm	Visited Stores XI Corps Truck re (1) Electric light (2) Beds for C.R.S. (3) Personnel for Baths.	
		4pm	Visited Red Cross Stores at HAM-EN-ARTOIS re Stores, Games etc. for Rest Station & Officers Depot.	
"	20th	1pm	Routine & Inspection of Confectio[n] Depot etc. Horses lined most indifferently - No Conveyancy and provided. Then main tents & Harness room is small & leaky.	
"	21st		Routine: Capt. LEITCH WILSON left for England & reported N.W.C. on completion of Contract and is struck off the strength accordingly. Capt. A GARRETLY posted i/charge of Skin Depot, Capt. B.M. ARMSTRONG leaving i/charge of Officers Rest Station, leaving 1st Lieut. DORAN U.S.A in charge self only for duty as Corps Rest Station. This number of Officers not sufficient. It is impossible to pay sufficient attention to administration of Officers Rest Station, Corps Rest Station and C/I Skin Depot, and at the same time do executive work in the Corps Rest Station.	
"	22nd		Routine, Inspect C.R.S. Inf. a case of Shell Gas Poisoning Attached to Corps Rest Station from No. 129 Field Amb. (Sergt. FAIR). Sent in Indents to C.R.C. XI Corps for Gratuities for Nursing 200 Hospl. beds. Capt. & F.A. NEILSON have reported from No 64 C.C.S.	
	23rd		Routine: Capt. NEILSON Admitted to the Corps Officers Rest Station	

WAR DIARY or INTELLIGENCE SUMMARY.

Army Form C. 2118.

(Erase heading not required.)

Instructions regarding War Diaries and Intelligence Summaries are contained in F. S. Regs., Part II. and the Staff Manual respectively. Title pages will be prepared in manuscript.

Place	Date	Hour	Summary of Events and Information	Remarks and references to Appendices
MERVILLE	24th		Routine: D.D.M.S. & I Corps visited Officers Rest Station & Corps Rest Station. Sanctioned application for 40 wire beds for Corps Rest Station. Nothing has yet been done re horse standings for the homeless.	N/L
	25th	7/am	Routine: Drainage of ditches round Corps Shower Billet being taken in hand. Submitted list of recommendations for Mont Honoré Gazette to H.Q. 1st & 2nd Divisions.	N/L
	26th	7/am	Routine: Inspected Officers Rest Station. Capt. H.W. FARROW A.S.C. 1st Army Area H.T. Coy. evacuated from Off. R. Station #54 C.C.S. with Scabies (chairmans + body/mesentery etc + abdominal case)	N/L
	27th	7/am	Routine.	N/L
	28th	"	Routine: D.D.M.S. & I Corps visited Corps Rest Station re provision of stoves for the homeless. Inspected C.B.B., Corps troops re practical for washing beds in C.R.S. and Horse Standings.	N/L
	29th	"	Routine: Capt. A.J. LANE M.O.I.C. returned from leave to U.K.	N/L
	30th	"	Routine: Remaining Officers R. Station 8. Corps Rest Station 185 – Shew Septet 57	N/L

Major Kinsman
L/Col. Kinsman
O.C. No. 100 Field Amb.

100TH FIELD AMBULANCE.

Appendix. 1.
War Diary 100 Field Ambce.

Admissions. Evac^{ns} etc. during month of Septr 1917.

100 Field Ambce 1/9/17 - 30/9/17.

	Admissions		Evacuations		Transfers		Duty	
	Off.	O.R.	Off.	O.R.	Off.	O.R.	Off.	O.R.
BRITISH	17	211	11	121	4	87	2	38
PORTUGUESE	1	79	1	79	—	—	—	—

XI Corps Rest Stn - Officers. 18/9/17 - 30/9/17

Admissions	Evacuations	Transfers	Duty
7	1	—	4

XI Corps Rest Stn - Other Rks 18/9/17 - 30/9/17

Admissions	Evacuations	Transfers	Duty
279	64	2	203

XI Corps Skin Depot. 18/9/17 - 30/9/17

Admissions	Evacuations	Transfers	Duty
62	11	—	34

Army Form C. 2118.

WAR DIARY
or
INTELLIGENCE SUMMARY.

(Erase heading not required.)

Confidential

War Diary of No. 100 Field Amb'ce

for October 1917.

Volume 24.

100TH FIELD AMBULANCE.
No. 2098/19
Date 1.11.17

COMMITTEE FOR THE
MEDICAL HISTORY OF THE WAR
Date —8 DEC. 1917

Army Form C. 2118.

WAR DIARY
or
INTELLIGENCE SUMMARY.
(Erase heading not required.)

No. 100 Field Ambulance

Instructions regarding War Diaries and Intelligence Summaries are contained in F. S. Regs., Part II. and the Staff Manual respectively. Title pages will be prepared in manuscript.

Place	Date	Hour	Summary of Events and Information	Remarks and references to Appendices
XI Corps Rest Station	1917 OCTOBER		Ref. Map. Sheet 36ᵃ (France) 1/40,000.	
MERVILLE (K 29)	1ˢᵗ		Routine: Capt. D.F.A. NEILSON R.A.M.C. (T.C.) takes over duty as M.O. & 22ⁿᵈ R. Fusiliers and attends officers of 1ˢᵗ./4ᵗʰ. E. F SCHMITZ. U.S.A. M.O.R.C. reported unit from temp. duty with 2ⁿᵈ Bn. Bucks L. Inf. Town of Merville bombed by enemy aircraft last night 3 civilians wounded. Visit from A.A. & Q.M.G. 2ⁿᵈ Division regarding Horse Standings for the Unit.	Fine
"	2ⁿᵈ	Thu	Routine. XI Corps visited Unit regarding the Provision of Hot Standing for the Unit and electric light. Early Eng. Ste. for the Corps Rest Station. Nothing has yet been fixed as regards these things and horses will probably be without shelter during bad weather.	Fine
	3ʳᵈ		Routine.	Nil
	4ᵗʰ		Routine. Capt. B.W. ARMSTONG Agnew R.C.) went on leave to U.K. Agnew 2nd S/O Of. Dahr R.3 reserve regarding Horses of Field Ambulances on 5ᵗʰ, 6ᵗʰ & 7ᵗʰ insts. on relief by Fd. Amb. Units of 25ᵗʰ Division. A.D.M.S. 2ᶜᵈ & 35ᵗʰ Divisions visited Corps Rest Station.	Rain.
	5ᵗʰ		Routine. Visited by A.C. No.87 Field Amb. preparatory to taking over charge of Corps Rest Station, Officers Rest Station & Light Skin Depot. 1 Sgt. attd. on 1 Pte. Relieve reported Unit from 2ⁿᵈ Divⁿ. Sig Staff School.	Nil
	6ᵗʰ	Thu	Handed over charge of XI Corps Officers Rest Station, Rest Station, and Skin Depot to No. 76 Field Ambulance & transferred the personnel of 73 B.A./R. 97/D. of 73 G.H. of 73 G.H. 130 B.O.R. transferred unit from temporary duty with No.54 C.C.S. and Skin Depot to No. 54 C.C.S.	Nil

Army Form C. 2118.

WAR DIARY
or
INTELLIGENCE SUMMARY.

(Erase heading not required.)

Instructions regarding War Diaries and Intelligence
Summaries are contained in F. S. Regs., Part II.
and the Staff Manual respectively. Title pages
will be prepared in manuscript.

Place	Date	Hour	Summary of Events and Information	Remarks and references to Appendices
AUCHEL C.27.I.6.4. (Hôtel de Ville)			Reference Map 36B 1:40,000 — C.27.I.6.4.	
	7th	9 am	Unit left MERVILLE	
		4 pm	Unit arrived at AUCHEL after 25 Kil. March in bad weather. Men billeted on march. Unit took over Hôtel de Ville and Pont Stes as billets.	Heavy rain in afternoon
"	8th	7/on	Cleaned billets — Parades — Physical drill. Billets in foul & leaky condition. Accommodation for about 10 slight cases. Sick collected from 99th Inf. Brigade in AUCHEL area. Sick then evacuated to 1st Corps Rest Station (FOUQUIÈRES or LA BEUVRIÈRE) & to No. 23 CCS LOZINGHEM.	Nil
	9th		Routine. Cadre drill etc.	Nil. Rain
	10th	6/pm	Routine. Field Amb. Reinforced. Checked R.B.T.C. sections	Nil
	11th	7/pm	Squad drill, Physical drill etc. and "Gas" drill. Visited A.D.M.S of Lieut. 4 a 2nd Lt. E.B.SNOWDEN detached from Leave to U.K. 1st Lieut. B.P.DORAN U.S.A M.O.R.C. to temp. duty as M.O.K. 2nd Bn. H.L. Inf.	Nil
"	12th		Routine, Squad drill, Stretcher drill, short march.	Rain.
	13th	5.30	Routine. Physical drill. Stretcher drill etc	
"	14th	"	Routine. Attended Conference of M.Os at A.D.M.S. office.	Nil
	15th	6/pm	Routine. Squad drill & Stretcher drill etc.	Nil.
"	16th	6/pm	Routine. Drills & lectures.	Nil.
	17th	6/pm	Routine. About 100 cases of Diarrhoea occurred in unit last night — all fed from Main Cookhouse — No cases really severe. Probable cause. Tinned Pork & Beans ration.	Nil.

A 7092 Wt. W125 g/M1293 750,000 1/17 D. P & L. Ltd Forms/C018/14

Army Form C. 2118.

WAR DIARY
or
INTELLIGENCE SUMMARY.
(Erase heading not required.)

Instructions regarding War Diaries and Intelligence Summaries are contained in F. S. Regs., Part II. and the Staff Manual respectively. Title pages will be prepared in manuscript.

Place	Date	Hour	Summary of Events and Information	Remarks and references to Appendices
AUCHEL	18th	6 p.m.	Routine – Light fatigues. Nearly all Brancheer cases received. Ration meat of inferior quality	
"	19th	6 p.m.	Physical & Company Drills etc. Lectures on "First Aid" to Bearers & Nursing Orderlies. Clipping of all Horses in the Unit nearly completed. Horse standings much improved.	
"	20th	6 p.m.	Drill & Physical & Company. 2nd Blankets issued to all O.R. Capt. B.W. ARMSTRONG R.A.M.C. (T.F.) Returned from leave to U.K.	
"	21st	5.30 p.m.	Routine: Unit resting. All articles considered essential to formation of Advanced Dressing Station during active operations packed in one limber ready for immediate use.	Appendix "B"
"	22nd	5.30 "	Routine: Drills, Kit Inspection.	
"	23rd	"	Routine: Drills & Fatigues etc. 1st Lieut. B.P. DORAN USA MORC returned from temporary duty at H.Q. 2nd Batt. H.L.I.	Rain
"	24th	4 p.m.	Routine: Route march, training.	
"	25th	6.30 p.m.	Routine: Drills & exercises	
"	26th	6 p.m.	Routine & Badminath – Mdrills. 1st Lieut. B.P. DORAN USA MORC left for Temporary Duty with No. 47 C.C.S., DOZINGHEM.	
"	27th	7 p.m.	Routine: Unit bathing – Drills, exercises etc.	
"	28th	–	Routine: No parades.	
"	29th	–	Route march for whole Unit, 9.30 a.m., Drills & Football, force 2nd Division visited Unit. Gilled this CO.Ol.	

Army Form C. 2118.

WAR DIARY
INTELLIGENCE SUMMARY.

(Erase heading not required.)

Instructions regarding War Diaries and Intelligence Summaries are contained in F. S. Regs., Part II. and the Staff Manual respectively. Title pages will be prepared in manuscript.

Place	Date	Hour	Summary of Events and Information	Remarks and references to Appendices
AUCHEL	30th	6 p.m.	Routine: Physical Drills + Demonstration of Pannier etc. 1st Lieuts. E.A. CURTIN + W.J. MIEHE, U.S.A. M.O.R.C. reported from Havre Base last night and taken on strength of Unit from 29th inst.	Rain
	31st	6 p.m.	Routine - Drills + Exercises.	Nil

Alfred Keogh
Lt. Col. M.C.
O.C. No. 100 Field Amb.

Army Form C. 2118.

WAR DIARY
or
INTELLIGENCE SUMMARY

(Erase heading not required.)

No. 100 Field Ambulance.

Appendix "A" - to Vol. 24. Oct. 1917.

Movement orders. during month.

2nd DIVISION MEDICAL ARRANGEMENTS No. 22.

[stamp: 100TH FIELD AMBULANCE. No......... Date..........]

7th October 1917.

-:-:-:-:-:-:-:-:-:-:-:-:-:-:-:-:-

Collection of sick on morning of 8th instant.

<u>No. 5 Field Ambulance</u> at LOZINGHEM will collect from units at

      LOZINGHEM.
      ALLOUAGNE &
      BURBURE AREA.

<u>No. 6 Field Ambulance</u> at ANNEZIN will collect from units at

      BETHUNE.
      LABEUVRIERE.
      LAPUGNOY &
      MARLES LES MINES.

<u>No.100 Field Ambulance</u> at AUCHEL will collect from units at

      AUCHEL &
      RAIMBERT.

                                                      [signature]
                                                      Colonel, A.M.S.,

                                        A.D.M.S., 2nd Division.

Copies to :-

      O's.C. Nos. 5.6.100 Field Ambulances.
      "G" 2nd Division.
      "Q" 2nd Division.
      H.Qrs., 5th, 6th & 99th Inf.Bdes.

SECRET.   SECRET   100TH FIELD AMBULANCE.

2nd DIVISION MEDICAL ARRANGEMENTS No. 2

4th October 1918

Sick will be collected during the move to the AUCHEL AREA as follows :-

Date	Unit	Location	Field Ambulance Collecting
OCT. 5th	99th Brigade.	BETHUNE I.	No. 6
6th	6th Brigade. 99th "	BETHUNE II) " I)	No. 6
7th	5th Brigade 6th "	BETHUNE I) " II)	No. 6
	99th Brigade) 2 Coy.Train)	AUCHEL.	No. 5
8th	5th Brigade 6th Brigade) 4 Coy.Train) 242 M.G.Coy.	BETHUNE I. BUREURE) LAPUGNOY)	No. 6 No.100.

NOTE :- BETHUNE Area No. I is :-
BETHUNE Barracks and ANNEZIN.

BETHUNE Area No. II is :-
Tobacco Factory.
Girls School.
BEUVRY.

COLONEL, A.M.S.,
A.D.M.S., 2nd DIVISION.

Copies to all concerned.

SECRET.

A.D.M.S., 2nd Div.No. 3653/54   4.10.17.

[Stamp: 100TH FIELD AMBULANCE. No ..... Date .....]

O's.C. Nos. 5.6.100 Field Ambulances.

      In continuation of 2nd Division R.A.M.C. Order No. 83 of even date, Field Ambulances will be billeted as follows :-

    No. 5 Field Ambulance........LOZINGHEM.
    No. 6 Field Ambulance........ANNEZIN.
    No.100 Field Ambulance.......HURIONVILLE.

H.Q.,2nd Divn.,
4th October 1917.

                          Colonel, A.M.S.,
                     A.D.M.S., 2nd Division.

SECRET

SECRET

100TH FIELD AMBULANCE.
No ....
Date ....

Copy No... 3

2nd DIVISION R.A.M.C. ORDER No. 83.

4th October 1917.

-:-:-:-:-:-:-:-:-:-:-:-:-:-:-:-:-

1. The 2nd Division will be relieved in the line by the 25th Division. Relief (less Artillery) to be completed by 6 a.m. on morning of 7th October.

2. Field Ambulances will be relieved and move in accordance with the attached table.

    Details of the relief of Advanced Posts to be arranged between Field Ambulance Commanders direct.

3. In handing over Regimental Aid Posts receipts will be taken for Primus Stoves, Tea urns, Thomas' splints, and other Trench stores.

4. No equipment surplus to mobilization tables will be removed by Field Ambulances.

5. Office of A.D.M.S. will close at LOCON at 10 a.m. on the 7th instant, and open at LABEUVRIERE the same hour.

6. ACKNOWLEDGE.

                                        H Herrick
                                        COLONEL, A.M.S.,
                                    A.D.M.S., 2nd DIVISION.

Issued at 12 Noon.

            Copy No. 1 --- O.C. No. 5 Field Ambulance.
                     2 --- O.C. No. 6   "   "
                     3 --- O.C. No.100 "   "
                     4 --- "G" 2nd Division.
                     5 --- "Q" 2nd Division.
                     6 --- D.M.S., First Army.
                     7 --- D.D.M.S., XI Corps.
                     8 --- D.D.M.S., I Corps.
                     9 --- A.D.M.S., 25th Division.
                    10 --- A.D.M.S., 46th Division.
                    11 --- H.Qrs., 5th Inf.Bde.
                    12 --- H.Qrs., 6th "   "
                    13 --- H.Qrs.,99th "   "
               14 - 16 --- Office and Records.

TABLE TO ACCOMPANY 2nd DIVISION R.A.M.C. ORDER No. 83 of 4.10.17.

Date.	No. of Field Ambulance.	Relieved by.	Move to	Remarks.
OCT. 5th	No. 6 F.A.	No. 75 F.A.		No. 6 F.A. remains at ANNEZIN. No. 75 F.A. take over ECOLE CATORIVE and Advanced Dressing Station at CAMBRIN CHURCH, with posts at HUMANITY, VERMELLES, and BARTS ALLEY.
5/6th	Bearers of No. 5 F.A.	No. 77 F.A. Advanced party.	ESPLAUX FARM.	Advanced bearers of No. 77 F.A. take over Advanced Dressing stations, TUNING FORK and LONE FARM, with Bearer Posts.
6th	No. 5 F.A.	No. 77 F.A.	ALLOUAGNE AREA.	Billets to be communicated later.
6/7th	No. 8 F.A.	No. 75 F.A.		Hands over Advanced Dressing station, HARLEY STREET with remaining posts of Canal Sector.
7th	No.100 F.A.	No. 76 F.A.	BURBURE AREA.	Billets to be notified later.

Army Form C. 2118.

WAR DIARY
INTELLIGENCE SUMMARY
(Erase heading not required.)

No. 100 Field Ambulance

Appendix "J" — to Nov. 24th Oct. 1917.

Miscellaneous:-

"List of Equipment required for Advd. Dressᵍ Stn. etc

List of Surgical & Medical Equipment Required for an Advanced Dressing Station in War Time

Articles	No. Required	Articles	No. Required	Articles	Required
Surgeons Roll	1	Wool White (Absorbent)	15 lb	Lamps Operating	1
Surgical Haversack	1	Bandages Roller	40 / 250	Lanterns	2
Artery Clips	6	Triangular	50	Hampers	1
Scissors Surg. Dressing	6 prs	Abdominal		Wool (Absorbent)	4 lbs
Forceps Dissecting	1 pr	Capelines (Head, Neck)	60	Boots Bacon	4
Scissors Strong	6 prs	Haversacks Shell	6	Sand Bags	
Razor Axilla	1	Splints Back		Sheets Mackintosh	10
Clippers Hair Size 0.0	1	Gooch	3 yds	Bandage Canvas (Apron)	1
Sterilizer (Complete)	1	Thomas (Thigh)		Cape Canvas	1
Tubes Tracheotomy	1	Cramer (Wire)		For Operator	1
Hyperd. Syringe (Glass)	1	Listons (Foot)		Petrol Tins Oil Waste	4
Syringe (20 c.c.)	1	Basins Washing	2	Brandy	1 bot.
Tourniquets (Samways)		Bowls Dressing	6	Bovril (2lb)	24 lbs
Bandage Web Elastic	3 yds	Trays Dressing D	2	Ryo Oxo Bovril (Dressing)	1 jar
Ligatures Silk (No 6)		Trays Dressing K.S.	2	Milk	6 tins
Cat-Gut (No 3)		Pans Bed	1	Tea	2 lbs
Infusion Apparatus	1	Urinals	2	Sugar	6 lbs
Bags (Linen for Excel)	1	Cups (Feeding)	2	Dishes Cloths	3
Medical Companion	1	Bottles Hot Water	4	A.T.S.	Medicine
Lysol	2 btls	Cramps (Pigskin)	4 prs	Linen Roller	4 lbs
Eusol	1 gall	Saucepans (Large)	2	Soft Cream Soap	2 gys
Aether (1lb)	1 bot.	(Medium)	6	Tissue	15 lbs
Sub. Metal	2 galls	Spoons Vertical		Aromatic	2
Novocain 2%	2 ozs	Stoves Primus			
Hyp. Morph. Sol 1/3 g.	1 oz btls	Oil (Paraffin)		Splint Box (Large)	1
Sod. Chloride		Soap	4 cakes	Towels	6
Capsules Gas	60	Brushes (Nail)	4	Needle Surgeons	6
Listers Ointment (Ammonium)	3 tins	Blankets	20	Dressing Trays	4
Paraffin (Wh.)	1 lb	Stretchers	5		6
Oxygen	50 c.f.	Gas Pipe		Tobacco	24

Bars supporting for Thomas Splints 2

A.D.M.S. 2ND DIVISION.

The following death(s) reported for your information:—

REGTL. NO.	RANK	NAME & INITIALS (IN BLOCK LETTERS)	COY	BATTN & REGT.	DATE OF DEATH.	*CAUSE OF DEATH.	SITE OF GRAVE	REMARKS

* State whether "Killed in Action", from "Wounds received in action", "Disease" or "Accidental Death", etc.

Date .... 191 .

O.C. No. 100 Field Ambulance.

Army Form C. 2118.

WAR DIARY
or
INTELLIGENCE SUMMARY
(Erase heading not required.)

Summary of Events and Information

No. 100 Field Ambulance.

Appendix "C" — to Vol. 24. Oct. 1917

Miscellaneous :-

Summary of Cases passing through 100 Fd. Amb. during month of October, 1917

"C" Appendix to War Diary, October 1917.

Summary of Cases passing through No.100 F. Amb.ce during month of October 1917.

No.100 F. Amb.ce

Officer			Other Ranks		
Admitted	Discharged to Duty	Discharged to C.C.S & C.R.S.	Admitted	Discharged to Duty	Discharged to C.C.S & C.R.S.
5.	–	5.	110.	4.	107.

XI Corps Rest Station 1/10/17 to 6/10/17 (inclusive)

Officers			Other Ranks		
Admitted	Discharged to Duty	Discharged to C.C.S & C.R.S	Admitted	Discharged to Duty	Discharged to C.C.S & C.R.S
–	1.	–	34.	38.	13.

Army Form C. 2118

WAR DIARY
or
INTELLIGENCE SUMMARY
(Erase heading not required.)

100TH FIELD AMBULANCE.
No. 2098/21
Date 3.12.17

COMMITTEE FOR THE
MEDICAL HISTORY OF THE WAR
Date 17 JAN 1918

Confidential

War Diary of
No 100 Field Ambulance
for November 1917

Volume 25

WAR DIARY

INTELLIGENCE SUMMARY

Army Form C. 2118.

No. 100 Field Ambulance

Instructions regarding War Diaries and Intelligence Summaries are contained in F. S. Regs., Part II. and the Staff Manual respectively. Title pages will be prepared in manuscript.

(Erase heading not required.)

Place	Date	Hour	Summary of Events and Information	Remarks and references to Appendices
AUCHEL (C 27.c.7.3)	Nov 1st		Map Reference: Sheet 36B France 1/40,000	
		9 am	Routine. Route march in morning. Got chamber with Gen. Bon Respirators for whole unit at 8pm.	Myths Numm
"	" 2nd	9am	Routine. Drills & Football. Leaving order for three in 5" Unit. Received from A375 @ 99th Brigade.	New
"	" 3rd	5.30pm	Drills & Physical Exercises. Demonstration of Tump line. Unit now only 1 under strength in O.R.	New
"	4th	7pm	Routine. March orders for next two days received from H.Q. 99th Inf. Bde. All arrangements made. Move to BUSNES tomorrow.	
BUSNES	5th	10.30am	Unit in left marching order left AUCHEL - Blankets + Packs in convoy, as rear unit of 99 Inf. Brigade	Nov
		1.30pm	Arrived at BUSNES - No casualties on march. G.O.C. 2nd Division inspected Unit on the march + expressed his satisfaction with Horses transport. Unit billeted in + about BUSNES Village full to tight. 1 man of Unit (Pte Hogg) evacuated this evening to No. 58 C.C.S. (Bronchitis?)	Fine
ESTAIRES Sheet 5A France 5 I	6th	11.35am	left BUSNES. Unit marched via ROBECQ o MERVILLE to ESTAIRES. No casualties on march.	Nov
		3.30pm	Arrived at ESTAIRES. Unit billeted in Pensionnat de Demoiselles.	Nov
EECKE	7th	9.25am	Unit left ESTAIRES marched in rear of 99th Inf Brigade via VIEUX BERQUIN + STRAZEELE to EECKE area	Nov
		3.30 pm	Unit arrived + billeted in a farm at Q.17 d 7.3. (Map Sheet 27 1/40,000). 2 men fell out on march.	
HERZEELE Area	8th	9am	Unit left billets marched in rear of 99th Brigade via STEEN VOORDE + WINNIZEELE to HERZEELE area. Unit billeted in farm in D.17. C.8.6. (Sheet 27. 1/40,000)	Nov

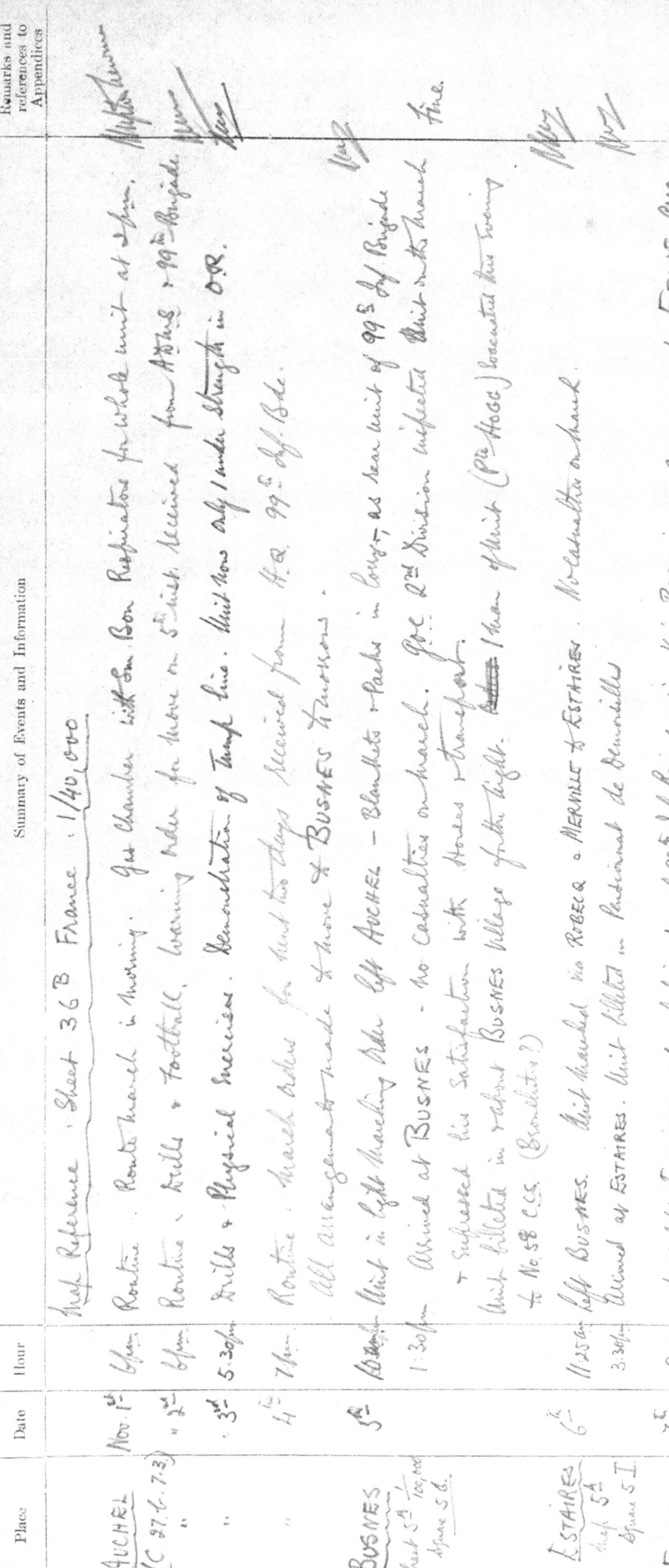

Army Form C. 2118.

WAR DIARY
INTELLIGENCE SUMMARY.
(Erase heading not required.)

Instructions regarding War Diaries and Intelligence Summaries are contained in F. S. Regs., Part II. and the Staff Manual respectively. Title pages will be prepared in manuscript.

Place	Date	Hour	Summary of Events and Information	Remarks and references to Appendices
HERZEELE Area (D.17.c 8.6)	Nov. 9th	11am	Ref. Map. Sheet 27 1/40,000 Unit Resting - fatigues - No parades. Billet surroundings v. hot and muddy. Sick being evacuated to No. 63 CCS at HARINGHE (sheet 5th A.1.50.10)	Nov.
	10th	4.30pm	Routine fatigues. Unit Resting. Bad weather. Kerns XVIII Corps Instructions received	Rain Rain
	11th	11am	Routine: Unit resting. Very bad weather. Camp v. wet muddy.	Very wet Rain
	12th	5.30pm	Routine: Unit Bathed 9am - 11am. Route march 2pm - 4 Large photos Ambulance Cars left at 7.30 am under orders received from A.D.M.S. to report to A.D.C. No. 31 M.A.C. at DUHALLOW M.D.S. (Sheet 28 - C.25. d. 3.0.) for duty.	Fine
	13th	6pm	Routine: Drills. Demonstration of YUKON PACK. 1st Lieut. W.J. MIEHE left for temporary duty at No. 12 C.C.S.	Nov.
,,	14th	6pm	Routine: Drills & Exercises.	Nov.
,,	15th	6pm	Routine: Route march. Inspection of marching order.	Nov.
,,	16th	6.15pm	Routine: Physical Drills etc. 2pm 2 officers & 100 men through Chlorine gas chamber at Div. gas school. Brabazon (Pte MARSH) slightly gassed (accid) and evacuated to No. 12 C.C.S.	Nov.
,,	17th	6.05	Routine: Inspection by A.D.M.S. & S.A.D.V.S. 1 officers & 100 men through chlorine gas chamber. Remainder of Unit went through Chlorine gas chamber 2.30pm.	Nov.

WAR DIARY or INTELLIGENCE SUMMARY

Army Form C. 2118

Place	Date	Hour	Summary of Events and Information	Remarks and references to Appendices
HERZEELE Area (D.17.e.& 6.)	Nov. 18th	6:30 a.m	Ref. Map Sheet 27 1:40,000. Routine. Under instruction from D.of T. 1 Ford Motor Amb. Car was Exchanged this morning at "S" 9 H.Q. Ammun. Park for 1 Sunbeam Motor Amb. This latter Car was not handed over in good running condition.	
"	19th	6 p.m	Routine. All M.T. Vehicles inspected at "B" Coy's Supply Column Workshops at 10 a.m. The Napier Car and one Vauxhall Car replaced by Sunbeam & Daimler Cars respectively. Unit now has 4 Sunbeam Cars, 2 Daimlers & 1 Ford.	
"	20th	7 p.m	Routine.	
"	21st	6 p.m	Routine. Capt. A. GAMETLY M.C. Reuse left for U.K. to report to W.O. on expiry of contract. 1st Lieut. W.J. MIEHE U.S.A. M.O.R.C. rejoined the Unit from temporary duty with No.12 C.C.S. Forwarded Returning Strength of Unit to A.D.M.S at Ghyn in reply to priority wire.	
"	22nd	6 p.m	Routine. 1st Lieut. B.P. DORAN U.S.A. M.O.R.C. rejoined Unit from temp. duty with No.47 C.C.S. Warning order for Entrainment received from H.Q. 99th Inf. Bde. Unit ready to Entrain at 2 hours notice from 6 p.m. tonight.	
"	23rd	4:15 p.m	Routine. Received Entraining orders for No. 24 Amb. Conditional following arrangements for Entrainment.	
Au Tan	24	2.15 p.m	Unit left HERZEELE area and marched to RESERVELBECQ where it Entrained at 5:30 p.m. to one train.	

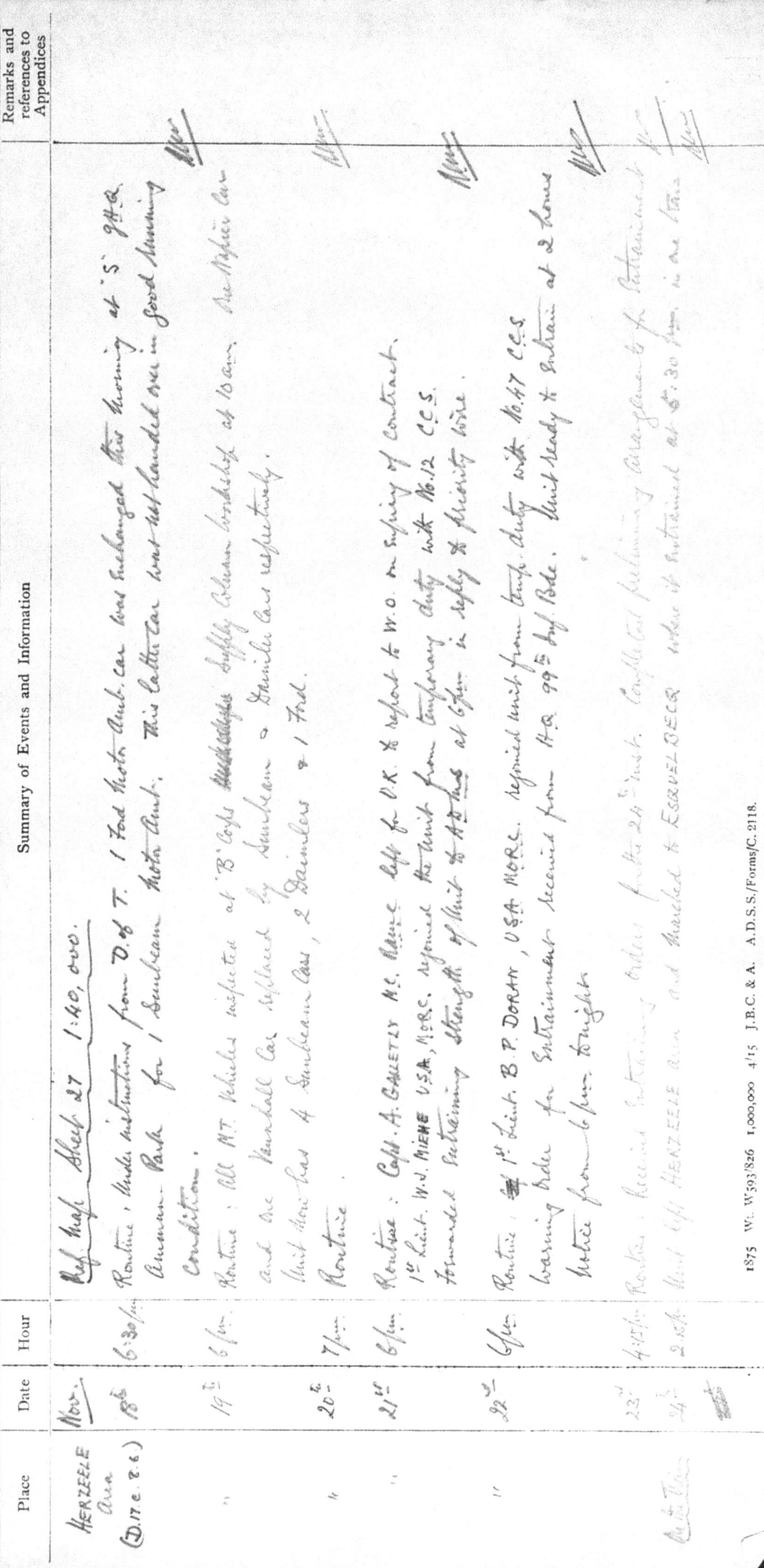

Army Form C. 2118

WAR DIARY
or
INTELLIGENCE SUMMARY
(Erase heading not required.)

Place	Date	Hour	Summary of Events and Information	Remarks and references to Appendices
			Reference Map. Sheet 57 C. 1/40,000	
BEAUMETZ Lez CAMBRAI (J.20.C)	25th	7pm	Unit Obtained at ACHIET-LE-GRAND at 10.30 am this morning, and travelled via BAPAUME and then CAMBRAI Road to BEAUMETZ-LEZ-CAMBRAI & arrived about 4:30 pm. Encamped for the night. No casualties & sick on journey from HERZEELE. 3 casualties (sick) dealt with soon after arrival.	MV
"	26th	10 a.m.	Sick evacuated to YPRES (P.20.D) Unit Resting	
		5 pm	Visited ADMS and got instructed re taking over A.D.S at HERMIES from a Unit of 36th Divn. Visited DADMS 36th Divn re taking over stretchers.	MV
HERMIES (J.29.a.3.0.)	27th	8.30am	Capt P.J. LANE M.C. and 98 Bearers left to relieve at W.W.C.P. HERMIES and takes over branch of line from No.108 Field Ambulance	MV
		9.30am	Unit (less 2 officers & Bearers as above) moved from BEAUMETZ to HERMIES. Officers + 1 Tent Subdivision took over A.D.S. at DEMICOURT (J.18.t.3.1) Remainder of Unit took over charge of Walking Wounded Collecting Post at HERMIES.	
"	28th	6:30 p.m	Visited Bearer Posts in HINDENBURG Line. Bearers so far chiefly employed in evacuation of 62nd Divn Wounded. Capt RENTON and 92 Bearers of No.5 Field Amb. Brought out evacuation in Rear area. Evacuation by night being carried out by Motor Amb. along Rear CAMBRAI Road. 3 Motor Amb. Cars from No.5 F.A. + 3 from No.6 F.A. attached to duty at W.W.C.P. (HERMIES) and A.D.S. DEMICOURT	MV

WAR DIARY

Army Form C. 2118

Instructions regarding War Diaries and Intelligence Summaries are contained in F. S. Regs., Part II. and the Staff Manual respectively. Title Pages will be prepared in manuscript.

(Erase heading not required.)

Place	Date	Hour	Summary of Events and Information	Remarks and references to Appendices
HERMIES	March 29	10.30 p.m.	ADS at DEMICOURT shelled during night. No casualties. Visit Bearer post in HINDENBURG Line during day. Evacuation from W. side of Canal easy and not interrupted. Evacuation from R.A.P. East of Canal difficult owing to heavy shelling. Neighbourhood of W.W.C.P. HERMIES shelled during afternoon. One wagon badly PE-HARRS hit & died of wounds at M.D.S. — One Amb. Wagon slight damage. Capt. A.C. FISHER M.C. Nurse (S.R.) deputed arrival yesterday with the Unit. 1 Officer & 30 Bearers from No.6 F.A. sent up for duty in evacuation area by A.D.M.S. Bearers of the two No.5 F.A. heavily worked and tired. Wrote A.D.M.S. 2nd Div. at 7 p.m. asking the transference of H.Bs from DEMICOURT & HERMIES.	
	30	10 p.m.	Heavy casualties in during night. Bearers v. hard worked and tired. 2 Officers & 90 Bearers of No.2 F.A. have now been sent by A.D.M.S. into the line & help.	
	31	2/h.	1 Ford Ambulance & A.S.C. transport moved from HERMIES and camped in P.3.c. Applied to A.D.M.S. 63rd Inf. Brigade for Infantry men to relieve tired Stretcher Bearers in the line. 1 Officer & 50 men 2nd H.L.I. sent up for about 12 hr daylight.	

Milne Thompson Major R.A.M.C.
OC. No.100 Field Amb.

Appendix to War Diary, Vol. 2¼ (?)

100th FIELD AMBULANCE

SUMMARY OF ADMISSIONS & EVACUATIONS ETC. FOR NOVEMBER 1917

DATE 1917	OFFICERS				OTHER RANKS			
	Admissions	To Duty	Evacuated	Died	Admissions	To Duty	Evacuated	Died
November 1	—				2		2	
" 2	—				2		2	
" 3	—				10		8	
" 4	—				7		4	
" 5	—				4	3	5	
" 6	1		1		2		3	
" 7	—				—			
" 8	1		1		8		8	
" 9	—				3		3	
" 10	—				3		3	
" 11	1		1		2		2	
" 12	—				7		7	
" 13	—				7		7	
" 14	—				7		7	
" 15	—				6		6	
" 16	—				5		4	
" 17	—				9		10	
" 18	1		1		4		4	
" 19	—				4		4	
" 20	1		1		10		9	
" 21	—				11		11	
" 22	—				7		8	
" 23	1		1		12		10	
" 24	—				—			
" 25	—				—			
" 26	—				8		6	
" 27	2		2		36	1	37	
" 28	—				—			
" 29	—				—			
" 30	—							
TOTALS	8	—	8	—	176	4	170	—

Army Form C. 2118

WAR DIARY No. 100 Field Ambulance

or

INTELLIGENCE SUMMARY

(Erase heading not required.)

Instructions regarding War Diaries and Intelligence Summaries are contained in F. S. Regs., Part II. and the Staff Manual respectively. Title Pages will be prepared in manuscript.

Place	Date	Hour	Summary of Events and Information	Remarks and references to Appendices
HERMIES J.24.a.3.0.	DEC 1st		Ad. Msh. Sheet 57.C. 1:40,000	
		4 a.m.	A.D.S. and Personnel removed from DEMICOURT to HERMIES. DEMICOURT heavily shelled and accommodation not sufficient or suitable.	
		3 p.m.	Reconnoitred Road of CANAL DU NORD from P.31.a. to Lock No.6. Unproposed evacuation route by Motor Ambulance. — Not yet satisfactory. Old evacuation route still continued for present. Beaver R. still not No block in evacuation.	
		9:30 p.m.	All available men including A.S.C. (H.T.), sent up to HINDENBURG line from Motor Ambs. for stretcher duty. — 4 Squads. No extra Bearers available from other Field Ambulances.	Night Ambulance Keep Mune
"	2nd	7:30 a.m.	Capt. SOMERVILLE Reave No.6 F.A. went up as Bearer officer with No.5 F.A. Bearers	
		10 a.m.	No.100 F.A. Bearers relieved in line by No.5 F.A. Bearers & returned for rest & transport lines	
		3 p.m.	A.D.S. locality HERMIES shelled. Many severe casualties from local units dealt with during the day. Evacuation by Motor Amb. Cars & DECAUVILLE railway to M.D.S. LEBUCQUIERE working satisfactorily	
"	3rd	10 a.m.	Bearers of No.6 F.A. relieved in line by Bearers of No.100 F.A. No.6 F.A. Bearers returning to rest in Transport lines	Nyer
			Evacuation proceeding satisfactorily. Average of 150 cases daily passing through A.D.S. & M.D.S.	
"	4th	12 noon	Visited A.D.M.S. & received instructions re Evacuation of Bearer Relay Posts in HINDENBURG Line in conformity with movements of Infantry tomorrow morning.	Yes
		4 p.m.	Issued necessary orders re Movement of Bearers	
		6 p.m.	Units (Class B) 5000 4/15 A.B.D. & A. Stat. S. 9/Forms/C2118/1 HERMIES to P.1.t.o.9. (VELU WOOD)	Nyer
		10 a.m.	No.5 F.A. Bearers relieved by No. 6 F.A. Bearers	Nyer

Army Form G. 2118

WAR DIARY
or
INTELLIGENCE SUMMARY
(Erase heading not required.)

Instructions regarding War Diaries and Intelligence Summaries are contained in F. S. Regs., Part II. and the Staff Manual respectively. Title Pages will be prepared in manuscript.

Place	Date	Hour	Summary of Events and Information	Remarks and references to Appendices
VELU WOOD P.I.6.6.9.	Dec. 5th	11.30a	Refresh Sheet 51E 1:40,000. Bearer Relay posts in HINDENBURG LINE etc. knocked. Bearers of No. 6 4700 F.As. fell back to HERMIES with Relay Posts in DEMICOURT (J18.6.3.0.) CHINESE wall (K.13.d.6.3.) and Brick Stack (K.15.a.3.4.). All casualties evacuated.	
		10am	Nº70 F.A. Bearers came out of line & returned to P.I.6.6.9. for rest.	
"	6th		Routine.	
"	7th			
"	8th			
"	9th			
"	10th			
"	11th			

1875   Wt. W593/826   1,000,000   4/15   J.B.C. & A.   A.D.S.S./Forms/C. 2118.

Army Form C. 2118.

WAR DIARY
or
INTELLIGENCE SUMMARY
(Erase heading not required.)

Instructions regarding War Diaries and Intelligence Summaries are contained in F. S. Regs., Part II. and the Staff Manual respectively. Title Pages will be prepared in manuscript.

Place	Date	Hour	Summary of Events and Information	Remarks and references to Appendices
HERMIES J.29.a.3.0.	Dec. 12th	4/pm	Ref. Trench Sheet 57.D. 1:40,000. Because Took over Evacuation of sick from Canal K.9.b.4.9. tributary K.11.c.9.0. (including two R.A.P.s) from Bearers of 4th London F.A. – 47th Division in addition to our line from K.7.a. of K.9.a. 1 Motor Amb. Car left at 47th Div. A.D.S. HAVRINCOURT (K.27.b.) until 8pm. to transport to our 2nd Div. cases coming through there. Neighbourhood of A.D.S. HERMIES shelled about 3pm. 1 Sunbeam Motor-Ambulance total damaged. Evacuation returned successfully via CHINESE WALL (K.14.b.) by day and along Bed of CANAL DU NORD by night. — only 5 wounded through during last 24 hours. Mostly sick.	/WW/
	13th	7/pm	A/Lieut. MIEHE U.S.M.C.R.C. sent for temp. duty as M.O. to 17th Bn The Middlesex Regt. vice Capt. FISHER R.A.M.C. (S.R.) Who rejoined No. 110 F.A.	/WW/
"		8/pm	Capt. A.G. FISHER M.C. (S.R.) from temp duty with 17th Middlesex Regt. rejoined this Unit early this evening. Lieut. T.P. DORAN U.S.M.C.R.C. sent to our on temp. duty with 1st Bn. K.R.R. Corps. Routine. Bearer officers in touch with all Reg.tl Aid Posts during day & night. Stretcher-bearer Bn and Hors. Rec. F.A. went round the subgroup talking over evacuation of sick & wounded.	/WW/
"	14th	8.30/a	Routine. Reg. line cases through A.D.S. Hermies fairly fast 24 hours. Bearers of No. 6 F.A. relieved Bearers of No. 100 F.A. in line at 4pm. (Bearers of No. 100 returned to Divnl. HQr. at P.I.Z.c.9 (VELU WOOD) at 7pm.	/WW/

Army Form C. 2118.

WAR DIARY
or
INTELLIGENCE SUMMARY

(Erase heading not required.)

Instructions regarding War Diaries and Intelligence Summaries are contained in F. S. Regs., Part II. and the Staff Manual respectively. Title Pages will be prepared in manuscript.

Place	Date	Hour	Summary of Events and Information	Remarks and references to Appendices
HERMIES J.29.a.3.c.	Dec. 15	4 pm	Routine. Baths &c. Hutting being erected for fluic at hits P.1.a.9.9. — 7 huts III Corps Pattern approved allotted. Evacuation passing through A.D.S.	fine
"	16	10 am	1st field E.F. SCHMITZ U.S.M.O.R.C left for temp. duty as M.O. 1/6 1st King's Regt.	fine
		2 pm	1st Lieut. E.A. CURTIN US MORC & 30 B.R. Ravine (hospital attendants) left for temporary duty at M.D.S. 59th Division ROYAULCOURT.	
	17	7 pm	Routine.	
	18	6 pm	Routine = 4 huts & flooring of Horse standings drawn from R.E.	
	19, 20, 21, 22, 23, 24, 25		Routine. All very frosty.	
	26	7 am	Routine. Casualties from 12 noon 15 day the evacuation from A.D.S. (HERMIES) to V Corps M.D.S. ROYAULCOURT Beaver fact at J.18.c.5.3. and Regtl Aid Post at K.7.c. Central handed over to a field Amb. of 51st Division Lieut. T.J. ARBUTHNOT M.R.C. U.S.A. joined for temporary duty	

WAR DIARY
INTELLIGENCE SUMMARY

Army Form C. 2118.

Place	Date	Hour	Summary of Events and Information	Remarks and references to Appendices
VELU WOOD (P.I.R. 99)	27th		Reference Map Sheet 57c 1:40,000. Unit moved from HERMIES A.D.S. to VELU WOOD - H.Q. of Unit. Routine. Major ARBUTHNOT M.O.R.C. - U.S.A. proceeded to No.6 Field Amb. according to A.D.M.S. Instructions. Corps Commander 7th Corps has awarded Military Medal to following men of this unit. No. 73193 a/Sjt J.T. SMITH & Pte & No. M²/133598 Pte F.A. JONES A.S.C. (M.T.) attached. 74440 Pte E.L. CALLARD 14th Bn & a Bar to the Military Medal to No. 66354 a/Sgt H.W. DUTTON R.A.M.C. No. M²/133586 Pte C.R. SHERRATT A.S.C.(M.T.) attached. To Bearers in the Field during operations on 29th - 30th Nov. 1st Dec.	State of award 24/12/17
"	28th		Routine:	
"	29th		Capt. P.W. LANE & 60 O.R. (Bearer Division) took over evacuation of front line from Bearers of No. 5 Field Amb. at 4/p.m. Evacuation by same route continues. By day via Sensation Road in K.19.a.& b. By night by photo Ambulance cars in half canal up to K.15.a.3.5. Sick of 2nd Division etc. now evacuated from A.D.S. HERMIES by Decauville Railway to BUS and hence to D.R.S. (N.H. Central) at 4 p.m. daily.	

Army Form C. 2118.

WAR DIARY
or
INTELLIGENCE SUMMARY
(Erase heading not required.)

Instructions regarding War Diaries and Intelligence Summaries are contained in F. S. Regs., Part II. and the Staff Manual respectively. Title Pages will be prepared in manuscript.

Place	Date	Hour	Summary of Events and Information	Remarks and references to Appendices
VELU WOOD (P.1.a.9.9.)	Dec. 30th	7am	Ref. map. Sheet 57c. 1:40,000. Routine. Motor Ambulance Cars there having been many casualties recently from frost & bad roads, as well as two casualties from shell fire. Ambulatory difficult to obtain. Frost has made roads almost impossible for Motor Ambulances.	Nil
	31st	5pm	A.D.M.S. 2nd & 17th Divisions visited Relay posts occupied by Bearers of this Unit preparatory to taking them over. 1 Bearer (Pte CALLARD M.M.) handed this morning & evacuated to M.D.S. S. Sergt. GRIFFIN Albert, evacuated from No. 3 C.C.S. to Base today sick.	Nil

2449 Wt. W14957/M90 750,000 1/16 J.B.C. & A. Forms/C.2118/12.

2ND DIVISION
MEDICAL

NO. 100 FIELD AMBULANCE

JAN - DEC 1918

1918 JAN - 1919 JUNE

Army Form C.2118.

WAR DIARY
~or~
INTELLIGENCE SUMMARY
(Erase heading not required.)

Confidential

War Diary of
No. 100 Field Ambulance
for January 1918
(Volume XI)

COMMITTEE FOR THE
MEDICAL HISTORY OF THE WAR
Date -4 MAR. 1918

Army Form C. 2118.

WAR DIARY
or
INTELLIGENCE SUMMARY

(Erase heading not required.)

Instructions regarding War Diaries and Intelligence Summaries are contained in F. S. Regs., Part II. and the Staff Manual respectively. Title Pages will be prepared in manuscript.

Place	Date	Hour	Summary of Events and Information	Remarks and references to Appendices
VELU WOOD	January 1/1918		Lt. Col. R.E.V. Newman M.C. R.A.M.C. departed on leave to the U.K. (2/1/18 – 1/2/18) & handed over command of the unit to Capt. B.W. ARMSTRONG R.A.M.C. (T.C)	Withanthorp Capt R.A.M.C.
FRANCE 57C (Edition 2) P.1.a.9.1.	2		Notified by A.D.M.S. that we should be moving to LECHELLE when Division is relieved to vacate F.A. site there which is at present occupied by two F.A's with no room for a third	B.W.A.
"	3		100th F.A. being relieved in the line by two of the 53rd F.A. The Field Subdivision at A.D.S. HERMIES replaced by a party from No 5 F.A. 1st Lieut B.P. DORAN. U.S.M.O.R.C. att. 100 F.A. T reinforcements (Privates) joined for duty. Orders received tonight to move to LECHELLE & to take over accommodation then occupied by 149th F.A. & to remain closed down. 1 Car belongs to No 5 F.A. injured by shell fire this evening between the "CHINESE WALL" & HERMIES. The driver wounded & the orderly & a patient killed.	B.W.A.
LECHELLE P.25.c.5.5.	4		Moved to LECHELLE this afternoon. heavy holding party at VELU to remain until the camp is taken over by 53 F.A. on Jan 6th 1st Lieut E.F. SCHMITZ reported from Temporary duty with the 1st KINGS (The Liverpool Regt)	B.W.A.

2449 Wt. W14957/Mgo 750,000 1/16 J.B.C. & A. Forms/C.2118/12.

WAR DIARY
INTELLIGENCE SUMMARY

Place	Date	Hour	Summary of Events and Information	Remarks and references to Appendices
LECHELLE 57C P25.C.5.5	Jan 5		A.D.S. HERMIES taken on by 5.1 F.A. Equipment withdrawn. 1st Lieut. B.P. DORAN U.S.M.O.R.C. rejoined.	MHA
"	6		1st Lieut. E.F. SCHMITZ A.S.N.O.R.C. departed on leave to Paris (6½ - 12½) a/Staff Sgt. W. STEPHENSON R.A.M.C. (No. 67914) evacuated to England 28/1/17 struck off the strength from 7/1/17	MHA MHA
"	7		Capt. P.J. LANE M.C. R.A.M.C. departed on leave to Paris (8½ - 14½)	MHA MHA
"	8		Routine	MHA
"	9		Routine	MHA
"	10		Routine	MHA
"	11		1st Lieut. B.P. DORAN U.S.M.O.R.C. departed for temporary duty as M.O. i/c 58 H.A. Bde. D.R.M.S. V Corps visited the camp this morning. Capt. A.G. FISHER R.A.M.C. (S.R.) departed on 14 days leave to the U.K.	MHA

Army Form C. 2118.

WAR DIARY
or
INTELLIGENCE SUMMARY
(Erase heading not required.)

Instructions regarding War Diaries and Intelligence Summaries are contained in F. S. Regs., Part II. and the Staff Manual respectively. Title Pages will be prepared in manuscript.

Place	Date	Hour	Summary of Events and Information	Remarks and references to Appendices
LECHELLE	Jan 12.		Lieut E.A Curtin USMARC + 29 O.R. reported event from temporary duty with I Corps M.D.S.	MMA
	13		Lieut E.F. SCHMITZ U.S.M.O.R.C. reported event from leave in Paris.	
			66167 S/Staff Sgt H.H GRIFFIN R.A.M.C + 86045 Sgt A.V. COLEMAN R.A.M.C Evacuated Sick to England Struck off the strength of the unit from 21/1/17 + 6/1/17 respectively	BMA
	14		Lieut W. HEBBS RAMC joined the unit today from leave later	BMA
			Capt P.V KANG M.C. reported event from leave in Paris	
	15		Lieut Curtin AV from the	BMA
	16		1st Lieut E.F. SCHMITZ U.S.M.O.R.C. departed to Third Army Sanitary Course at ARRAS.	BMA

WAR DIARY
or
INTELLIGENCE SUMMARY

Army Form C. 2118.

Place	Date	Hour	Summary of Events and Information	Remarks and references to Appendices
LECELLE	Jan 17		1st Lieut E.A. CURTIN U.S.A.O.R.C departed for temporary duty with the 17th Bn Royal Fusiliers	MMA
	18		Lieut & Quar. Master E.B. SNOWDEN R.A.M.C. departed on leave to the U.K. (18/1/5 - 1/2/18) Capt. P.S. LANE M.C. R.A.M.C. detailed for temporary duty with C.R.E. 3rd Div. No 46292 Sergt B. GOOCH R.A.M.C. to be acting Staff Sergeant & 66304 Pte (A/L/Sgt) J.H. THOMAS M.M. R.A.M.C. to be Sergeant. Such appointments with any duty from this Authority D.G.M.S. 8/143 8/1/1943 date 16/1/18	MMA
	19		1st Lieut F.F. SCHMITZ U.S.M.O.R.C. rejoined from III Army School of Sanitation Rouen	MMA BMA
	20			

Army Form C. 2118.

WAR DIARY
or
INTELLIGENCE SUMMARY

(Erase heading not required.)

Instructions regarding War Diaries and Intelligence Summaries are contained in F. S. Regs., Part II. and the Staff Manual respectively. Title Pages will be prepared in manuscript.

Place	Date	Hour	Summary of Events and Information	Remarks and references to Appendices
LECHELLE	Jan 21		Routine	NUA
"	22		Routine	NUA
"	23		1st Lieut. E.F. SCHMITZ U.S.M.O.R.C. detailed for temporary duty with No 5. F.A.	
			No. 64641 a/Sgt. FARTHING. J.E. R.A.M.C. promoted to a/staff Sergt from 21/12/17 } authority	
			No. 64650 a/Cpl. GUTHRIE. W. R.A.M.C. " a/Sgt. from 21/12/17 } DA445/B1	
			No. 53570 a/L.Cpl. MUNN. A. R.A.M.C. " a/Cpl. from 21/12/17 }	
			No. 64982 a/Pte. WOOD. R.W. R.A.M.C. " a/L.Cpl. from 6/12/17 } 1/14504/11963	
"	24		Routine. Field Ambulance horse transport inspected by Lt Col. E.W. BROOK a/20. 1.18. D.S.O. A.S.C. O.C. 2nd Div. Train	NUA
"	25		Routine	NUA
"	26		1st Lieut. E.F. SCHMITZ U.S.M.O.R.C. reported from No 5. I.F.A.	NUA
"	27		1st Lieut. E.A. CURTIN. U.S.M.O.R.C. reported from 17th F.E. Capt. P.J. KANE. M.C. R.A.M.C. reported from 2nd Div. R.E.	NUA
"	28		1st Lieut. E.A. CURTIN U.S.M.O.R.C. departed for temporary duty with 2nd S. Staff. Regt. (Capt. P.J. KANE. M.C. R.A.M.C. departed on leave to U.K. (29/18 - 12/2/18) Capt. A.G. FISHER. M.C. R.A.M.C. reported unit. from leave to U.K.	NUA

2449   Wt. W14957/M90   750,000   1/16   J.B.C. & A.   Forms/C.2118/12.

Army Form C. 2118.

WAR DIARY
or
INTELLIGENCE SUMMARY

(Erase heading not required.)

Instructions regarding War Diaries and Intelligence Summaries are contained in F. S. Regs., Part II. and the Staff Manual respectively. Title Pages will be prepared in manuscript.

Place	Date	Hour	Summary of Events and Information	Remarks and references to Appendices
LECHELLE	Jan. 29		Capt. N.G. FISHER M.C. R.A.M.C. proceeded today 6/7th 2nd South Staffordshire Regt. in relief of 1st Lieut. E.A. CURTIN who rejoined the F.A.	BMA
"	30		1st Lieut. E.A. CURTIN U.S.M.O.R.C. departed to attend Third Army Sanitary Course at APPOMS.	BMA
"	31		Routine	W.Armstrong Capt. M.C. O/c 100 F.A.

2449 Wt. W14957/M90 750,000 1/16 J.B.C. & A. Forms/C.2118/12.

Army Form C. 2118.

WAR DIARY
or
INTELLIGENCE SUMMARY

(Erase heading not required.)

CONFIDENTIAL

WAR DIARY
OF
No. 100 FIELD AMBULANCE
from 1st FEBY. 1918. to 28th FEBY. 1918.
(VOLUME 28)

COMMITTEE FOR THE
MEDICAL HISTORY OF THE WAR

Date —8 APR. 1918

Vol 21

WO/2784

Army Form C. 2118

WAR DIARY
or
INTELLIGENCE SUMMARY

(Erase heading not required.)

Instructions regarding War Diaries and Intelligence Summaries are contained in F. S. Regs., Part II. and the Staff Manual respectively. Title Pages will be prepared in manuscript.

Place	Date	Hour	Summary of Events and Information	Remarks and references to Appendices
LECHELLE	February 1918			
	1		Routine	Mr Armstrong Castradle
Lens 57.c.	2		1st Lieut. G.A. Curtin, U.S. M.O.R.C. reported for duty from Third Army. School of Sanitation, ARRAS.	PMA
P.25.c.5.5	3rd		Routine. Lieut Col. R.E.U. NEWMAN DSO returned from leave to U.K. and assumed command of Units	Mr McNTewman DSO
"	4		Routine. 1st Lieut. E.A. CURTIN M.O.R.C. USA left for temporary duty as M.O. to 41st Bde R.F.A.	Mr
"	5		Routine. Cleaning up of Camp + Good lines and Building of Stables being proceeded with. Most of Units Huts have protected from floods by sink pouches.	Mr
"	6		Routine	Mr
"	7		Routine. 1st Lieut J.O. PARRAMORE M.O.R.C. USA reported for duty + taken on the strength.	NZ
"	8		Routine	NZ / Mr / NZ
"	9			
"	10		Routine. Capt R.W. ARMSTRONG Reserve left on 1 months leave to U.K. 1st Lieut E.F. SCHMITZ M.O.R.C. USA left on 14 days leave to Paris.	RSpears / NZ
"	11		Construction of Latrine + improvement of Camp Toilets proceeding. Routine.	

WAR DIARY or INTELLIGENCE SUMMARY

Army Form C.2118

Place	Date	Hour	Summary of Events and Information	Remarks and references to Appendices
LECHELLE P.25.c.5.5	12th		Ref. map Sheet 57.C. Routine: 1 N.C.O. & 8 men proceeded for temp. duty at No. 21 C.C.S. YPRES in addition to 18 O.R. already there.	Fine
"	13th		Routine: 1st Lieut. J.O. PARRAMORE M.R.C., U.S.A., left to attend Course of Instruction at 3rd Army School of Sanitation ARRAS. Capt. P.J. LANE M.C. R.A.M.C. reported back from leave to U.K.	Fine
"	14th		Routine: Capt. A.G. FISHER M.C. R.A.M.C. rejoined the unit from temporary duty as M.O.i/c 2nd Bn. The S. Staffordshire Regt.	Rain
"	15th		Routine: Anti-vermin Inspection of huts, followed by mud baths & sandbags, finished.	" V. Cold
"	16th		Routine: 1st Lieut. J.O. PARRAMORE returned from 3rd Army School of Sanitation.	"
"	17th		Routine: Billeting area bombed by Enemy Aeroplanes from 7.30 to 9.30pm last night. 62 bombs fell near Noble Lines — no damage.	" V. Cold
"	18th		Routine	"
"	19th		Routine: Capt. A.G. FISHER M.C. R.A.M.C. & temporary duty as M.O.i/c 10th D.C.L.I.	"
"	20th		1st Lieut J.O. PARRAMORE M.O.R.C. U.S.A. to No.21 C.C.S. for temporary duty. Routine	"
"	21st		Routine: Party of 20 O.R. working at R.E. dump, YPRES. Returned at 3pm today and immediately sent on to No.5 F.A. at METZ for work on dugouts in R.E.C. (Sheet 57 c).	"

Army Form C. 2118.

WAR DIARY
or
INTELLIGENCE SUMMARY

(Erase heading not required.)

Instructions regarding War Diaries and Intelligence Summaries are contained in F. S. Regs., Part II. and the Staff Manual respectively. Title Pages will be prepared in manuscript.

Place	Date	Hour	Summary of Events and Information	Remarks and references to Appendices
LECHELLE P.25 c.0.5.	Feb.		Ref. Map. Sheet 57 C. 1:40,000.	
"	22nd		Routine: 1st Lieut. J.O. PARRAMORE MORC USA returned from 21 CCS. A.D.M.S. 2nd Division inspected Camp.	
"	23rd		Camp inspected by D.M.S. 3rd Army - & D.M.S. 2nd Corps at 12.30 pm.	
"	24th		Routine: 1st Lieut. J.O. PARRAMORE to temp duty as M.O. K. 1st R. Berkshire Regt.	
"	25th		Routine: Above canteen is being fixed up in Camp.	
"	26th		Routine: 1st Lieuts E.F. SCHMITZ & E.A. CURTIN reported back from leave to Paris.	
"	27th		Routine: T/Capt. R.M. ARMSTRONG & P.J. KANE recommended to promotion to rank of Major under G.R.O. 3448 d/ 23/2/18.	
"	28th		Routine: 1st Lieut. J.O. PARRAMORE MORC USA returned from temporary duty as M.O. K. 1st R. Berkshire Regt. 1st Lieut. E.F. SCHMITZ temp. duty as M.O. K. 2nd Bn. Oxf. & Bucks L.I.	

[signature]
Lt. Col. Field Ambulance
O.C. No. 100

Army Form C. 2118.

WAR DIARY
or
INTELLIGENCE SUMMARY

(Erase heading not required.)

Instructions regarding War Diaries and Intelligence Summaries are contained in F. S. Regs., Part II. and the Staff Manual respectively. Title Pages will be prepared in manuscript.

Place	Date	Hour	Summary of Events and Information	Remarks and references to Appendices

CONFIDENTIAL

CONFIDENTIAL

WAR DIARY

OF

No. 100 FIELD AMBULANCE

from 1st March, 1918 to 31st March, 1918

(VOLUME 29)

140/2400

COMMITTEE F...
MEDICAL HISTOR...
Date -6 JUN 1918

2449 Wt. W14957/M90 750,000 1/16 J.B.C. & A. Forms/C.2118/12.

Army Form C. 2118.

WAR DIARY
or
INTELLIGENCE SUMMARY
(Erase heading not required.)

Place	Date	Hour	Summary of Events and Information	Remarks and references to Appendices
LE CHELLE P.25.c.5.5.	March 1918		Ref. Map: Sheet 57 C. 1:40,000	
	1st		Routine: Ambulance still at rest. Detached Parties = 27 O.R. at Corps M.D.S. 24 O.R. at 21 C.C.S. ROYAUXCOURT. 23 O.R. with No. 5 F.A. Enlarged on Bright construction = 1 Officer & 27 O.R. on leave to U.K. Remainder of unit employed chiefly on improvement of billets & Camp.	Weather Summary A. & E. Report
	2nd		Routine: 16 O.R. rejoined unit from No. 5 Field Ambulance. Leave for the men. 2nd Lieut A.J.K. Young Campbell & Capt. P.J. Lane the Nance & 2 O.R. H.Q. 5 F.A. for temporary duty. 1st Lieut. B.P. Doran U.S. M.O.R.C. proceeded to medical charge of 158th H.A. group & struck off strength of this unit.	Met
"	3rd		Routine: 16 O.R. returned from duty with No. 5 Field Ambulance (Bright construction)	Met
"	4th		Routine: 27 O.R. returned from duty with No. 21 C.C.S.	Met
"	5th		Routine: 1st Lieut. R.F. Schatz USA M.O.R.C. reported from temporary duty with 2nd Batt. No Infant Manche. Z.J.	Met
	6th		Routine: Attended Conference of F.A. Commanders at Astrue office	Met
	7th		Routine: Inspected with Sen Beam officer of Divn, proposed new Barracades routes from Rear H.Q.S. 1st Lieut E.A. Curtin U.S. M.O.R.C & M.O. Intrenching Battalion for temporary duty.	Met
	8th		Routine: 10 Reinforcements (Pte Rance) arrived — 3 Category A — 1 Cat B.i — 5 B.ii — 1 B.iii. Majority have had little training & took unable to bearing a sketcher 100 yds. Medical Arrangements for 5th Duf I Corps front received from Corps Scheme - Defence Scheme	Met

2449 Wt. W14957/M90 750,000 1/16 J.B.C. & A. Forms/C.2118/12.

Army Form C. 2118.

WAR DIARY
or
INTELLIGENCE SUMMARY

(Erase heading not required.)

Instructions regarding War Diaries and Intelligence Summaries are contained in F. S. Regs., Part II. and the Staff Manual respectively. Title Pages will be prepared in manuscript.

Place	Date	Hour	Summary of Events and Information	Remarks and references to Appendices
LECHELLE P.25.c.55	March 9th		Routine: Capt. A.G. FISHER M.C. reune reported to Unit from temp. duty with 10th D.C.L.I. Bon Respirators worn by Unit from 1 hour today & duties performed with S.B.Rs. adjusted Unit now up to strength except for 1 M.O. & 1 O.R. A.S.C. M.T.	Very fine
"	10th		Routine: Major P.J. LANE M.C. to temporary duty at A.D.M.S. Office, 2nd Division. 1st Reinf. E.A. CURTIN, U.S. M.O.R.C., reported from temporary duty with 10th D.C.L.I.	Fine
"	11th		Routine	Fine
"	12th	1.20 pm	2nd Lieut. E.F. SCHMITZ U.S. M.O.R.C. to 1st Bn. The R. Berkshire Regt. for temporary duty vice Capt. ORRIT slightly gassed.	Fine
"	"	5 pm	1st Lieut. E.A. CURTIN & 5.D. O.R. Stretcher Bearers to No. 5 Field Ambulance at METZ for duty in the line. Reported that Sgt. THOMAS M.M. R.A.M.C. & 18 other ORs of this Unit have been evacuated today from No. 48 C.C.S. to the base wounded (Shell gas). Division & Highland Divisions (63rd) have had casualties during night from shell gas. All available Moto Ambulances gone for duty at No. 5 F.A. (A.D.S.) Major P.J. LANE M.C. R.A.M.C. returned from temporary duty at A.D.M.S office.	Fine & hot
"	13th		Routine: 42 O.R. of No. 6 Field Amb. arrived at 10 am today for duty in the line as Stretcher Bearers & regunit. 1 M.T. Driver & 1 Pte R.A.M.C. of the Unit admitted this afternoon "Gassed" "Shell & Personal". Total no. of Casualties ("gassed") in the Unit since Zero Hour G.M.T. personal short. yesterday = 24.	Mild

2449 Wt. W14957/M90 750,000 1/16 J.B.C. & A. Forms/C.2118/12.

Army Form C. 2118.

WAR DIARY
or
INTELLIGENCE SUMMARY

(Erase heading not required.)

Instructions regarding War Diaries and Intelligence Summaries are contained in F. S. Regs., Part II. and the Staff Manual respectively. Title Pages will be prepared in manuscript.

Place	Date	Hour	Summary of Events and Information	Remarks and references to Appendices
METZ Q.19 & 9.1	14	9 am	Ref. Map: Sheet 57ᴱ 1:40,000. At 9 am Unit moved from LECHELLE to METZ, an order received from A.D.M.S. 2nd Div. last night, & not took over Advanced Dressing Station METZ and evacuation of line held by 2nd Div from No 5 Field Ambulance, who handed in to day S.Bearer from "Mustard Gas". 40 O.R. of No. 6 F.A. also brought up from LECHELLE for duty in this unit, under Capt. CATFIELD, Adjutant of No. 6 F.A. Major O.J. LANE i/c No.100 F.A. in charge of Walking Bearers. 21 OR of this Unit (S.Bearers) evacuated to day "Wounded – Shell Gas". 5 Motor (light Car) Drivers evacuated from 2nd Div Supply Col. to replace casualties. Many Casualties (nearly all "gassed") passed through A.D.S. during day.	Fire...
	15		Unit "Stood to" twice during night to "gas alarm". METZ shelled with gas shell at 9 am lightly. Gas Casualties still passing through A.D.S. to M.D.S at RUYAULCOURT by Motor Ambulances & Lorries. Over 100 gas casualties through this morning. Gas Casualties still occurring in Stretcher Bearers. This Unit has already lost 54 men, no Reserves left. All gas casualties seen v. light cases, have b/n sent to Corps M.D.S. Have arranged to do it by Train (Becourville) chiefly, starting tomorrow. S.B.s of this unit to the line now reduced to 16 — with 40 S.B.s of No. 6 F.A.	

WAR DIARY
or
INTELLIGENCE SUMMARY

Army Form C. 2118.

(Erase heading not required.)

Place	Date	Hour	Summary of Events and Information	Remarks and references to Appendices
METZ R.19 B.9.1.	March 16th		Capt. CHATFIELD returned No.6 F.A. returned Road work today slightly gassed. Stream of gas casualties has now ceased. Total gas casualties in this unit from 13th inst to present time now = RAMC : 60 / M.T.A.S.C. : 4. No reinforcements yet received.	Fine Cold at night
"	17th		Major B.W. ARMSTRONG R.A.M.C. reported with today from leave to U.K.	
			1st Lieut. MOSER U.S.M.O.R.C. arrived in place of Capt. CHATFIELD Major No.6 F.A. and took over duty as liason officer at VILLERS PROUICH with Major P.J. KANE. No more casualties from this unit. The Casualties arrived for Ambulance Car — Unit still 3 Ambs short. 2 M.T.A.S.C. Reinforcements arrived for Ambulance Car — Unit still 3 Ambs short. Capt. Lieut E.F. SCHMITZ Regmnd hands over temp. duty with 1stBn. Royal Berkshire Regt.	
"	18th		Lieut SCHMITZ took over charge of Stretcher Bearers & Hqrs. in VILLERS PROUICH from Major P.J. KANE who who has rejoined H.Q. of unit in METZ.	
			1st Lieut. J.H. GRAFF U.S.M.O.R.C. joined unit from Base Reinforcements & / reported duty. (1st part of day.) 2nd — Bn's Gas Consulting Course through — a few delayed gas cases — Mild to those admitted. Sent down gassed — have died — 1st + 3 O.C.S (Pte S. BOWDEN) and 1 at ROUEN (Pte G.A. CROCKER).	Fine Dry

WAR DIARY or INTELLIGENCE SUMMARY

Army Form C. 2118.

Place	Date	Hour	Summary of Events and Information	Remarks and references to Appendices
METZ Q.19.d.9.1.	March 19th		Took over 5th London F.A., his heavy officers & Bearers & 3 ADMS 47th Division. Round Bearer Relay Posts & R.A.P.s between 11am & 3pm preparatory to handing men evacuation of Divisional Front & A.D.S. over to 5th London F.A. tomorrow. Few casualties come through ADS — Gas cases have almost stopped. Reinforcements arriving from Base to replace casualties in the Unit. Capt A.G. FISHER & Lieut. RAINE returned from leave to Paris.	Rain. APPENDIX "A"
ROCQUIGNY O.21.c.9.4.	20th		Handed over evacuation of line taken over by 47th Division to O.C. 5th London Field Ambulance. Adv Dressing Stations METZ & VILLERS PLOUICH, also handed over at 2pm. Unit moved in 3 parties, with Stretcher Bearers of No 6 F.A. from METZ to ROCQUIGNY at 4pm., and took over Field Ambulance Site from 6th London F.A. Stretcher Bearers of No 6 F.A. rejoined their Unit at N.11 Central.	
	21st		Routine: Cleaning & reclothing of Equipment. Under Urgent Orders from ADMS 2nd Division Capt. A.G. FISHER and Lieut. RAINE & 1st Rent. W.H. GRAFF U.S. Army with 27 O.R. left to duty at 48 C.C.S. YPRES at 11am. Germans attack on 5th Corps Front seems to be developing. 1st Lieut. J.O. PARAMORE U.S. Army & 13 O.R. RAINE (Stretcher Bearers) left & join No. 8 Field Ambulance at LECHELLE to duty of reinforced at 3pm. ROCQUIGNY Shelled during day. There are now 27 O.R. — 10 O.R. suffering from Gas Shell in Camp with the 2nd 1st Lieut CURTIN reported here from Temp duty with KRR Corps	

Army Form C. 2118.

WAR DIARY
or
INTELLIGENCE SUMMARY
(Erase heading not required.)

Instructions regarding War Diaries and Intelligence Summaries are contained in F. S. Regs., Part II. and the Staff Manual respectively. Title Pages will be prepared in manuscript.

Place	Date	Hour	Summary of Events and Information	Remarks and references to Appendices
ROCQUIGNY Q.27.C.9.4	MARCH 22nd		Units collecting kits from 5th & 6th A/ Brigade Groups at BARASTRE and HAPLINCOURT, to which places their Brigades moved during the night. A few local casualties dealt with. Camp shelled during today. No casualties. A few of the lightly 'gassed' casualties returning to duty. 80th & 32nd O.R. Names deficient.	Fine
COURCELETTE N.25.6.73			Received orders to move from ROCQUIGNY to BEAULENCOURT N.15.a. (Site of 21 C.C.S.) at 3.30 a.m. Which arrived at 6 a.m. — Progress slow as roads full of transport.	Fine
		9/am	Unit moved from BEAULENCOURT to COURCELETTE via LE BARQUE and main BAPAUME — ALBERT Road. Arrived at COURCELETTE at 4 p.m. All horse ambulance cars sent to No. 6 F.A. for duty at main Dressing Station. Considerable difficulty in carrying equipment (200 blankets, pyjamas, bedsocks etc.) Duplicate Mobilization Tables as the extra transport has been provided and all Ambulance cars have been withdrawn for duty elsewhere. G.S. wagons have to make double journeys + horses are getting tired. Transport has been allotted to F.A. to carry the Equipment. Authorised of F.A. are asked to carry a large amount of extra Equipment, then extra transport should be provided also.	
		10am	1st Lieut. E.F SCHMITZ. M.O.R.C. U.S.A. left for temp. duty with 1st Bn. The King's Regt. early this morning.	Fine
	24 E	5/pm	2 Ambulance cars struck by bomb at PUCHVILLERS last night (a Sunbeam + a Daimler). Car [struck?] driver of Sunbeam missing — feared killed. Daimler car destroyed.	*Since identified — wounded + prisoner
			Received orders to move to BEAUMONT — HAMEL.	

Army Form C. 2118.

WAR DIARY
or
INTELLIGENCE SUMMARY
(Erase heading not required.)

Instructions regarding War Diaries and Intelligence Summaries are contained in F. S. Regs., Part II. and the Staff Manual respectively. Title Pages will be prepared in manuscript.

Place	Date	Hour	Summary of Events and Information	Remarks and references to Appendices
BEAUMONT HAMEL H.5 -75.03	March 25th		Reference Map LENS Sheet 11. 1/100,000.	
		10 am	Unit arrived from COURCELETTE at 11:30 pm last night. 1 Ambulance & 1 Bearer bn. broken down at AVELUY, unable to move and abandoned. Ambulance Car was carrying part of A.D.M.S. office documents forward. Unit now 4 large cars short.	Fin
		12 noon	Unit moved to Road Junction Sec. of MAILLY - MAILLET (S.H. 1.9.) & packed with Nos 5. & 6 F.A. off road. 1st Lieut. J.O. PARAMORE & 12 Stretcher Bearers reported here on his 7/march. Major P.J. LANE & 7 O.R. left at BEAUMONT HAMEL about 10am for duty in this line in formation MIRAUMONT	
		4:30 pm	Unit moved to BEATRAM COURT and arrived at 5:30 pm	
LOUVENCOURT (S.F. 95.10)		7 pm	Unit moved to LOUVENCOURT at 9pm & billeted with No.6 Field Amb. in chateau. Major LANE and also Stretcher Bearers reported state being hospital in convention & line held by 2nd Division	Afm
ARQUEVES G.F. 65.87.	26th	2 pm	Unit left LOUVENCOURT and arrived at ARQUEVES at 3pm. Confused on outskirts of village. Major S.W. ARMSTRONG & 5 O.R. left Kform. Adv. Dressing Station at BEAUSSART (S.G. 95.00.)	.
		5 pm	1 Section of unit sent up to BEAUSSART for duty in relief of other Amd. Bearers	
		10 pm	1st Lieut. E.A. CURTIN with further supply of Medical Comforts & Dressings joined party at Adv. Dressing Station. Men not yet recovering from leave. Two reinforcements coming up.	
"	27th	.	Unit resting Majors B.W. ARMSTRONG, P.J. LANE, and 1st Lieut. CURTIN with 1st O.R. reported from duty at Adv. Dressing Station BEAUSSART	Afm

249 Wt. W14957/Mg0 750,000 1/16 J.B.C. & A. Forms/C.2118/12.

Army Form C. 2118.

WAR DIARY
or
INTELLIGENCE SUMMARY

(Erase heading not required.)

Instructions regarding War Diaries and Intelligence Summaries are contained in F. S. Regs., Part II. and the Staff Manual respectively. Title Pages will be prepared in manuscript.

Place	Date	Hour	Summary of Events and Information	Remarks and references to Appendices
ARGUEVES (C.F. 65.87)	March 28th		Ref. Map. LENS Sheet 11. (1/100,000)	
		7/am	Unit's meeting. ADS for Division opened by No.2 F.A. at ENGLEBELMER (G.H. 30.75) with M.DS. at HEDAUVILLE. ADS sent from this unit for duty at W.W. Collecting Post at CLAIRFAYE (G.G. 25.63). 2 clerks sent from this unit for duty at M.DS. HEDAUVILLE. 2 remaining large cars to duty at M.DS. HEDAUVILLE.	Rain
"	29th	7/am	Unit meeting. 2 large Amb. cars back from duty at M.DS. followed Workshops Unit now short of M. Transport. Men now billeted in barns.	Rain
"	30th		Unit meeting. 2 Motor Bicycles to Workshops (LONGUEVILLERS – a long way away) for repairs. 2 Field Feature ROLLS and 6 G.S. Panniers containing Advance Equipment (Bulls Eye Lanterns, Flags, Signal, Corrected Set) which had never been used and which it was lately refused during this war, handed over to Railhead A.O.D Officer, BELLE EGLISE Railhead, and receipt obtained. There is now more down at Longpré. Only useful Equipment Cars Blankets + 100 suits of Pyjamas had little abandoned at BEAUMONT HAMEL on 25th inst owing to lack of Motor Transport + inability to find anyone to carry them.	Rain
"	31st		Unit meeting. Routine & cleaning.	

Lists attached (Appendix "A") Stores & Equipment which this Contained might well be attended with during present time.

[signature]
O.C. No. 100 Field Amb.

(APPENDIX A)

Reference - G.R.O. 3472 d/ 25-2-18

List of Articles of Equipment for a Field Ambulance recommended to be dispensed with.

A. MEDICAL EQUIPMENT	
Reserve F.M. Panniers (Sec No. 8 Med Stores) prs	1
F.M. Panniers No 2 (- do -)	3
Fracture Boxes (- do -)	3
Operating Table (portable) Sec No 7 Med Stores	1

B. MOBILIZATION STORE TABLE. G1098

Section 2 - A	
Flags, distinguishing (to be replaced by tin flags)	2
Lanterns, tent	6

Section 5 - A	
Breechings, straps, extending	40
Girths, pieces, extending	10

Section 5 - B	
Bags, entrenching tool	3
Covers, 6ft x 6ft F.A.	9

Section 6 - A	
Straps, extending	20

Section 6 - B.	
Saddle - trees	2
Straps, girth v attachment	18
- do -, releaseable	6
Washers, No 6 S.W.G	16

Section 8 - C	
Flags, signal, army	12

Section No 11	
Lanterns bull's-eye	36

Section No 12	
Boxes, cash, G.S.	2
Clippers, hair	4
Covers, tin, 6¼ inch	60
Cups, spitting, enamelled	12
Feeders, enamelled	8
Funnels, tin ½ pint	9
Panniers, general service	12
- do - Medical Comforts	3
Pans, bed enamelled	12
Stools, close, F.A., nest of 4	3 nests
Urinals, zinc	6

Section 13 - A	
Cases, bolster, tent (straw usually not available)	150

Section 13 - C	
Flags, union 6ft x 3ft	2

Pimlico Section No 30	
Brushes, shaving	9
Combs, hair	4

Rifles and ammunition carried by A.S.C. H.T. personnel attached to Field Ambulance.

Army Form C. 2118.

WAR DIARY
or
INTELLIGENCE SUMMARY
(Erase heading not required.)

CONFIDENTIAL

Instructions regarding War Diaries and Intelligence Summaries are contained in F.S. Regs., Part II. and the Staff Manual respectively. Title Pages will be prepared in manuscript.

JBC 23

140/29/30.

4

CONFIDENTIAL

WAR DIARY

OF.

No. 100 FIELD AMBULANCE

from 1st April 1918 to 30th April 1918.

(VOLUME 30)

-6 JUN 1918

Place	Date	Hour	Summary of Events and Information	Remarks and references to Appendices

CONFIDENTIAL

Army Form C. 2118.

WAR DIARY or INTELLIGENCE SUMMARY

(Erase heading not required.)

Instructions regarding War Diaries and Intelligence Summaries are contained in F.S. Regs., Part II. and the Staff Manual respectively. Title Pages will be prepared in manuscript.

Place	Date	Hour	Summary of Events and Information	Remarks and references to Appendices
	April		Reference Map LENS: Sheet 11: 1/100,000	
ARQUEVES (6.F 6.9)	1st	7 p.m.	Routine Unit resting. Capt. A.G. FISHER M.C. R.A.M.C. 1st Lieut. J.H. GRAFF is here + a party of 27 O.R. reported here ready this morning for duty with 48 CCS. (No. 3 Canad. Stat. Hospl. DOULLENS)	Summary M. Col.
ORVILLE S.E. 93 42.	2nd	7:30 p.m.	Received orders at 5 a.m. from Attres to proceed to ORVILLE with 99th Inf. Bde this morning. Left ARQUEVES 9:30 a.m. arrived ORVILLE at 11:30 a.m. 99th Inf. Bde in the meanwhile attached to BEAUVAL (S.D.) Unit camped beside No. 138 F.A. (41st Div. at ORVILLE) Fire Unit still deficient of 52 O.R. R & 4 large motor ambul. cars.	
REBREUVE (3.E.05.15)	3rd	2 p.m.	Received orders from 99th Inf. Bde. that dismounted portion of Unit was to proceed in advance.	Morg.
		3:10 p.m.	Dismounted portion of unit embussed on outskirts of DOULLENS & went to PREVENT, Marched from there to REBREUVE arriving at 6:45 p.m. Transport proceeded via HALLOY & LUCHEUX to REBREUVE arriving at 8 p.m.	Morg.
"	4th	7 a.m.	Unit resting + getting cleaned up. Sick of 99th Inf. Bde in villages around collected and evacuated to PREVENT. Greater part of unit bathed & changed clothes today.	Summary
"	5th	7 p.m.	Routine. Capt A.G. FISHER M.C. R.A.M.C. posted a/s 4.0. & 2nd Battn. King's M.C. Rifles and attached off. strength The Regt. & reinforcements reported duties tonight.	Ane Appx
	6th	7:30 p.m.	Routine. Attached - M. Col. E.F. SCHMITZ M.R.C. LSA posted for duty a/s 2nd Bn. The King's Regt. and attached off. strength. 64 O.R. Reinforcements reported tonight. 1st Lieut. G.F. ROBINS - US M.C. reported from No.B.F.A. and Lieut... 65 O.R. Reinforcements arrived from Base Depot.	Morg.

2449 Wt. W14957/Mgo 750,000 1/16 E.F. SCHMITZ M.R.C. LSA J.B.C. & A. Forms/C.2118/12.

Army Form C. 2118.

WAR DIARY
or
INTELLIGENCE SUMMARY
(Erase heading not required.)

Instructions regarding War Diaries and Intelligence Summaries are contained in F. S. Regs., Part II. and the Staff Manual respectively. Title Pages will be prepared in manuscript.

Place	Date	Hour	Summary of Events and Information	Remarks and references to Appendices
REBREUVE 3.E.66.15	Aug 7th	4 pm	Ref. Map. LENS Sheet 1/100,000	MW
	8th		Routine. Unit training	MW
			Routine. Major P.J. LANE, the Rebus was on 8 days special leave to U.K.	MW
	9th		Routine. Capt M.L. STIERS A.A.M.C. joined Unit from England for duty & taken on strength	MW
CANETTEMONT J.E. 40.35	10th	9.30 pm	Unit moved from REBREUVE to CANETTEMONT via HOUVAL at 1.30 pm. under orders from 2nd Div. C.H.S. June: A.99 Unit billeted in village. Ready to move at 2 hours notice with 99th Inf. Brigade Group, to which it is at present attached. Unit now over strength in Rank. O.R. Personnel. Still 3 large Motor Ambulance cars deficient.	MW
WARLUZEL 4.F.65.75	11th	2 pm 5.30 pm	Unit moved from CANETTEMONT with 99th Inf. Brigade. Arrived at WARLUZEL. Ready to move at short notice.	MW MW
GRINCOURT J.F.93.99	12th	1.30 am 4 am	Unit left WARLUZEL with 99th Inf. Brigade Group. Arrived GRINCOURT 1 from billets for men. 99th Inf. Bde. some distance away at LAHERLIÈRE. 23 Evacuations from Bde. Group & to Corps Rest Station at GOUY-EN-ARTOIS and 18 to C.C.S. at DOULLENS. One Infectious Case (Measles) to AUXI-LE-CHATEAU. MEASLES occurring in 99th Inf. Brigade — imported by new draft from England. 3 #1 R.A.M.C. Personnel of Unit evacuated today.	MW

Army Form C. 2118.

WAR DIARY
or
INTELLIGENCE SUMMARY

(Erase heading not required.)

Instructions regarding War Diaries and Intelligence Summaries are contained in F. S. Regs., Part II. and the Staff Manual respectively. Title Pages will be prepared in manuscript.

Place	Date	Hour	Summary of Events and Information	Remarks and references to Appendices
GRINCOURT S.F.93.99	12th		Lt. Arcolo sent Sheet II 1/40,000	
		2pm	Medical meeting. Visited IIth Corps Main Dressing Station at LE BAC DU SUD preparatory to taking over from No 3 Field Amb (Guards Divn) on 15th inst.	
		7pm	Lt Colonel Sudlow billeted down to CARNOY Corps 5 CAMBRAI Group from Q & 2nd Division.	
		8am	Capt GRACOVICH arrived.	
LAVENTIE 46.X.C	13th		Visited various CARNOY and PILOT ? farms for sick.	
		7pm	Visit lecture on Advance Party - Majors G.W. ARMSTRONG + H.D.B. BLINE - up for IInd Corps M.A.S. at BAC de SUD at 9pm preparatory to taking our functions.	
			Lt-Col. Blair S.F.S ADC now.	
LE BAC DU SUD E.32.4.S.C	15th	10am	Met LT. KNIGHT at 9.30am, arrived LE BAC DU SUD at 10.15am. Take over IIth Corps Main Dressing Station at 10.15am from 3rd Field Amb. (Guards Divn.) 1 Field 3rd Division for 6th Canal Field Amb. & 93rd Field Amb. attached for duty. The wounded from 6th Corps were received.	
	16th	7am	Routine of Main Dressing Station. 30 S.N.C.C. & 4 lorries returned for wounded & Americans. 150 - from 79th Div for later attached for Evacn Duty 1 PAU form 45 Frenchman Regiment. 1 LAD - ER Sick - hour duty pared through Carry from 12 hours - 15/4/18 - 8 am	

Army Form C. 2118.

WAR DIARY
or
INTELLIGENCE SUMMARY

(Erase heading not required.)

Instructions regarding War Diaries and Intelligence Summaries are contained in F. S. Regs., Part II. and the Staff Manual respectively. Title Pages will be prepared in manuscript.

Place	Date	Hour	Summary of Events and Information	Remarks and references to Appendices
LE BAC DU SUD Q 32.a.5.0	April 18		Position: Officers {killed 1, wounded 3} O.R. {killed 6, wounded 116} passed through C.M.D.S. between 6 p.m. last night & 6 p.m. tonight.	Showery.
			3 large Daimler cars have now joined the unit completing establishment	
			3 Cars are at present doing duty with No. 6 F.A. at Adv. Dress. Station.	
			...wounded coming in in good condition & owing to presence of 30th M.A.C. can be got away quickly.	
"	19	6 p.m.	Routine. a quiet day. Officers {S. 3, W. 2} O.R. {S. 58, W. 45} passed through C.M.D.S. in last 24 hours.	
			... visited C.M.D.S. & expressed satisfaction with improvements already carried out. A large quantity of "passed" clothing sent & steam disinfected after prolonged exposure in open air.	
			Major R.V. LANE temp. O.C. rejoined unit from special leave to U.K.	
"	20		Routine. Evacuation passing through Officers {W. 7, S. 1} O.R. {W. 37, S. 71} in 24 hours.	V. cold. Sleet.
			Lieut. Major R.V. LANE inc. 1st Lieut. PARRAMORE U.S.A. M.R.C. ... M.O. transferred from R.A.P. to A.D.S.	
			...with s/m ... today. Officers {W. -, S. -} O.R. {W. 36 +1 Pof war, S. 46}	

Army Form C. 2118.

WAR DIARY
or
INTELLIGENCE SUMMARY

(Erase heading not required.)

Instructions regarding War Diaries and Intelligence Summaries are contained in F. S. Regs., Part II. and the Staff Manual respectively. Title Pages will be prepared in manuscript.

Place	Date	Hour	Summary of Events and Information	Remarks and references to Appendices
LE BAC DE SUD Q.33.A.50	21st	6 p.m.	Ref. Trench sheet 51 C 1:40,000 Routine. Officers {W.2 S.1} + O.R. {W. 45 S. 46} through H.Q.R.S. 6 p.m. to 6 p.m. tonight	
"	22nd	7 p.m.	Routine. Officers {W.5 S.—} + O.R. {W. 38 S. 47} through HQRS in last 24 hours. Gas treatment used working satisfactorily, several cases of men gassed by our own gas at over 1000 yds. distance have come in. Symptoms in most cases fairly severe. Referred to Corps inspector MGRS.	
"	23rd	7 p.m.	Routine. Issued from distinctive treatment of W.F.O. (gas?) + lightly gassed cases is being developed. One case passing through in 24 hrs before yesterday 24 hr period today. Officers {W.2 S.1} O.R. {W.48 S.51}	True
"	24	7 p.m.	Routine. Officers {W.1 S.1} + O.R. {W.48 S.51} through in last 24 hours	
"	25	7 p.m.	Routine. Officers {W.1 S.1} + O.R. {W.40 S.51} in last 24 hours. (also three German (MO) lightly gassed in charge)	
"	26	7 p.m.	Officers {W.1 S.3} + O.R. {W.55 S.75} dealt with in past 24 hours.	Thunderstorm Rain
			NYE (W.4) + lightly gassed cases are now being distributed hospital trains to empty. Imported out to Shorch thoroughly sound a type well trialled in direct. Quite a delightful girl, being that the return arrived at CCS. Coffee and beaux light are two particularly excellent. All field units not specially great. A.D.S. ADMD Shall Paris Supplements or Thingham in	

2449 Wt. W14957/M90 750,000 1/16 J.B.C. & A. Forms/C.2118/12.

Army Form C. 2118

WAR DIARY
or
INTELLIGENCE SUMMARY
(Erase heading not required.)

Instructions regarding War Diaries and Intelligence Summaries are contained in F. S. Regs., Part II. and the Staff Manual respectively. Title Pages will be prepared in manuscript.

Place	Date	Hour	Summary of Events and Information	Remarks and references to Appendices
Le TBAC DU SUD	1/3/17		Ration Strength 31 O. 1,140 O.Rs.	
Q.32.a.5.0.	27	1/pm	Routine. D.D.M.S. inspected Unit. D.M.S. 3rd Army inspected Chiefly Sanitary.	
			Admitted { W.H. 4 O.R. { W. 47 Recall units in first 24 hours	
			{ S. 7 { S. 7	
			Admitted R.Smyth all others Ambulance cases with —	
			{ 1 Thomas Splint Buttock 1 Head Severe Humerus Splint & 1 M.S. Fresh Gelatine }	
			{ Thomas Splint Splints 1 Humerus Leg Splint }	
			Noted that the arrangement Work of any practical Value of the Splints are	
			not ready known in R.A.Ps + A.D.Ss etc. They will last be applied not at best.	
		15/2	1/pm Pts. Lieut. G.F. RoBinson Invac to N.S.F. evacuated sick to No 3 General. S.F.t. Hosp. Time	
			Balleul	
			{ W.H. 2 O.R. { W. 47 through R.A.S. in first 24 hours	
			{ S. 1 { S. 59	
	29	1/pm	R.A.M.C. GE Murray Rank No.5 F.A. Joined for temporary duty	
			{ W.H. 1 O.R. { 88./62 Passed through in 24 hours Upper Upper	
			{ S. — { S. 43	
			Invac. y Major Bremer Stated shelled by HMA Heavy fire (11") — no casualties	
3.5	1/3		Rout. (Strength & Prt. as above) 16.H. 34 hours Admissions { W.H. 53 O.R. { W. 53	
			{ S. 3 { S. 33	

M.H. [signature] U.C.A. C...
O.C. No.100 Field Amb.

Army Form C. 2118.

WAR DIARY
or
INTELLIGENCE SUMMARY

(Erase heading not required.)

Vol 24

140/2983.

COMMITTEE
MEDICAL HISTORY OF THE WAR
Date 9 JUL 1919

CONFIDENTIAL

WAR DIARY
OF
No 100 FIELD AMBULANCE
from 1st MAY 1918 – 31st MAY 1918.
(VOLUME 31)

Army Form C. 2118.

WAR DIARY
or
INTELLIGENCE SUMMARY
(Erase heading not required.)

Instructions regarding War Diaries and Intelligence Summaries are contained in F. S. Regs., Part II. and the Staff Manual respectively. Title Pages will be prepared in manuscript.

Place	Date	Hour	Summary of Events and Information	Remarks and references to Appendices
LE BAC DU SUD	Aug 1st	7am	Ref. Trench Sheet 51c 1:40,000 Routine. Officers {Wounded — O.R. {W.32, S.52} passed through in last 24 hours	
			Lieut. V. JAMIESON R.A.M.C. (C.S.) Age 41. Joined this unit for duty. Strength from England —	
Q 33.a.5.0	2nd		E.S.L. Routine. Lieut. S.F. MURRAY leave No.3 F.A. returned to this unit from temporary duty at C Coys A.D.S. Vicinity of subs. shelled lightly during the night — no casualties	Fine weather
			Officers {W.2, S.2} — O.R. {W.55, S.61} passed through Clubs in past 24 hours	
			Arrangements made for Medical Statistical Cards from all Divisions in the Corps Hosp. from Feb 1st to be sent (and have been so) to Dental Surgeon at FREVENT 1st Aug.	
	3rd	7pm	Routine. R.M.S. 3rd Army Info. Officer and A.A. Hosp. El Capt. reported having sustained gunshot wounds	
			Officers {W.1, S.7} — O.R. {K.110, W.64, S.47} passed through Clubs in past 24 hours	
	4th	7am	Routine. Officers {W.2, S.4} — O.R. {W.64, S.45} passed through in past 24 hours	

Army Form C. 2118.

WAR DIARY

or

INTELLIGENCE SUMMARY

(Erase heading not required.)

Instructions regarding War Diaries and Intelligence Summaries are contained in F. S. Regs., Part II. and the Staff Manual respectively. Title Pages will be prepared in manuscript.

Place	Date	Hour	Summary of Events and Information	Remarks and references to Appendices
LE BAS DU SUD Q.32.a. 5.0	May 5th	6.30pm	Ref. Map Sheet 51ᶜ - 1:40,000 Routine: A "Haldane's" 4 way apparatus has been put in Gas treatment word for administration of oxygen. Officers {W.2 S.6} & O.R. {W.55 S.23} through M.O.S in past 24 hours. All inter blankets, leather jerkins & winter underclothing in unit has now been called in	Showery
"	6th	6.30pm	Routine: Officers {W.2 S.7} & O.R. {W.37 S.53} passed through C.M.D.S in past 24 hours	
"	7th	2pm	Routine: D.D.M.S II Corps & A.D.M.S. Guards, 2nd & 32nd & 2nd Canad. Div. visited C.M.D.S for Conference. Officers {W.1 S.3} & O.R. {W.45 S.39} through C.M.D.S in past 24 hours. A Nissen hut for detention & treatment of lightly gassed cases has been erected & is ready for use.	
"	8th	6pm	Routine: Horse Transport inspected by OC. 2nd Div Train, who expressed opinion that it was "a very good turn-out". Visited WARLUZEL (O.27.b.) with D.D.M.S II Corps and A.D.M.S 2nd Division to inspect proposed site of "Reserve" Main Dressing Station. Officers {W.5 S.2} & O.R. {W.47 S.42} passed through C.M.D.S in past 24 hours. Reported to A.D.M.S on Equipment dumped at Roo BELLE EGLISE on 30/3/18.	Fine

2449 Wt. W14957/M90 750,000 1/16 J.B.C. & A. Forms/C.2118/12.

WAR DIARY
or
INTELLIGENCE SUMMARY
(Erase heading not required.)

Army Form C. 2118.

Instructions regarding War Diaries and Intelligence Summaries are contained in F.S. Regs., Part II. and the Staff Manual respectively. Title Pages will be prepared in manuscript.

Place	Date	Hour	Summary of Events and Information	Remarks and references to Appendices
LE BAC DU SUD Q.22.c.8.8	May 9		Routine. O.C. 91 F.A visited Church preparatory to taking over on 11th inst.	Nil
		7pm	HRRQRS {W.6 / S.3} 9 BR. {W.83 / S.38} passed through Church on foot 26 hours	
			A Party of Unit Stn + 25 hands to WARLUZEL to prepare site for Reserve M.D.S.	
"	10	12 noon	Routine. Officers {W.1 / S.2} + F.R. {W.47 / S.64} passed through Church on foot 26 hours	Nil
			Visited WARLUZEL and inspected preparations for Reserve Camp – Both purposes	
			Capts Young + BIDDLE of No 91 F.A. + 20 OR. arrived here assisting as Advance Party.	
WARLUZEL O.27.C.8.8	11	9am	Advance Parties of II Corps M.D.S. Bac Do Sud to OC No 91 Field Ambulance at 9 am	R.A.C. Fogna Nil
		12 noon	Rest of Unit left Bac Du Sud	
		1.30pm	First arrival at WARLUZEL. No time fell out on march. 4 sick Matients brought by Car.	
			All Ranks in Camp etc. Baths functioning on base Reserve M.D.S.	
"	12	6 pm	Unit settling + work on M.D.S proceeding	Nil
"	13	6 pm	Unit on 1 hour notice 8 am to 12 noon and 3 hours notice 12 noon to 8 am. Visit from Arthur + C.R.E. 2nd Division, and DDMS II Corps. 2 Motor Ambulances lent to Am American Troops on arrival at MONDICOURT	Nil

2449 Wt. W14957/M90 750,000 1/16 J.B.C. & A. Forms/C.2118/12.

Army Form C. 2118.

WAR DIARY
or
INTELLIGENCE SUMMARY

(Erase heading not required.)

Instructions regarding War Diaries and Intelligence Summaries are contained in F. S. Regs., Part II. and the Staff Manual respectively. Title Pages will be prepared in manuscript.

Place	Date	Hour	Summary of Events and Information	Remarks and references to Appendices
MARUZEL O.27.c.8.8	May 14th	7 hr.	Ref. Map 57c. 1/40,000. Routine: Motor Ambulance sent at intervals from 7hm last night to 1 pm to-day to MONDICOURT to meet & convey sick & incoming American troops (308th Regt.)	Nil
	15th	5.30 p.m.	Routine. Party of 12 O.R. went to No. 9 Field Amb. (Guards Div.) at RAMPART (X.7.C) to assimilate a French hut for transference to this Site (Chipo.). Visited by N.B. Officer. I lifted H.Q. to water supply of site for Camps in village — will have to contract with Civilian to carriage of water. Work of laying roads not available. At present 6th of American Battn. in this village. SOMBRIN workshop succeeded through Motorized.	Nil
"	16th		Routine. Work on M.D.S. progressing.	Neighbour
"	17th	1 pm	Lt. Col. No. F. B. SNOWDEN Range rejoined Unit after 1 month's leave to U.K. Party of 2 O.R. having completed lathing down of hut at RAMPART rejoined Unit. 15 small Hosp. Marquees received from Ordnance & with but will be first of here. Conference at A.D.M.S. 2nd Division.	Nil
"	18th	9 am	Routine. Lieut J. JAMIESON Raune (T.C.) left for temporary duty with 45th Labour Group. Visited H.Q. 99th Inf. Brigade & arrange for underground for Bearers in case of heavy fighting. Have had no definite instruction from Division yet. B.D.M.S. II Corps & A.D.M.S. 2nd Division visited Unit. Two old inefficient Motor Ambulance drivers from the 2nd Div. M.T. Coy. Ambulance Cars will benefit accordingly.	Nil

2449 Wt. W14957/M90 750,000 1/16 J.B.C. & A. Forms/C.2118/12.

Army Form C. 2118.

WAR DIARY
or
INTELLIGENCE SUMMARY.
(Erase heading not required.)

Instructions regarding War Diaries and Intelligence Summaries are contained in F. S. Regs., Part II. and the Staff Manual respectively. Title pages will be prepared in manuscript.

Place	Date MAY	Hour	Summary of Events and Information	Remarks and references to Appendices
WARLUZEL O.27.C.8.8.	19th	7pm	Routine. Visit from A.D.M.S. VI Corps.	Very hot.
"	20th	6.30pm	Routine. Party of 8 O.R. went to 32nd Div: A.D.S. at BLAIRVILLE to dismantle 3 Nissen huts & load up at WARLUZEL	
"	21st	7pm	Routine. Nothing to note. Capt. Skinn went to No. 3 C.C.S. for the week for work on	
"	22nd	7pm	treatment of "Shock". 21/5/18.	
"	23rd	7pm	Routine. Lieut. J. JAMIESON RAMC. rejoined unit from temporary duty with 45th Labour Group. Fine & foggy. Unit attended inspection of 99th Inf. Brigade Group at LA CAUCHIE by G.O.C. VI Corps.	
"	24th	7pm	Routine. 3 more small Nissen huts have been brought in from A.D.S. at BLAIREVILLE and are to be erected here.	Rain
"	25th	8pm	1st Lieut. J.O. PARRAMORE M.O.R.C. U.S.A. temporary duty with 72nd Army Bde. R.F.A. The Unit held its "Annual Sports" and won the Divisional Ambulance Relay Race & for Fringe given by A.D.M.S. 2nd Division.	
"	26th	7pm	Routine.	
"	27th	"	Lieut. J. JAMIESON temporary duty with 1st R. Berks Regt.	
"	28th	"	Routine.	
"	29th	6pm	Routine.	
"	30th	6pm	Routine. Transport inspected by G.O.C. 2nd Division, who expressed himself as very pleased with the turnout.	
"	31st	6pm	Routine.	No 100 Field Amb.

Clifton Thompson Lt.Col. O.C. No 100 Fd. Amb.

Army Form C. 2118.

14

WAR DIARY
or
INTELLIGENCE SUMMARY

(Erase heading not required.)

Instructions regarding War Diaries and Intelligence Summaries are contained in F. S. Regs., Part II. and the Staff Manual respectively. Title Pages will be prepared in manuscript.

JJ 25
160/306.

Place	Date	Hour	Summary of Events and Information	Remarks and references to Appendices
June 1918.				

CONFIDENTIAL

WAR DIARY
OF
No. 100 FIELD AMBULANCE
from 1st JUNE 1918 to 30th JUNE 1918
(VOLUME 32)

2449 Wt. W4957/M90 750,000 1/16 J.B.C. & A. Forms/C.2118/12.

Army Form C. 2118.

WAR DIARY
or
INTELLIGENCE SUMMARY
(Erase heading not required.)

Instructions regarding War Diaries and Intelligence Summaries are contained in F. S. Regs., Part II. and the Staff Manual respectively. Title Pages will be prepared in manuscript.

Place	Date	Hour	Summary of Events and Information	Remarks and references to Appendices
WARLUZEL O.27.c.88.	JUNE 1st	7 am	Ref Map 51 c 1:40,000 Routine. Nothing to note	Fine
	2nd	7 am	Routine. Nothing to note	Fine
"	3rd	6 pm	Routine. 1st Lieut. J. O. GRAFF M.O.R.C. USA rejoined from temporary duty with 17th R. Fusiliers. E. Corps Advanced Dressing Station & F.A. & and expressed himself as very pleased with work done. A.D.M.S. 2nd Division also visited Unit. 2 large French tents, 3 small Wilson tents & 10 marquees (6m. Hospl.) have been erected during past 3 weeks, and are now ready for use as Main Dressing Station & Rest Station.	M.Wks Water White
"	4th	6 pm	Routine: Received 2nd Bn. Reserve Order No. 99 last night regarding relief of Field Ambce. of Guards Divn by F.As. of this division. Visited No. 9 F.A. at RANSART & BERLES-AU-BOIS this morning preparatory to taking over A.D.S. & W.W. Collecting Posts there.	M.W.
"	5th	4:30	Routine: Visited with Major Lane Roque & Bearer Staff Sergt. the R.A.B. & Left Centre Brigades of Guards Division preparatory to taking over Stretcher Bearer Posts & line.	M.Wks Fine
"	6th	6 pm	Routine.	M.W.

Army Form C. 2118.

WAR DIARY
or
INTELLIGENCE SUMMARY
(Erase heading not required.)

Place	Date	Hour	Summary of Events and Information	Remarks and references to Appendices
RANSART X.7.6.B.2	June 7th	9 am	Ref. Map 1:40,000 BUCQUOY (Contoured Sheet) Unit left WARLUZEL handing over F.A. site to advance party of No.9 Field Amb. travelled via BAC-DU-SUD (left A.D.S.) to BERLES-AU-BOIS and RANSART. Major P.J. LANE A/c + 7 SPuds Beared took over evacuation of RAPs left + centre Brigades from No.9 Field Amb.	Very hot.
		4 pm	Major CURTIN A/c R.C. and 1 tent subdivision took over A.D.S. RANSART from No.9 F.A. Remainder of Unit + Transport t/c Major B.W. ARMSTRONG took over site at W.14.d.1.9. from No.9 Field Ambulance. 1 Moto Ambulance damaged by shell fire at Car Post ADINFER X.21.d.3.9. soon after arrival.	[illegible]
RANSART	8th	11 am	H.Q. + Transport of Unit moved from W.14.d.1.9. BERLES-AU-BOIS (an unsatisfactory site, exposed + frequently shelled) to W.13.d.5.7. under canvas. Visited Car Post in ADINFER. Bearer Relay Posts + R.A.Ps at F.4.b.8.5. (DOUCHY), two in Sunken Road in X.29.c. And one at X.24.c.3.9, and Relay Post (2 Spuds) at X.28.b.5.5. Most of the Relay Posts not good + require more work to make suitable accommodation + shelter. Lieut J.O. PARRAMORE M.O.R.C. U.S.A. reported from temporary duty with 72nd Army Bde. R.F.A. Lieut J.H. GRAFF M.O.R.C. U.S.A. posted to 72 Bde. R.F.A. remaining at M.O.H. + struck off strength	Hot. [illegible]
	9th	7 am	Routine	[illegible]

Army Form C. 2118.

Instructions regarding War Diaries and Intelligence Summaries are contained in F. S. Regs., Part II. and the Staff Manual respectively. Title Pages will be prepared in manuscript.

2449 Wt. W14957/M90 750,000 1/16 J.B.C. & A. Forms/C.2118/12.

Army Form C. 2118.

WAR DIARY
or
INTELLIGENCE SUMMARY.
(Erase heading not required.)

Instructions regarding War Diaries and Intelligence Summaries are contained in F. S. Regs., Part II. and the Staff Manual respectively. Title pages will be prepared in manuscript.

Place	Date	Hour	Summary of Events and Information	Remarks and references to Appendices
RANSART (X.7.b.3.2.)	JUNE 10th	7hr.	Routine. 1st Lieut. E.A. CURTIN to 24th R. Field Med for temporary duty as M.O. 1/c. An epidemic of the Influenza of a mild type in many of the Regts of the Division. After cases also in this Unit. Symptoms — usually 2 days Fever, coryza & malaise with sore joints & seem to be very infectious. It is not trench fever, and in no one case there has been no soreness.	Still. a little Rain
"	11th	6hr.	Routine. Lieut. V.O. PARRAMORE from H.Q. to A.D.S. to replace Lieut. CURTIN. Casualties through A.D.S. 8 O.R. Relieve to VI Corps. Rec. D.S. for temporary duty.	New
"	12th	7/m	Routine. 12 Graves who went into the Relay Posts on 7th inst. have been relieved tonight by 12 Field Bearers.	New
"	13th	7/m	Routine. A.D.M.S 2nd XXDS inspected M.O. & Transport Cart at W.13.d. 5.7.	New Fine
"	14th	7/m	Routine. Bearers in the Line changed by fresh bearers. Influenza still continues in Regts in this Unit.	New Still
"	15th	6/m	Routine. Capt. N.L. SPEIRS A.A.M.C. rejoined at A.D.S. from temporary duty ("Shock" work) at 3 C.C.S.	New

Army Form C. 2118.

WAR DIARY
or
INTELLIGENCE SUMMARY
(Erase heading not required.)

Instructions regarding War Diaries and Intelligence Summaries are contained in F. S. Regs., Part II. and the Staff Manual respectively. Title Pages will be prepared in manuscript.

Place	Date	Hour	Summary of Events and Information	Remarks and references to Appendices
RANSART (X.7.c.2.3)	16th	7pm	Routine. Visited R.A.P.s & Relay Posts. Influenza continued. A freshwater system in the trench, both in relay Posts continued. Cellars of A.D.S. also being strengthened with help of R.E. Gas protection (anti-gas pts) also improved. Capt Speirs thought trial with his considerable quantity of sterilised gauze for treatment of "shock" cases. Several cases have already been done by this with good results. Visited A.D.Ss re provision of "Reserve" A.D.S. in the event of heavy fighting on this front. 1st Lieut E.A. CURTIN adjoined from temp. duty with 26th R. Fusiliers.	Still some rain
"	17th	4pm	Routine. Reconnoitred track for "walking wounded" from ADINFER to BEALES-AU-BOIS	
"	18th	9:30pm	Raid by a Batln of left Brigade at midnight last night. 11 Motor Ambulances left in readiness at R.A.P. had all wounded back at A.D.S. within 20 mins after getting to R.A.P. – Gauze given to cases of "shock" with very good results by Capt. SPEIRS, R.A.M.C. Routine. Visited A.D.S.s re evacuation from New R.A.P. in the Support System. There are now 22 cases of Influenza in the Trench, all kept under canvas & treated at H.Q.	Fine
"	19th	7pm		
"	20th	9pm	Routine. Visited R.A.P.s & Relay Posts. 28 more of the trench down with Influenza.	

2149 Wt. W14957/M90 750,000 1/16 J.B.C. & A. Forms/C.2118/12.
Capt. W. L. SMYTH U.S.A. M.O.R.C. joined Unit for duty.

WAR DIARY
or
INTELLIGENCE SUMMARY

Army Form C. 2118.

(Erase heading not required.)

Instructions regarding War Diaries and Intelligence Summaries are contained in F. S. Regs., Part II. and the Staff Manual respectively. Title Pages will be prepared in manuscript.

Place	Date	Hour	Summary of Events and Information	Remarks and references to Appendices
RANSART (X.7.t.9.2)	June 20th (Contn)		Officers of Unit attended lecture by Consult. Surgeon III.rd Army at II Corps Hr.Qrs. G.O.C. & D.A.A.G. 2nd Divn inspected H.Q. Camp & Transport Lines at BERLES-AU-BOIS this morning. Sergt. Major F.W. JEFFRIES awarded M.S.M. (King's Birthday Honours Gazette)	Some Rain
"	21st	7/pm	Routine : Major Miller, Lieut MOSER and 2 N.C.Os. N.C. F.A. took over Mortar Sorties of Evacuation at present in use by the Field Amb. from Left & Centre Brigades. Influenza still continues throut throut limits of the Division affected. No few Casualties occurring in this Sector. 2 Gassed Cases (Yellow X) today yesterday.	Dull.
"	22nd	9/pm	Routine.	
"	23rd	7/pm	Routine : weather continued dry & there is no difficulty in evacuation of the line.	Fine

Army Form C. 2118.

WAR DIARY
or
INTELLIGENCE SUMMARY
(Erase heading not required.)

Instructions regarding War Diaries and Intelligence Summaries are contained in F. S. Regs., Part II. and the Staff Manual respectively. Title Pages will be prepared in manuscript.

Place	Date	Hour	Summary of Events and Information	Remarks and references to Appendices
RANSART	June 24th	9 a.m.	Routine : Nothing to note. 8 O.R. Nunn received as reinforcements from Base	Fine
"	25th	7 a.m.	Routine : Visited R.A.P.s & Relay Posts. Village lightly shelled during night. No damage to A.D.S. Bearers are now relieved in the line every 7 days — 7 days in & 5 out. Sgt. FARROW Num. evacuated to C.C.S. suffering from (N.Y.D. Mental?)	Fine Fine Very bright
"	26th	9 a.m.	Routine	Warm
"	27th	6.30 a.m.	Routine : Village lightly shelled — No damage done. 2 Leave spaces in line relieved by fresh bearers. 1st Lieut. E.A. CURTIN M.R.C. U.S.A. to 17th R. Fusiliers for temporary duty vice Capt. MOIR Royal Army "sick". Capt. N.L. SPEIRS rejoined unit from Hospital (Influenza).	Warm Fine
"	28th	7 a.m.	Routine : Arrangements made at A.D.S. for Separate Statement of "Gassed" cases in a small French Hut	Very Fine
"	29th	7 a.m.	Routine : Visited R.A.P.s & Bearer Relay Posts.	Very
"	30th	8 p.m.	Routine : Village lightly shelled during afternoon — slight damage — none to A.D.S. Lieut. E.A. CURTIN 1st R.C. U.S.A. rejoined from temporary duty with 17th R. Fusiliers	Very

Milton Thompson
Lt. R.A.M.C.
o.c. No.100 Field Amb.

WAR DIARY or INTELLIGENCE SUMMARY

Army Form C. 2118.

Place	Date	Hour	Summary of Events and Information	Remarks and references to Appendices
	June 30th 1918		WAR DIARY : No. 100 Field Ambulance APPENDIX "A" Table of "Sick" + "Wounded" passed through A.D.S. RANSART from 7th to 30th July inclusive. (attached) Summary Officers { Sick 19 { Wounded 2 Other Ranks { Sick 464 (Prev. Disease . Influenza) { Wounded 112 Wyllie Turner Lt. Col. O.C. No. 100 Field Amb.	

TOTALS S + W. OFFICERS + OTHER RANKS

	Officers		Other Ranks	
	Sick	Wd	Sick	Wd
June 7		1	4	4
8	1	—	5	7
9	—	—	25	2
10	1	1	25	4
11	7	—	44	2
12	—	—	25	6
13	2	—	30	7
14	—	—	20	12
15	—	—	26	6
16	—	—	10	7
17	—	—	12	8
18	—	1	28	11
19	1	—	10	2
20	—	—	11	6
21	2	—	25	2
22	—	—	36	5
23	—	—	13	2
24	—	—	13	1
25	—	—	12	12
26	1	—	16	—
27	4	—	18	—
28	—	—	22	3
29	—	—	21	—
30	—	—	13	3
	19	2	464	112

Army Form C. 2118.

WAR DIARY
or
INTELLIGENCE SUMMARY.
(Erase heading not required.)

CONFIDENTIAL

WAR DIARY

OF

No. 100 FIELD AMBULANCE

from 1st JULY 1918 TO 31st JULY 1918

(VOLUME 33)

Army Form C. 2118.

WAR DIARY
or
INTELLIGENCE SUMMARY.
(Erase heading not required.)

Instructions regarding War Diaries and Intelligence Summaries are contained in F. S. Regs., Part II. and the Staff Manual respectively. Title pages will be prepared in manuscript.

Place	Date	Hour	Summary of Events and Information	Remarks and references to Appendices
RANSART (X.7 & 8.2)	July		Ref. Map BUCQUOY (contoured sheet) 1:40,000	
	1st	7ᵃᵐ	Routine: Work very light - very few casualties owing to "Influenza" "Epidemic" elsewhere.	Nufford Aylmer W.O.2. at No. 102 F.A.
"	2nd	9ᵃᵐ	Routine: Unit won Eliminating Competition for Field Ambulance Transport to represent 2nd Division at Corps Transport Show on July 10th. Unit also won all 3 prizes given by A.D.M.S. 2nd Division for (1) Best group of 2 ambulance wagons (2) Best group of 2 G.S. wagons and (3) Best group of 2 water carts. Transport Show consisted of 1 Mounted Officer (Major Bro. Armstrong, Branch to Transport Officer) 1 mounted N.C.O. N.C.C., 2 G.S. wagons, 2 water carts and 1 maltese cart with strong horses and wagon orderlies.	Fine Busy New
"	3rd	7ᵃᵐ	Routine: visited R.A.Ps a Bearer Relay Posts. Work on new dugouts for Bearer Posts proceeding slowly but good work is being done.	Fine New Cool
"	4	8ᵃᵐ	Routine.	New
"	5	7ᵃᵐ	1st Lieut. E.A. CURTIN M.R.C. U.S.A. to temporary duty with 2nd Battⁿ Highland Light Infantry. Routine.	New
"	6	7ᵃᵐ	Routine: visited R.A.Ps & Bearer Relay Posts. Gas protection for dugouts being improved. Gave Lectures & demonstrations to Nursing & Dressing Staff on "Gas poisoning - treatment etc.	Fine Warm New

Army Form C. 2118.

WAR DIARY
or
INTELLIGENCE SUMMARY.
(Erase heading not required.)

Instructions regarding War Diaries and Intelligence Summaries are contained in F. S. Regs., Part II. and the Staff Manual respectively. Title pages will be prepared in manuscript.

Place	Date	Hour	Summary of Events and Information	Remarks and references to Appendices
RAMSKRT (N.Z.E.S.)	July 7th	11 am	Ref. map — BUCQUOY (equidistant sheet) 1:40,000. Adj. Maj. present. 1st Lieut. 1. BURNS, M.R.C. USA. arrived. Unit for duty & taken on strength	V. Urban
"	8th	9 pm	Routine. i/ Vicinity of AMS. lightly shelled with gas shell about 8.30 pm. — No damage	Nil
"	9th		Routine.	Nil
"	10th	8 pm	Went 1st & 2nd lines to Field Ambulance. Transferred at H.Q. Corps Transport Sheds. Battery being treated by 10th Canadian Field Ambulance. Most of the H.Sc. (H.T.) Drivers down with "Influenza"	Fine, cool.
"	11th			Nil
"	12th	7 am	Routine. Nothing to note.	
"	13th			Nil
"	14th	11 am	Capt. M.L. SPEIRS. AAMC. left for duty at No. 1 Australian General Hospital and struck off strength of the Unit. 1st Lieut. S.E. BURNS M.O.R.C USA to temporary duty with Rear HQ. 99th Inf. Brigade. Visited AMS. An unusual number of N.C.Os "posted to this unit from the Base recently when any RDD Offices go down "sick" they are duly returned to the Unit. When ask'd for permission to make "phahe" "f/laughs". I am sad strange and Mostly Useless NCOs from the Base. My men are practically all New Army men. Seldom get a offer of promotion, and I get other peoples "2nd" NCOs. Result — universal dissatisfaction. There is some bad Administration somewhere.	W

A6945   Wt. W14422/M1160   350,000   12/16   D. D. & L.   Forms/C./2118/14.

WAR DIARY
or
INTELLIGENCE SUMMARY.

(Erase heading not required.)

Army Form C. 2118.

Place	Date	Hour	Summary of Events and Information	Remarks and references to Appendices
RANSART (X.7.c.8.2.)	July 15th	4pm	Ref. map Ordnance Survey BOCAVOT 1:40,000. 1st Batt. The "Bufs" Regiment made a raid last night on Enemy Trenches. Motor Ambulance was taken down to R.A.P. in DOUCHY and all casualties got back to A.D.S. in short time. 8 British casualties (nearly all slightly) after the raid. Capt. W.L. SMITH M.O.R.C. USA left to report to A.D.M.S. 31st Divn for duty & struck off strength of Unit. There are now 9 or 10 men in this Unit who have not been on leave for more than 18 months.	Cloudy. Showers.
	16th	8pm	Routine — Nothing strict — work for Stretcher Bearers very light — most R.A.Ps. can be evacuated by wheeled stretcher.	Very hot. Thunderstorm.
"	17th	9am	Routine.	Very hot. Muggy.
	18th	3pm	R.A.P. of Sth Stafford Regt in DOUCHY was shelled suddenly this morning. Capt WILLIAMS & all R.A.P. staff gassed. 1st Lieut. J.C. PARRAMORE M.R.C. U.S.A. and 1 nursing orderly sent immediately to R.A.P. through B.H.Q DOUCHY & the light of the line. About 16 gas casualties (Yellow X shell) through A.D.S. during the day. Several other serious cases through during the day.	Very hot. Very keen.

WAR DIARY
or
INTELLIGENCE SUMMARY.

(Erase heading not required.)

Army Form C.2118.

Place	Date	Hour	Summary of Events and Information	Remarks and references to Appendices
RANSART (X.7.b.8.2)	July		Ref Map :– BUCQUOY (Combined Sheets) 1:40,000	
	19th	10 a.m	Routine. Men slightly gassed last (Mustard Gas) brought in from Neighbourhood of DOUCHY. Visited all Coys. Visited Arras. He leaves for Africa personnel.	
"	20th	9/-	1st Lieut. N.L. WASHBURN M.R.C. U.S.A. joined for duty from 31st Division and taken on Strength. Bad local Scouts have caused many casualties in back areas and strings of Motor ambulances etc. They have been in workshops.	Five Coys
"	23rd	10 p.m.	Held Kit Inspection of Unit – a very good Show throughout. Routine. Influenza epidemic seems to be here. Few cases now coming in. Wired to A.D.M.S. to point out bad results of the System of Sending up N.C.Os from the base to fill up vacancies in Establishment. Men of this unit who have been with change of Front are crept to Spearhead in their service. At last I have had all Nursing Sisters & 2 senior NCOs leave since problem of big vacancies filled I had on to the vacancies but demanded Reinf from Base to fill the vacancies. Keep the men out Ref :– Lots of Influenza & dysentery in 3 good men.	Five Coys

WAR DIARY or INTELLIGENCE SUMMARY.

Army Form C. 2118.

Place	Date	Hour	Summary of Events and Information	Remarks and references to Appendices
RANSART	JULY		Ref. Map: BUCQUOY (Confined Sheet) – 1:40,000	
(X.7.b.8.2.)	22nd	9/pm	Routine. Visited R.A.P.s, Beaver Posts. Village shelled during night. No damage to A.D.S.	Fine, warm
			Gas bombardment (Yellow X gas) to troops of French Division on immediate left of this Division. Getting through this A.D.S. during the day. Lung symptoms of moderate severity present.	N.V.
"	23rd	7/pm	Routine. A few heavy casualties through A.D.S. during last night & today. Heavy "Mustard" Gas Casualties from French Division. Enemy Artillery fairly active.	Heavy Rain. Thunderstorm N.V.
"	24th	7/am	Routine. Village shelled during early morning – no damage to A.D.S. All blankets in R.A.P. & Relay Posts exchanged and others sent for disinfection. Gas protective measures for troops in dug-outs & Relay Posts being overhauled.	Fine N.V. N.V.
"	25th	9/am	Routine	Showery N.V.
"	26th		Village shelled during night. One shell fell in A.D.S. Motor Car but no damage done. Artillery Officer over this A.D.S. Motoring looking for site for 15" gun – wished to put gun near A.D.S. Objected. Routine – few casualties through	Fine. N.V.

A6945 Wt. W11422/M1160 350,000 12/16 D. D. & L. Forms/C./2118/14.

Army Form C. 2118.

WAR DIARY
or
INTELLIGENCE SUMMARY.
(Erase heading not required.)

Instructions regarding War Diaries and Intelligence Summaries are contained in F. S. Regs., Part II. and the Staff Manual respectively. Title pages will be prepared in manuscript.

Place	Date	Hour	Summary of Events and Information	Remarks and references to Appendices
RANSART (X.7.6.8.9.)	July 27th	8/am	Routine. Nothing to note. Village shelled night of 26th & 27th. Two shells fell in A.D.S. on night of 27th. – No damage done.	N.F.
	28th			
	29th	7/am	Routine.	N.F. Showery
	30th	3/pm	Routine. Raid & Sweep lines by 1st/8th King's Regt. last night. Ambulance Car taken down to R.A.P. at DOUCHY and all casualties (7) brought back to A.D.S. (RANSART) in very short time.	Fine. Very warm
	31st	7/am	Several severe local counter attacks preceded in this sector – caused by local shelling. 2 men severely wounded died shortly after admission. During whole month has been very light during past months – weather fine & invigorating. At the time held by 5th & 6th A.F. Brigade has been easy. A lot of work has been done in strengthening & improving cellars in the A.D.S. (RANSART) and in making dugouts for Bearer Posts in the line. The Influenza "Epidemic" has been the chief factor in the sick rate.	

[signature]
Lt. Col.
O.C. No. 100 Field Ambulance

Appendix to Vol. 33.

Number of Officers and Other Ranks who passed through the ADS Ransart. (X.7. B 8.2) Bucquoy Combined Sheet 1/40,000.

	Officers		Other Ranks	
	Sick	Wounded	Sick	Wounded
July 1st			16	1
" 2nd	1		22	-
" 3rd			20	4
" 4th	1	1	11	2
" 5th		1	18	1
" 6th		1	16	-
" 7th			8	6
" 8th	1		-	5
" 9th			7	9
" 10th			12	3
11th	2	1	10	5
12th	1	1	8	3
13th			12	2
14th			12	12
15th		2	14	5
16th			16	1
17th			14	2
18th		2	13	14
19th			11	14
20th	1	-	17	5
21st			14	13
22nd	1		12	11
23rd		1	16	18
24th			13	3
25th			14	2
26th			11	3
27th			4	6
28th			8	4
29th			13	7
30th			10	14
31st		1	17	12
Totals.	8	11	389	187

CONFIDENTIAL

WAR DIARY
of
N° 100 Field Ambulance

from 1st August 1918 to 31st August 1918

(Volume 34)

WAR DIARY
or
INTELLIGENCE SUMMARY
(Erase heading not required.)

Army Form C. 2118.

Place	Date	Hour	Summary of Events and Information	Remarks and references to Appendices
RANSART (X.7.b.8.2.)	AUGUST 1st	Noon	Ref. Map: BUCQUOY (combined sheet) 1:40,000 Unit distributed as follows — Evacuating line held by 5th & 6th Inf. Brigades. Bearer Posts at F.4.c.5.8. Advanced Dressing Station RANSART (X.7.b.8.2.) H.Q. & Transport lines at W.13.d.5.7. Routine: a few American wounded (320th Inf. Regt.) passing through A.D.S. There are 3 motor ambulance cars now in workshops. 1st Lieut. W.L. WASHBURN M.R.C. U.S.A. left to rejoin A.E.F. & struck off strength of unit.	Very fine. Hot.
"	2nd	8/am	Routine: A third large Amb. Car. gone to workshops today. Another large one temporarily attached from No.6 Field Amb. for duty. Have now 3 officers only doing duty with unit — 2 at A.D.S. + 1 at H.Q. Have applied to A.D.M.S. for at least one officer the returns permit.	Wet.
"	3rd	7/am	Routine: Village shelled fairly heavily about 9-10 p.m. last night. Several local casualties through A.D.S. IIIrd Army "Notes for Regimental Medical Officers" issued today. Would have been useful 2 years ago.	

Army Form C. 2118.

WAR DIARY
or
INTELLIGENCE SUMMARY

(Erase heading not required.)

Instructions regarding War Diaries and Intelligence Summaries are contained in F. S. Regs., Part II. and the Staff Manual respectively. Title Pages will be prepared in manuscript.

Place	Date	Hour	Summary of Events and Information	Remarks and references to Appendices
RAMSART (X.7.b.8.2.)	August 4th	9 p.m.	Ref. Map BUCQUOY (Combined Sheet) 1:40,000 Routine: Visited all R.A.P's — Renew Postn. Worked on Brigade preceding satisfactorily. A fourth large ambulance car went into workshops yesterday, but one replaced work today, leaving 3 large cars with unit.	Fine & warm
"	5th	7 p.m.	Routine: Lieut. J. JAMIESON Royal Service unit from temporary duty as M.O. ?c. 1st R. BERKS Regt.	[signature] [signature]
"	6th	7 p.m.	Routine: Huyshe animation passing through A.D.S. Unit second in 2nd Division Eliminating Competition to III Corps Horse Show in Class "B" Best turned out pair of light Draught Horses in G.S. or R.E. limbered wagon " — 16 entries Major H.B. ARMSTRONG R.A.M.C. left on Short leave in France.	Showery [signature]
W.13.d.9.7.	7th	6 a.m.	Routine: 1st Lieut. E.S. HUGGINS M.R.C. U.S.A. joined unit from the Base for duty and taken on the strength accordingly. Lt. Col. R.E.C. NEWMAN turned from A.D.S. RAMSART to W.13.d.9.7. during absence on leave of Major B.M. ARMSTRONG.	[signature] Fine
"	8th	9 a.m.	Routine: Wagon Lines A.D.S.	[signature] Fair
"	9th	7 p.m.	Routine.	[signature]
"	10th	6 p.m.	Routine: [illegible] returned from M.T. workshops yesterday & 1 large car & 1 Ford Van [illegible]	Fine [signature]

2449 Wt. W14957/M90 750,000 1/16 J.B.C. & A. Forms/C.2118/12.

WAR DIARY
or
INTELLIGENCE SUMMARY

Army Form C. 2118.

Place	Date	Hour	Summary of Events and Information	Remarks and references to Appendices
W13 d 2.7.	August		Ref. Map. BUCQUOY (contoured sheet) 1:40,000.	
	11th	7 p.m.	Routine. 1st Lieut S.J. BURNS M.R.C. USA. deputed went from temporary duty as high 1st Batt'n K.R.R. Corps. A few American casualties 319th Inf. Regt. passing through A.D.S.	Very warm
	12th	8 p.m.	Routine. All lorries overhauled etc. Motor-buses in work shops. Both motor cycles in workshops. 1 Officer & 20 OR. M Sanitary Train 319th Regt. of U.S. Army joined ADS. RAMSART last night for instruction in "Beaver Hunts" Shuttle Service. Established Evacuges Relief Post in The line	Very fine
	✗			Nil
	13th	7 p.m.	Routine. 1st Lieut. H.J. BAKER M.R.C. USA joined unit for duty.	Nil
			1st Lieut. J.C. PARRAMORE " " Rejoined from Temp. duty with 2nd Batt'n S.Stafford Regt.	
			1st Lt. S.J. BURNS " " " " appt in footing as M.O.K.	
			1st Lieut. E.A. CURTIN " " " Rejoined unit from leave to U.K.	
	14th	6 p.m.	Raid made by 1st Batt'n The King's Reg. on enemy outpost line in early morning. Ambulance Car taken up halfway between ADINFER & R.A.P. in DOUCHY. A few light casualties which passed swiftly through A.T.R. Vista ack R.A.B. new dugouts for Beaver Relief Posts nearing completion. Lieut. J. JAMIESON returned to 24th R. Fus. for temporary duty.	Very hot.
				Nil
	15th	6 p.m.	Routine. 1st Lieut. J.O. PARRAMORE left for the weekly instruction at 3rd Army Shock Centre at No 3 C.C.S. 8 P.B.I. Codes (thousand) from 1st Batt'n The King's Regt. through ADS. in Trent Sd. forward.	Nil

Army Form C. 2118.

WAR DIARY
or
INTELLIGENCE SUMMARY
(Erase heading not required.)

Instructions regarding War Diaries and Intelligence Summaries are contained in F. S. Regs., Part II. and the Staff Manual respectively. Title Pages will be prepared in manuscript.

Place	Date	Hour	Summary of Events and Information	Remarks and references to Appendices
W.13.d.9.7	Aug. 16th	6 p.m.	Ref. Map - BUCQUOY (Combined Sheet) 1:40,000	
			Routine visited A.D.S. etc. "Influenza" cases again occurring in 2nd Battn H.I.I.	Hygroma
"	17th	6:30 p.m.	Routine. 1st Lieut E.S. HUCKINS M.R.C. U.S.A. to 2nd Battn H.I.I. for temporary duty.	Cloudy - cool. Wet
RANSART (X.7.C.8.3)	18th	7 a.m.	Major W.B. ARMSTRONG having returned from leave in France O.C. moved mess up to Adv. Dressing Station RANSART.	Fine & cool. Wet
"	19th	7 a.m.	Heavy American Casualties (320th Inf. Regt. U.S.A.) through A.D.S. during night. Buried with inguinal severe. 1 case (comp. fracture vault of skull) died in A.D.S.	Fine & cool.
"	20th	8 a.m.	1st Lieut J.C. PARAMORE M.R.C. U.S.A. rejoined unit from temp. duty No.3 C.C.S. 1st Lt E.S. HUCKINS " " " " " 2nd Battn H.I.I.	Fine & cloudy
			All preparations being made at Beaver Relay Posts and A.D.S. for N coming offensive operations by the Division.	
			Major P.J. LANE M.C. R.A.M.C, 1st Lieut E.A CURTIN and 1st Lieut SPROUL to DOUCHY and AVETTE Beaver Relay Posts. 2 new Beaver Posts established in	

A VETTE

Army Form C. 2118.

WAR DIARY
or
INTELLIGENCE SUMMARY
(Erase heading not required.)

Instructions regarding War Diaries and Intelligence Summaries are contained in F. S. Regs., Part II. and the Staff Manual respectively. Title Pages will be prepared in manuscript.

Place	Date	Hour	Summary of Events and Information	Remarks and references to Appendices
RAMSART (S.7.c.2.2)	AUGUST 21	9 p.m.	Ref. Map — BOCROY (Confidential Sheet) 1 in 40,000. II Corps attacked enemy positions at dawn. 23rd R. Fusiliers & Gordon Regt. of 99th Inf. Bde. were in attack. This Unit responsible for collection of casualties from 23rd R. Fusiliers & 5th Inf. Bde. Bearer Posts established last night at F.11.c.2.4 & F.11.a.J.7. Ambulance cars brought to DOUCHY at 7 a.m. and to F.11.a.5.7. at 8 a.m. About 400 cases through A.D.S from 8 a.m. to 8 p.m. Grenad. 2nd & 3rd Divisions all evacuations done by cars of this unit with help of Stray lorries blocked on road. Two lorries sent from II Corps HQ about 7pm. too late to be of much use. Lieut Mealy to have [?] forward at short notice. Major Rev Armstrong to 1st Field. BAKER with U.S.A. Lent to No. 5 F.A. for duty at A.D.S MONCHY during [?].	Appendices
"	21st	7 p.m.	All casualties cleared from F.A. units during the night. Major P.J. HANE and Bearer Division in DOUCHY during last night and to-day. Heavy German wounded through A.D.S during the night. H.Q and transport still [?] at W.13.A.9.7.	

WAR DIARY
or
INTELLIGENCE SUMMARY

Army Form C. 2118.

(Erase heading not required.)

Place	Date	Hour	Summary of Events and Information	Remarks and references to Appendices
A.15.a.11. (COURCELLES)	August 23rd	8 am	Adv. HqRs. BUCQUOY (trench sheet) 1/40,000 Major P.J. LANE MINN and 170 Bearers No.100 Field Ambulance and Major MILLAR RAMC No. 6 Field Ambulance assembled at A.15.a.11., Bearers of No.6 F.A. coming under command of O.C. No.100 Field Ambulance.	Fine
		12 noon	A.D.S. Party (roughly 2 tent Subdivisions with 1 Binber, 1 waterCart + 1 Amb. Wagon) Moved up from RANSART to A.15.a.11. and placed A.D.S. and Walking Wounded C.P. in trench at A.15.a. and 1 Battn 99th Inf Bde attacking ERVILLERS, 5th Inf Bde and 1 Battn 99th Inf Bde attacking BEHAGNIES + SAPIGNIES.	
			Bearers of No.100 F.A. clearing 6th Inf. Bde. Casualties from R.A.P's in Railway Embankment about A.16.b.6.4 and Bearers of No.6 F.A. clearing 5th Inf. Bde. Casualties from R.A.P. in Embankment about A.28.c.9.6. These R.A.Ps between Journed to about G.6.a.7.5. in Co[unter] Attk except through Sunken Roads in COURCELLES through "Cavy." on Right Bde Front very long	
		1 pm	Capt ACKLAND + 60 Bearers of No.5 Field Ambulance arrived. Some of these used on Rt. Bde. front.	
		7 pm	Very heavy Stretcher Cases (including German P. of W. Wounded) Evacuated during afternoon. Ambulance Cars of Unit working continuously and driven very hard. Tonight moved from W.13.d.9.7. at RANSART during the day. 1st Lieut. E. S. HOCKINS M.C.C. U.S.A. to temporary duty with 2 Lt Battn Oxf. & Bucks L.I. Pte BENNETT, D. Killed in action. Pte W.H. JAMES Wounded, Pte W. & CAVEY MOKM, and Pte LESLIE Gassed — all Evacuated to CCS.	

WAR DIARY or INTELLIGENCE SUMMARY

Army Form C. 2118.

Place	Date	Hour	Summary of Events and Information	Remarks and references to Appendices
A.15.a.11.	Aug. 24th	1/am	Ref. map: BUCQUOY (Combined Sheet) 1:40,000. Many cases through A.D.S. during the night. Cleared to III Corps M.D.S. by motor cars. No.5 Field Amb. opened M.D.S. for 2nd Div. at F.11.a.2.9. about noon and cases then cleared to them. A.D.S. kept fairly clean during day. COURCELLES Roads shelled this morning and cars taken up to Railway Embankment at A.16.6.6.4 and A.28.c.9.6. [illegible notes] 1st Lieut. E.A. CURTIN A.R.C. U.S.A. temp. duty with 2nd Batt. H.L.I. vice Capt. SOMERVILLE sent invalid. Pte TICKER & WHITTLE, car orderlies, wounded by enemy bombs and evacuated to C.C.S.	
"	25th		6th Inf. Bdes & 99th Inf. Bde relieved by 62nd Div. last night. Majors LANE and Capt. ACKLAND and Bearers of No.100 & 5 Field Ambulances returned to their respective units. 5th Inf.Bde. & Major MILLER and Bearers of No. 6 Field Amb. sent to the line at BEAUGNIES and SAPIGNIES, which they attached this morning. Ford Cars taken up to about C.6.a. & b. Evacuate wounded - walking. Horse Ambulances also working up to A.28.c.9.6. (Rly. Embankment) & evacuate wounded. Sitting cases sent back in limit cars to M.D.S. at F.11.a.2.9. Walking wounded to Corps W.W. C.P. at BELLACOURT (X.1.6.)	

WAR DIARY
or
INTELLIGENCE SUMMARY

(Erase heading not required.)

Army Form C. 2118.

Place	Date	Hour	Summary of Events and Information	Remarks and references to Appendices
A.S.a.l.l.	Aug.		Ref. Map: BUCQUOY (Contoured sheet) 1:40,000	
	26th	8 am	Handed over W.C.P. here to 2/2 W. Riding Field Amb.	
		11 am	5th Inf. Bde. having been withdrawn this morning Major MILLAR our Bearer of No.8 F.A. returned here — 1 Sqnd of S.Bs left with Each R.M.O. of 5th Inf. Bde.	
			A.D.S. here Still kept open during day for any wounded sick of 2nd Division	
		6 pm	1st Lieut H.J. BAKER M/Rc USA reported from temporary duty with No.5 Field Amb.	Nil
	27th	7/15	Bearer & A.T.S. Staff Meeting.	
			HQ & Transport moved this morning from RAMSART to AYETTE (F.10.d.8.6.) Many stretchers blankets have been lost during recent operations. Also very hard to get back. (when the water bottles from the B.S.)	Nil
	28th	7 pm	Much talking & getting cleaned up.	Nil
	29th	7 pm	Staff Meeting. Following Equipment returned to Advance + A.D. of Med. Stores today by order of A.D.M.S. This Equipment has never been replaced during this war.	Nil
			Reserve & Fixed Panniers Nos 1 & 2 from A Section	
			Field water Bottles — — — — 13	Bags interesting 3
			Haversacks B — 3	Stools, Mess 4
				Lamp, Orderly 6
				Med. Comfort Panniers 4

WAR DIARY
or
INTELLIGENCE SUMMARY

(Erase heading not required.)

Army Form C.

Instructions regarding War Diaries and Intelligence Summaries are contained in F. S. Regs., Part II. and the Staff Manual respectively. Title Pages will be prepared in manuscript.

Place	Date	Hour	Summary of Events and Information	Remarks and references to Appendices
A 15. a. 1.1.	Aug. 30th	7p.m.	Ref Map – BUCQUOY (Contoured Sheet) 1:40,000 Unit resting. Equipment cleaned up. Deficiencies replaced	N/S
"	31st	7p.m.	Unit resting; local sick only being attended to. Since Aug. 21st Unit has had hard work. Many casualties (Chamber Ambulatrice) have been evacuated. Our Bearers Stretcher Ambulance drivers have had very little rest between 21st and 28th August inclusive. Unit Casualties during recent fighting { 1 O.R. Killed { 5 O.R. wounded Members listed & fit and in good form.	

Clifton Leonard
Lt. Col. R.A.M.C
O.C. No. 100 Field Ambulance

Army Form C. 2118

WAR DIARY
or
INTELLIGENCE SUMMARY
(Erase heading not required.)

Vol 28

40/3259

CONFIDENTIAL.

WAR DIARY
of
No. 100 FIELD AMBULANCE.

From 1st Sept. 1918 to 30th Sept. 1918.

(VOLUME 35)

COMMITTEE FOR THE
MEDICAL HISTORY OF THE WAR
Date 9 NOV 1918

WAR DIARY or INTELLIGENCE SUMMARY

Army Form C. 2118.

Place	Date	Hour	Summary of Events and Information	Remarks and references to Appendices
A.15.a.1.1.	Sept. 1st		Ref Map :- BUCQUOY (Central Sheet) 1:40,000	Fine. Cool.
		9 pm	Division still resting. Unit Actuary Closed except for evacuation of sick of division. Bearers & A.D.S. Staff of No.100 F.A. + Major MILLAR and Capt. CHATFIELD and 60 bearers of No. 6 Field Ambulance staff at A.15.a.1.1. Remainder of Unit at AYETTE. Visited 45th C.C.S. at BAC-DU-SUD and brought back 50 Blankets & stretchers for future operations.	MV
		11:30pm	Received Op. Order D.38 from 63rd Brig.D.V.N. 1 Squad of SBs detailed & be ready to move with each Regt. of 6th Inf. Bde. tomorrow morning.	
"	2nd	6:30am	1 Squad of S.Bs. No.100 F.A. moved up towards BEHAGNIES with each R.M.O. of 6th Inf. Bde.	
		8:30am	1st Lieut J.O. PARRAMORE with U.S.A and 2 Squads of S.Bs. No.100 F.A. left in 2 and from 62nd Bde A.D.S. BEHAGNIES to deal with any casualties from 6th Inf. Bde.	
B.20.b.3.7.		2 pm	A.D.S. Party and remainder of Bearers moved to B.20.b.3.7. near El Cojul W.M.C.P. and bivouacked for the night, preparing to forming A.D.S. when division attacks tomorrow morning. Transport H.Q. moved from AYETTE to GOMIECOURT (A.23.c.)	NV

Army Form C. 2118.

WAR DIARY or INTELLIGENCE SUMMARY

(Erase heading not required.)

Place	Date	Hour	Summary of Events and Information	Remarks and references to Appendices
B.29 Cent.	1918 Sept. 3rd		Ref. Map – Sheet 57c. 1:40,000	Fine Showery
		5.30am	Bearers (No.5, 6 & No Field Ambs.) & A.D.S. party left B.20.b.37 and marched to B.29 cent. A.D.S. opened there under canvas at 6am. Bearers No.5 F.A. to 6th Inf. Bde. Bearers No.6 F.A. & 5th Inf. Bde. (in Reserve) and Bearers No.100 F.A. & 99th Inf. Bde.	
		8am	and sent forward to R.A.P. at C.26.c.7.4. and along VAULX–MORCHIES Road. Cars up to there have been left in in outskirts of VAULX.	
			Enemy bombed by 62nd Division. Formed German wounded. 6th & 99th Bdes Bearers attached MORCHIES about 5.30am — Not much opposition.	
		2pm	Cars forward to MORCHIES – roads had tracks found in places – few interruptions	
MORCHIES		4pm	A.D.S. moved from B.29 central to MORCHIES (I.11.d.5.2) Division had turned in towards DEMICOURT & HERMIES	
		5pm	Cars forward to DOIGNIES V.16.a.2.4.	
		7pm	Small A.D.S. established at V.13.b.3.1. in hut of old German Field Hospt. Blotton Cars have also been evacuated to No.5 F.A. at ERVILLERS whilst M.D.S. is being evacuated by No.5 Field Amb.	

Pte WHITTAKER Name Killed this afternoon.

WAR DIARY or INTELLIGENCE SUMMARY

Army Form C. 2118.

(Erase heading not required.)

Place	Date	Hour	Summary of Events and Information	Remarks and references to Appendices
MORCHIES (I.11.b.5.a)	1917 Sept 4th	8am	Ref. Arras Sheet 57 c 1:40,000. Main Dressing Station opened by No. 5 Field Amb. at MORCHIES at 5am. All walking cases evacuated to MORCHIES by cars of this unit. Car Relay Posts established in DOIGNIES (J.16.a.2.4), BEAUMETZ and MORCHIES. Bearers of No. 5 Field Amb. still in line with 6th Bde. No. 100 F.A. Bearers in support with 99th Bde. and No. 6 F.A. Bearers in reserve with 5th Inf. Bde.	First summer.
		10am	A.D.S. at BEAUMETZ closed for the present — cases evacuated straight from this Station. Difficulty of finding a water.	
		5pm	Car post established at J.17.b.2.6. Bearer Relay Post at same point. Very few casualties.	N/-
MORCHIES	5th	7pm	Major LANE, Lieut PARRAMORE and Lieut. No. 100 Field Amb. took over evacuation of line etc. from Bearers of No. 5 Field Amb. Often but light from Beaumetz of about. Only 2 R.A.Ps in line at present, both in DEMICOURT (J.18.b.3.1. and J.12.d.9.6.) Car Post abandoned at J.17.b.2.6. Very few casualties. H.Q. + Transport at I.4.d.3.3.	Very heavy Thunder Shower in evening. N/-

WAR DIARY
or
INTELLIGENCE SUMMARY

Army Form C. 2118.

Place	Date	Hour	Summary of Events and Information	Remarks and references to Appendices
MORCHIES	Sept 6	9/15	9th S.F. Bde. and Bearers of 16.100 Field Ambulance staff in position. [unclear] family [unclear] light & workshop bearers left for base. Received orders this morning from A.D.M.S. to follow a bit them EMILLERS for a Divisional Rest Station. the advance by three trucks or 8" truck. Examination of time of ambulance near to H.C. No.6 Field Amb. motorcycle. Site at B.M.A. 7.3 selected. H.Q. & transport meanwhile there from MORCHIES at 12 noon. Col. JONES W.M.S. and Lieut. TROMEY W.M.E. U.S.A. joined the trip. Set off on with from the BASE. [unclear] further there going well.	New
"	7"	12 noon	All Ranks Rev. from MORCHIES being to join H.Q. at EMILLERS. Rev Rest Station the found intact to A—6R Hospl. Unit [unclear]	
		6/15	Visited H.Q. at EMILLERS — B.M.S. already open & lacteals in, including Scabies Cases. Ambulance Car Borrowed by shell fire at Car Post last night	New

Army Form C. 2118.

WAR DIARY
or
INTELLIGENCE/SUMMARY.
(Erase heading not required.)

Instructions regarding War Diaries and Intelligence Summaries are contained in F. S. Regs., Part II. and the Staff Manual respectively. Title Pages will be prepared in manuscript.

Place	Date	Hour	Summary of Events and Information	Remarks and references to Appendices
MORCHIES	7.9.17		Ref. Map: Sheet 57c 1:40,000	Col. Hornby
	8	2/-	Handed over Evacuation of wounded by 2nd Division E of DEMICOURT & HERMIES to O.C. No 6 Field Ambulance.	
			Staff of both Collecting Posts at BEAUMETZ and Dressing Staff at DEMICOURT relieved by No 6 Field Amb. & returned H.Q. at ERMILLERS	
			Major S. LANE Med. & Lieut. J.O. PARRAMORE - Bearers of Motorist and 8 Relieved in the line by Bearers of No 6 F.A. Tonight. And returns to MORCHIES (in reserve) on relief.	
ERMILLERS B.19.a.9.4.	9	A.M.	Reformed H.Q. at ERMILLERS	New
	9		Lt. Col. R.E.P. NEWMAN M.C. R.A.M.C. departed on leave to the U.K. (Sept 10th - Sept 24th). Temporary command assumed by Major B.W. ARMSTRONG R.A.M.C.	B.W. Armstrong Major R.A.M.C.
	10		Major R.J. LANE M.C. R.A.M.C. departed on leave to the U.K. (Sept 11 - Sept 24th)	
	11		D.D.G.M.S. & Major General Sir ROBERT JONES A.M.S. inspected the D.R.S.	

2449 Wt. W14957/M90 750,000 1/16 J.B.C. & A. Forms/C.2118/12.

Army Form C. 2118.

WAR DIARY
or
INTELLIGENCE SUMMARY
(Erase heading not required.)

Instructions regarding War Diaries and Intelligence Summaries are contained in F. S. Regs., Part II. and the Staff Manual respectively. Title Pages will be prepared in manuscript.

Place	Date	Hour	Summary of Events and Information	Remarks and references to Appendices
ERVILLERS	Sept 12th		D.M.S. 3rd ARMY inspected D.R.S.	B.W.A.
Biq.d.T.H	13th		Routine	B.W.A.
"	14th		1st Lieut. S.N. TROCKEY. M.C.USA departed to 2nd Ox. & Bucks. L.I. area	M.W.A.
"	15th		1st Lieut. E.S. HUCKINS M.C.USA. evacuated to C.C.S. (still of W.) 1st Lieut J.O. PARRAMORE + the beary of the F.A. returned to HQ on to relief of the division in the line	M.W.A.
"	16th		D.D.M.S. VI Corps inspected D.R.S.	B.W.A.
"	17th		Routine.	M.W.A.
"	18th		Lieut S.E. MURRAY R.A.M.C. posted for duty to this F.A. from 24th R.F. + proceeded to No.29 C.C.S. for temporary duty.	B.W.A.
"	19th		19 O.R.s (1 tent subdivision) proceeded to No 29 CCS for temporary duty.	B.W.A.
"	20th		Capt. E.L. JONES R.A.M.C. posted to 2nd H.K.I. in relief of 1st Lieut. E.A. CURTIN USA.M.C. who appoint F.A. Lieut J. JAMIESON R.A.M.C. appointed unit from 24th R.F. on relief	B.W.A.

2449 Wt. W14957/M90 750,000 1/16 J.B.C. & A. Forms/C.2118/12.

Army Form C. 2118.

WAR DIARY
or
INTELLIGENCE SUMMARY

(Erase heading not required.)

Instructions regarding War Diaries and Intelligence Summaries are contained in F. S. Regs., Part II. and the Staff Manual respectively. Title Pages will be prepared in manuscript.

Place	Date	Hour	Summary of Events and Information	Remarks and references to Appendices
ETRILLERS	Sept			
B.iq.d.74.	20st		S/sergt B. GOOCH, L/cpl. L.S. HAMMER, & Pte J. BARRY R.A.M.C. decorated Military Medals for gallantry in recent operations	MM
	21st		Routine	MM
	22		Routine	MM
	23rd		Routine	MM
	24		Routine	MM
	25	9pm	Routine: Lieut. Col. R.E.V. NEWMAN Reeve reported from leave U.K. and attained command of unit - 2nd 5/r R.S.	Fair Nil
	26	6pm	Operation orders received from A.D.M.S. 2nd Division today in view of forthcoming operations. 3-9 cases to C.C.S. - 38 cases to B.Stop. D.D.M.S. & Brig. Gen. GORGAS of U.S. Army visited the B.R.S. A.D.M.S. II corps visited B.R.S. during the morning. 1st Lieut. E.A. CURTIN M.R.C. U.S.A. with H. Mess - 12 Bearer Squads joined 99th Inf. Bde. in concentration area. 1/6, 7/6, 8/6, 13th, 17th Coys 4 Motor Amb. Cars + 2 Horse Amb. Wagons. Infantry & active operations	Nil

2449 Wt. W14957/M90 750,000 1/16 J.B.C. & A. Forms/C.2118/12.

Army Form C. 2118.

WAR DIARY
or
INTELLIGENCE SUMMARY
(Erase heading not required.)

Instructions regarding War Diaries and Intelligence Summaries are contained in F. S. Regs., Part II. and the Staff Manual respectively. Title Pages will be prepared in manuscript.

Place	Date	Hour	Summary of Events and Information	Remarks and references to Appendices
ERVILLERS B.19.d.7.4.	Sept 27	7 pm	Routine. No walking wounded so far arrived at S.R.S. from the line. 1st Lieut. J.O. PARRAMORE U.S.A. left at 9 pm. last night for temporary duty with 2nd H.g. Batt. 1 Case N.Y.D. (Dysentery?) & 9 Cases of Diarrhoea Evacuated to No. 2 C.C.S. 4 days. 4 Cases Evacuated to No. 19 C.C.S. (Ordinary)	Nil
"	28th	6 pm	Routine: Visited Bearers in the line. 1st Lieut. J.O. PARRAMORE from temp. duty with 2nd H.G. Batt'n rejoined. Bearer Party forced to Divisional M.D.S. has moved forward to HAVRINCOURT - Very few 3 cases to C.C.S. (Diarrhoea) Bearer Sthty.	Showing in morning cold
"	29th	6 pm	Routine. Have been warned by A.D.M.S. that following a successful operation will probably be moved forward tomorrow. 2 Cases to C.C.S. (N.Y.D.M.) 9 patients discharged Thty.	Nil Showing v. cold.
"	30th	6.30 pm	Routine: Visited site of German Field Hosp. at BEAUMETZ with a view to establishing S.R.S. there. Site at present occupied by No. 3 & No. 8 Field Amb. Visited A.D.M.S. at FLESQUIERES - Bearers of No. 100 F.A. still in line Evacuating from 99th Inf. Bde. 1st Lieut. J.O. PARRAMORE M.R.C. U.S.A. to temp. duty with 2nd Batt. H.I.J. vice Capt. E.L. JONES killed in action this morning. Major B. O. Armstrong left to take over Command of Bearer Party No. 100 F.A.	Fine. Very cold

Multfff Armstrong
o/c No. 100 Field Amb.

Army Form C. 2118

WAR DIARY
or
INTELLIGENCE SUMMARY
(Erase heading not required.)

160/3601

CONFIDENTIAL

War Diary

of

N°. 100. Field Ambulance

from October 1st 1918 to October 31st 1918

(Volume 36.)

Army Form C. 2118

WAR DIARY
or
INTELLIGENCE SUMMARY

(Erase heading not required.)

Instructions regarding War Diaries and Intelligence Summaries are contained in F.S. Regs., Part II. and the Staff Manual respectively. Title Pages will be prepared in manuscript.

Place	Date	Hour	Summary of Events and Information	Remarks and references to Appendices
ERVILLERS B.19.d.7.4	October		Map Ref. Sheet 57c. 1:40,000	
	1st	18:30	Routine: Patients now in D.R.S. = 58. 10 Patients Discharged to Duty. 6 Cadre to C.C.S. "Continental Clock" comes into force in B.E.F. to-day.	Fine. Cold
"	2nd	17:30	Routine: Part of the Reinforcement of D.R.S. moved to BEAUMETZ by lorries this evening. Remainder of D.R.S. stationed tomorrow.	Showery
"	3rd	15:45	Routine. 28 Cases Evacuated to C.C.S. (Mostly Chronic Cases of I.C.T.) 4 Discharged to Duty. All remaining patients c/c Lieut. J. JAMIESON & Small Party Advance moved by M.T. Cars to new D.R.S. at BEAUMETZ. Remainder of Unit moved to BEAUMETZ tomorrow. "Leave" going well for unit — 2 per day U.K. at present	Fine.
BEAUMETZ J.13.b.2.1	4th	19:00	Unit left ERVILLERS at 09.15 to-day and arrived at BEAUMETZ at 12.45. D.R.S. now established at BEAUMETZ. beside No.3 Field Amb. General Distr. Patients accommodated in Huts, most of which require repair, and tents.	
BEAUMETZ LEZ-CAMBRAI (J.13.b.2.1)	5th	19:10	Routine: D.R.S. in process of arrangement. Hut construction & repair of huts required. Tents also being put up. Visited Beaumont Route NOVELLES.	

No. 46942. Lt. M. O'HARA Awarded D.C.M. by Commander-in-Chief for conspicuous Gallantry in the Field

1875 W.: W593/826 1,000,000 4/15 J.B.C. & A. A.D.S.S./Forms/C. 2118.

WAR DIARY
or
INTELLIGENCE SUMMARY
(Erase heading not required.)

Army Form C. 2118

Instructions regarding War Diaries and Intelligence Summaries are contained in F.S. Regs, Part II. and the Staff Manual respectively. Title Pages will be prepared in manuscript.

Place	Date	Hour	Summary of Events and Information	Remarks and references to Appendices
BEAUMETZ J.13.C.2c	Oct.		*Map Ref Sheet 57ᵉ 1:40,000*	
	6ᵗʰ	18:00	Routine: Three tents erected for patients & stores fixed into wards. Cases admitted today = 18. To C.C.S. = 3. To duty = 2. In Hospl tonight = 57. "Winter Time" came into force at midnight last night.	Cold. Showers
"	7ᵗʰ	15:30	Routine. Admissions today = 12. Evac. to C.C.S. = 10. To duty = 4. In Hospl. = 58. The single line G.S. Marquees with which the Rest Station is provided are not satisfactory. They blow cold & light shines through at night. Saw G.O.C. today and asked him to help me in getting Hospital double lined Marquees.	New Showery
"	8ᵗʰ	19:00	Routine. Another hut repaired & ready for use. Admissions today = 3. Evacs. to C.C.S. = 7. To duty = 10. In Hospl. = 54.	New Fine Cold.
"	9ᵗʰ	19:00	Routine. 2ⁿᵈ Division withdrawn from the line for rest today. Major B.S. ARMSTRONG RAMC, 1ˢᵗ Lieut E.A. CURTIN and Bearers of No. 100 Field Amb. rejoined their Unit by 8 pm. Bearers transferred 4 Casualties during Operations from 27ᵗʰ Sept. to date. Pte Mills, House & Lewis slightly wounded + Pte READE badly shaken N.Y.D.(N). 2ⁿᵈ Divn Concert Party gave a concert to patients in Rest Station this afternoon - much appreciated	New Fine
"	10ᵗʰ	19:00	Routine: 1ˢᵗ Lieut. TROCKEY, M.R.C. U.S.A. rejoined unit from temporary duty with 2ⁿᵈ Battn 52ⁿᵈ Light Inf. Remaining in Hospl. Same today = 51.	New Fine.

1875 Wt. W593/826 1,000,000 4/15 J.B.C. & A. A.D.S.S./Forms/C. 2118.

WAR DIARY
or
INTELLIGENCE SUMMARY

(Erase heading not required.)

Army Form C. 2118

Place	Date	Hour	Summary of Events and Information	Remarks and references to Appendices
BEAUMETZ (J.13.b.2.1)	Oct. 11th	18.15	Routine: Another hut taken into use for bread. To 9 am today — Admissions 18 (including 2 P. of W.) To CCS = 7. To duty = 6. Remaining in Hospl. = 66.	Cloudy, mild
"	12		Under Orders from A.D.M.S. 2nd Division. 1st Lieut. E.A. CURTIN M.R.C. 2.S.O. O.R. (Bearer Party) with 2 Horse Amb. Wagons + 1 Motorcar Reported to O.C. No. 5 Field Amb. at K.15.b.5.3 at Eleven. 18 hours today preparatory to moving forward with 99th Inf. Bde to SERANVILLERS area tomorrow. Admissions yesterday = 17. Evac. to CCS = 4. To duty = 6. Remaining 9 hrs today = 73	Showery & cool.
"	13	17.00	Routine. Major O.J. KANE M.C. having returned from leave Br.U.K., joined Bearer Party at RUMILLY. All patients evacuated from A.R.S. preparatory to a move forward.	
NOYELLES (L.11.b.2.7)	14	19.00	Unit moved at 9.30 am & reached NOYELLES at 13.40. Billeted in buildings for the night. Lieut. G.H. GWYNN M.R.C. U.S.A. taken on strength of Unit from 27th Sept., + doing temp. duty with 2nd Infy. Batt'n. from same date to present time.	Fine.

1875 Wt. W593/826 1,000,000 4/15 J.B.C. & A. A.D.S.S./Forms/C. 2118.

Army Form C. 2118

WAR DIARY
or
INTELLIGENCE SUMMARY
(Erase heading not required.)

Instructions regarding War Diaries and Intelligence Summaries are contained in F. S. Regs., Part II. and the Staff Manual respectively. Title Pages will be prepared in manuscript.

Place	Date	Hour	Summary of Events and Information	Remarks and references to Appendices
LA TARGETTE. (H. 15. C. 2. 2.)	Oct. 15th	9:00	Ref. Map. 57 B. 1:40,000. Unit moved from NOEUX-LES-MINES + reached billets in LA TARGETTE at 12:30. Bearer Party reported Unit here. Personnel in billets. No accommodation for sick at present except in tents, which have not yet been erected. Practically all equipment, clothing, blankets, stretchers, stores etc. for S/B. have been dumped under Guard at BEAUMETZ as no further transport has as yet been available from the Division.	Fine
"	16th	16:00	Major R.W. Armstrong went on leave to U.K. 1st Lieut. S.N. TROCKEY M.R.C. U.S.A. to 49th C.C.S. for temporary duty vice Lieut. S.E. Murray. Reine rejoining Unit. A few marquees (Hosp. + G.S.) erected & accommodate sick from Towners. Bas H.Q. during this afternoon and succeeded in having a big barn in rear of our billets allotted to the Unit for accommodation of Divisional sick.	Wet Rain. Cold.
"	17th	17:45	Routine. Another large attack taken over forces of Div. R.A.S.	Wet
"	18th	18:00	Routine. Admissions = 20. Evacuated = 13. In Hosp. = 8. 9am 17th & 9am 18th. 10 wounded (Accid. Bout wounds) admitted this afternoon from 17th R. Fus. 2 died after admission	Wet Fine
"	19th	18:00	Routine: Lieut. S.E. Murray Reine to temporary duty as M.O. k. 23rd R. Fusiliers. Admitted = 43. To C.C.S. = 12. Remaining = 37	Wet Fine

Army Form C. 2118

WAR DIARY
or
INTELLIGENCE SUMMARY
(Erase heading not required.)

Instructions regarding War Diaries and Intelligence Summaries are contained in F.S. Regs., Part II. and the Staff Manual respectively. Title Pages will be prepared in manuscript.

Place	Date	Hour	Summary of Events and Information	Remarks and references to Appendices
LA TARGETTE (H.15.c.2.2.)	Oct 20	18.00	Major P.J. LANE, 1st Lieut. E.A. CURTIN and Bearer Party of 30 O.R. with 2 Ambulance Wagons, 1 Water Cart & A.D.S. Limber left at 09.00 hours with 99th Inf.Bde. for CATENIERES. Remainder of Unit (1 Officer - O.C.) left behind in charge of Divn Rest Station. Capt. F.R. LEBLANC. Relieve No.6 F.A. Finished at 16.00 for temp. duty. Many patients from the Division evacuated during the day. Preparatory to possible move. Remained = 37. Admitted = 4. Evacuated = 12. To duty = 2. Remaining at 09.00 hours = 47.	Heavy Rain
"	21	17.00	Routine. Bearer Party still with 99th Inf.Bde. at CATENIERES. 0900 20/15 to 0900 h. 21 10/15 { Remained = 47, Evacuated = 44, Admitted = 29, To Duty = 9, Remaining = 23 } 1 New Sunbeam Motor Ambulance received instead of 1 Daimler Car Evac. to date	Fine showers Nil
"	22nd	19.00	Routine. Lieut. J. JAMIESON R.A.M.C on Expiry of 6 months Contract & Struck off Strength of Unit Admitted 39. Evac. 20. To Duty 2. Remaining 40. 9am 21st to 9am 22nd	Nil
"	23rd	19.00	Routine. Visited 29 C.C.S & 46 C.C.S. Re delivered of enter Equipment Admitted 37. Evac. 37. To Duty 5. Remaining 35. 9am to 9am 23rd Inst.	Nil
"	2			Nil

Army Form C. 2118

WAR DIARY
or
INTELLIGENCE SUMMARY
(Erase heading not required.)

Place	Date	Hour	Summary of Events and Information	Remarks and references to Appendices
ST PYTHON (V.30.c.7.4)	24th	1800	Map Ref. Sheet 51A 1:40,000. Under orders from ADMS 2nd Division Unit moved at 10 a.m. from LATARGETTE to site at St VAAST lately vacated by No. 5. Further orders received & unit moved on to ST PYTHON to site vacated yesterday by No. 6 F.A. Bearers still in line. All cases unable to return to duty evacuated yesterday & today & roll cleared. Evacuated To CCS = 10. To Corps Rest Station (CARNIÈRES) = 16. To duty = 9. Remaining = Nil. Some surplus ordnance & Red X stores yesterday handed over to No. 19 CCS.	Fine
"	25	1940	Routine. This Unit now serving local sick of ST PYTHON. Sick cases detained but most Bearers of unit still in line card to Corps Rest Station at CARNIÈRES. Bearers of which stretcher of 99th Inf. Bde. work has been light in character of last 4 days. All Surplus Equipment collected while running Div. Rest Station is being handed over so that unit may be able to move forward with Division.	Cold. Some rain
"	26th	1900	Routine. 99th Inf. Brigade in Reserve. Bearers of this Unit are therefore now resting. All ambulance attached to No. 6 F.A. rejoined unit this evening. A large number of cases of Influenza (in light form) now occurring amongst the Units	Fine Cool

WAR DIARY or INTELLIGENCE SUMMARY

Army Form C. 2118

(Erase heading not required.)

Place	Date	Hour	Summary of Events and Information	Remarks and references to Appendices
ST PYTHON (V.30.c.7.w)	27th	17:30	Map ref Sheet 57A 1/40,000. Routine. Vicinity of billets shelled with shrapnel by enemy during morning. No casualties in unit. 1 Officer & 1 O.R. of other units brought in wounded. Many French civilian sick left behind in German retirement are being attended. Capt LEBLANC R.A.M.C. No 6 F.A., at present attached, very helpful in looking after these cases. His is a French Officer. Chief thing required is medical comforts for the children. Under orders just issued by G.S. 2nd Div, 99th Inf Bde. & Bearers of No. 110 F.A. move to billets in SOLESMES tonight.	Rain till 16:00.
"	28th	11:00	Routine. Bearers of unit resting in billets in SOLESMES. Many local sick being seen at H.Q. ST PYTHON.	Wet
"	29th	17:30	Major P.J. LANE, Lieut. CURTIN & Bearers left for ESCARMAIN with 99th Inf Bde at 11:00. H.Q. & Transport of unit remain at ST PYTHON.	Wet
"	30th	19:15	Routine. A large number of French civilians still under treatment.	Fine
VERTAIN W.15.a.9.8	31st	18:15	Under orders from A.D.M.S. H.Q. & Transport left ST PYTHON 11:00 and moved to VERTAIN under treatment. 1st Lieut. E.A. CURTIN M.R.C. U.S.A. & temp duty as M.O. 2/23rd R. Fusiliers. Lieut S.E. MURRAY R.A.M.C. transferred to 62nd Division & struck off strength of Unit.	Rain

1875 Wt. W5593/826 1,000,000 4/15 J.B.C. & A. A.D.S.S./Forms/C. 2118.

Signatures

Instructions regarding War Diaries and Intelligence Summaries are contained in F.S. Regs., Part II. and the Staff Manual respectively. Title Pages will be prepared in manuscript.

Army Form C. 2118

WAR DIARY
or
~~INTELLIGENCE SUMMARY~~
(Erase heading not required.)

Instructions regarding War Diaries and Intelligence Summaries are contained in F. S. Regs., Part II. and the Staff Manual respectively. Title Pages will be prepared in manuscript.

CONFIDENTIAL.

WAR DIARY
OF
Nº 100 FIELD AMBULANCE

FROM 1ˢᵗ NOVʳ 1918 TO 30ᵗʰ NOVʳ 1918

VOLUME 37.

Army Form C. 2118

WAR DIARY
or
INTELLIGENCE SUMMARY
(Erase heading not required.)

Instructions regarding War Diaries and Intelligence Summaries are contained in F.S. Regs., Part II. and the Staff Manual respectively. Title Pages will be prepared in manuscript.

Place	Date	Hour	Summary of Events and Information	Remarks and references to Appendices
VERTAIN W.I.S.a.9.8.	Nov. 1st	18.15	Michelin Sheet 51 L 1:40,000. Routine: Unit standing by in huts for tonight. Warning order for move received from A. D. M. S. G.O.C. 2nd Division visited unit at 10.00 this morning. All hosps being shifted.	Fine
"	2nd	18.00	Division relieved in line this afternoon 99th Inf. Bde. & to St HILAIRE, but this unit remained in same area, still in tents. Major P.J. LANE M.C. & Bearer hypnied unit at 16.30	Rain.
"	3rd	1800	Routine.	
"	4th	1900	Routine: Division unit resting. Kit Inspections etc.	
"	5th	18.00	Unit Ready to move at short notice. Under orders of A.D.M.S 2nd Division Major B/C. Armstrong name to temporary duty at I Corps Rest Station CARNIERES. Two Officers (Majors LANE & Self) left for duty with unit.	Heavy Rain
"	6th	18.10	Routine. Unit resting in billets in village, all tentage struck	War Heavy Rain
"	7th	1800	Routine Unit resting. Sick of 5th Inf Bde, 2nd T.M.C. & 2nd Div. Train being collected. Still many cases of Influenza.	Wet

WAR DIARY
or
INTELLIGENCE SUMMARY
(Erase heading not required.)

Army Form C. 2118

Place	Date	Hour	Summary of Events and Information	Remarks and references to Appendices
VILLERS-POL L.34.d.6.6.	Nov. 8th	12:30	Ref. Map Sheet 51A. 1.40,000 Unit left VERTAIN under orders of O.C. 5th Inf. Brigade, and marched via RUESNES arriving at VILLERS POL at 1400 hours. Billeted in School. Under orders from A.D.M.S. 2nd Division unit is to open a Divisional Rest Station here. Under present circumstances + accommodation this is likely to prove difficult.	Rain
"	9th	18:00	Opened D.R.S. in School. Most of later on "Influenza" and have the Evacuated. Major B[n] ARMSTRONG Rams. rejoined unit from II Corps Rest Station, now closed.	N/W Fine
"	10th	18:00	Routine: Heavy "Influenza" cases still coming in from Division. Sick today, and third car used to assist to transport Volksdeutschen had to Evacuate as many as possible. M.A.C. failed to Evacuate	N/W Fine
"	11th	18:00	Announcement of Cessation of Hostilities from 1100 hours today. Routine. Influenza cases still continue of course.	N/W
"	12th	18:00	Routine. 3 M.A.C. Cars stationed at D.R.S. to help in Evacuation of sick.	N/W Fine Cold

WAR DIARY
or
INTELLIGENCE SUMMARY

(Erase heading not required.)

Army Form C. 2118

Place	Date	Hour	Summary of Events and Information	Remarks and references to Appendices
VILLERS-POL L.34.d.6.6.	Nov. 13th	1800	Ref. Map. Sheet 51 A : 1:40,000. Routine: G.O.C. 2nd Division inspected unit.	Fine
"	14th	1830	Routine: Unit preparing to accompany Division on march Eastwards - All surplus equipment & stores being handed back to N.N.S & & etc.	New Fine
"	15th	1815	Routine: Many sick & "crocks" being evacuated. Capt C.S. TENNANT R.A.M.C joined unit from 2nd Division preparatory to march to the Rhine. 1st Lieut TROCKEY & 15 O.R. at 34 C.C.S. 1st Lieut TROCKEY & temp. duty with 2nd Div. Receipt from temp. duty	New Fine
"	16th	1820	Routine: Motor Amb. Cars kneeing all day traversing the "croché"	Fine - No fold.
"	17th	1800	Routine: Sick evacuations diminishing. 4 M.A.C. Cars from 30th M.A.C. now attached. Unit for evacuation work.	New
			Ref. Map. VALENCIENNES, Sheet 12, 1:100,000	
LA LONGUEVILLE 3.K.24.50	18		Unit left VILLERS POL with 99th Inf. Bde. at 1200. Marched via COMMIGNIES & BAVAI and arrived LA LONGUEVILLE at 4.30 pm. Billeted in farm to right. No casualties on march.	Fine New

Army Form C. 2118

WAR DIARY
or
INTELLIGENCE SUMMARY
(Erase heading not required.)

Instructions regarding War Diaries and Intelligence Summaries are contained in F.S. Regs., Part II. and the Staff Manual respectively. Title Pages will be prepared in manuscript.

Place	Date	Hour	Summary of Events and Information	Remarks and references to Appendices
LONGUEVILLE 3.K.24.80	19th	18.00	Ref Map: VALENCIENNES, Sheet 12, 1:100,000. Unit resting.	Nil
ELESMES 3.A.15.71.	20th	18.00	Ref Map: NAMUR Sheet 8, 1:100,000. Unit left LA LONGUEVILLE with 99th Inf. Bde at 08:15. Marched via MAUBEUGE to ELESMES arriving about 11:45. Unit in good billets in village. Inspected by G.O.C. 2nd Division on the March. G.O.C. expressed himself as very pleased with turn out. All ranks of Division being evacuated to M.S. C.C.S. at SOUS-LE-BOIS.	Cold. Foggy. Nil This cold Nil
"	21st	18.45	Unit resting & road cleaning. Routine	Nil
"	22nd	"	" " "	Fine
"	23rd	18.00	" " Education Scheme Explained to men of Unit by Major Bro Armstrong MC	Nil Fine
RESSAIX I.C. 30.60	24th	17.20	Unit left ELESMES at 07:20 and marched in rear of 99th Inf Bde via BIVRY and BINCHE to RESSAIX where it is well billeted. Weather inclement. Arrived at RESSAIX at 12:30 hrs. Unit now collecting kit of 99th Inf. Bde only. Fine.	Nil

Army Form C. 2118

WAR DIARY
or
INTELLIGENCE SUMMARY
(Erase heading not required.)

Instructions regarding War Diaries and Intelligence Summaries are contained in F.S. Regs., Part II. and the Staff Manual respectively. Title Pages will be prepared in manuscript.

Place	Date	Hour	Summary of Events and Information	Remarks and references to Appendices
MARCHIENNE AU-PONT E.2.75.88	Nov. 25th	1800	Ref. Map NAMUR Sheet 8 - 1:100,000. Unit left RESSAIX at 10.30 and marched with 99th Inf. Bde. to present Billets in MARCHIENNE-AU-PONT arriving at 3.30 p.m. Unit marched very well. Billets. Stragglers picked up on march. Whole Brigade enthusiastically received. Sick evacuated to No. 55 CCS CHARLEROI.	Misty
"	26th	1800	Unit resting. "Influenza" beginning in A.S.C. M.T. personnel - 2 cases have already occurred	Misty Fine Cold
"	27th	1810	Unit resting. 2 Returned British POWs evacuated to CCS. 15 Returned French POWs sent on to French Frontier (MAUBEUGE) by Amb. Cars. Active routine work.	Misty Showers
CHATELET (2.G.35.82)	28th	1740	Unit left MARCHIENNE-AU-PONT with 99th Inf. Brigade at 10.20 hrs. and marched through CHARLEROI to CHATELET arriving at 1300. No stragglers from Brigade. Unit billeted in the town.	Misty Rain
SART-ST-LAURENT 2.I.90.83	29th	1745	Unit left CHATELET at 09.20 with 99th Inf. Bde. and marched via PRESSES & FOSSE to SART ST. LAURENT arriving about 2 p.m. 1 man of Unit fell out on the march. Unit billeted in the village. Ordinary Sick to CHARLEROI. Urgent cases only to NAMUR (44 CCS)	Misty Fine
"	30th	1820	Unit resting in billets	Misty

Capt. C.S. TENNANT. Above evacuated with to No. 44 C.C.S. (NAMUR) last night
J.B.C. & A. A.D.S.S./Forms/C. 2118.

[signature] Lieut. Col. Comdg.

Army Form C. 2118

WAR DIARY
or
INTELLIGENCE SUMMARY
(Erase heading not required.)

Instructions regarding War Diaries and Intelligence Summaries are contained in F. S. Regs., Part II. and the Staff Manual respectively. Title Pages will be prepared in manuscript.

WAR DIARY

OF

No 100 FIELD AMBULANCE

From 1-12-18 To 31-12-18

(VOLUME No 38)

—CONFIDENTIAL—

146/3481

COMMITTEE FOR THE MEDICAL HISTORY OF THE WAR
6 MAR 1919

Army Form C.

WAR DIARY
or
INTELLIGENCE SUMMARY
(Erase heading not required.)

Instructions regarding War Diaries and Intelligence Summaries are contained in F.S. Regs., Part II. and the Staff Manual respectively. Title Pages will be prepared in manuscript.

Place	Date	Hour	Summary of Events and Information	Remarks and references to Appendices
SART - ST LAURENT 2.I. 90.83	December 1918 1st	1800	Ref. Map. Sheet 8 NAMUR - 1:100,000 Unit resting: Routine. Rations rather short for past 5 days owing to transport difficulties. A few cases of Influenza still occurring amongst A.S.C. (H.T.) drivers. Most of the cases in division have occurred amongst transport drivers.	Fine. Cold.
"	2nd	1900	Unit resting. Routine	Misty. [illeg] L/Col. [illeg]
"	3rd	1810	Unit resting: Routine. By permission of G.O.C. 99th Inf. Bde. Unit had been allowed to march in "fighting order", the packs being carried on lorries. Concession much appreciated.	Wet. Fine. [illeg]
MARCHE - LES - DAMES 14.55.78	4th	1750	Unit left SART ST LAURENT at 09.40 with 99th Inf. Bde. and marched via BUZET - NAMUR & MARCHE - LES - DAMES arriving about 1500. Transport left at 09.33 and moved with Bde. transport via FLOREFFE & NAMUR & MARCHE-LES-DAMES arriving about 1400. Unit billeted in Village. A long march. All rather tired. 2nd Lieut E.A. CURTIN to 1st Battn KRR Corps for temporary duty as M.O. vice Capt C.S. TENNANT KRRC reported unit from No. 44 CCS (sick).	Rain. Foggy. [illeg]
"	5th			Wet. [illeg]
SEILLES 6.A.93.00	5th		Ref. Map: Sheet 7 LIEGE - 1:100,000 Unit left MARCHE -LES-DAMES at 1045 hours & marched in rear of 99th Inf. Bde. via ANDENNE to SEILLES arriving about 1315 hours. A short march. Unit billeted in Chateau. Sick of 99th Inf. Bde & 2nd Bn N.Q.C. evacuated sick at HUY.	Fine [illeg]

1875 W. W.593/325 1,000,000 4/15 J.B.C. & A. A.D.S.S./Forms/C. 2118.

Army Form C. 2118

WAR DIARY
or
INTELLIGENCE SUMMARY
(Erase heading not required.)

Instructions regarding War Diaries and Intelligence Summaries are contained in F.S. Regs., Part II. and the Staff Manual respectively. Title Pages will be prepared in manuscript.

Place	Date	Hour	Summary of Events and Information	Remarks and references to Appendices
			Ref. map Sheet No.9 MARCHE — 1:100,000	
ST VITO I.E.20.82.	Dec. 6th	1800	Unit left SEILLES at 09.15 hours and marched with 98th Inf. Bde. to HUY. Here personnel & Transport separated. Personnel marched direct to ST VITO via STREE arriving at 15.20 hours. Transport marched via BARSE — VIERSET — BARSE to ST VITO arriving about 16.30 hours. Unit billeted in chateau ST VITO. A long & tiring march. 38 men of different units fell out during march. Had these collected rations at CCS. (11 from 99th Inf. Bde. and 27 of the 2nd Bn. M.G.C.)	Fine Cold.
ONEUX I.H.77.68	7th	1720	Unit left ST VITO at 08.40 and marched with 99th Inf. Bde. to ONEUX arriving about 15.30. A long march, with 1 hours halt for dinners. Unit billeted in village. Three in the church needed rest Tomorrow. Boots getting worn & leather cord be got ex-horse Base. Sick of Bde. still evacuated to CCS at HUY. One of the M.A.C. cars attached Sent three afternoon to No.6 Field Amb. for duty.	New Fine
	8th	1800	Unit Resting.	Wet Fine
JOHOSTER I.J.37.72	9th	18.15.	Unit left ONEUX at 09.50 and marched in rear of 99th Inf. Bde. via AYWAILLE, REMOUCHAMPS and BELLEVAUX to JOHOSTER arriving about 16.15. One very long & steep hill, trying for Horse transport. 2 men fell out during march. Several motor ambulances in workshops, being stiffly country & lack of lubricating oil. Unit billeted in chateau.	New Rain New

Army Form C. 2118

WAR DIARY
or
INTELLIGENCE SUMMARY
(Erase heading not required.)

Instructions regarding War Diaries and Intelligence Summaries are contained in F.S. Regs., Part II. and the Staff Manual respectively. Title Pages will be prepared in manuscript.

Place	Date	Hour	Summary of Events and Information	Remarks and references to Appendices
JOHOSTER 1J 37 72	Dec. 10th	1800	Ref. trench sheet No. 9 MARCHE – 1:100,000. Unit resting. One horse (H.B.) died of gas gangrene following on wound received (slashed).	Rain
STER 1.L. 47 47	11th	1900	Unit left JOHOSTER at 0900 in rear of 99th Inf.Bde. Marched through SPA. 1 hour dinner halt 2 K East of Spa. Arrived at STER (Station) about 14.30. Unit billeted in Station. Heavy Rain during march.	Rain
			Ref. Map GERMANY 1M. 1:100,000	
LAGER EISENBORN 1. F.	12th	1900	Unit left STER at 0915 with 99th Inf.Bde. Crossed German Frontier and arrived at EISENBORN Barracks about 1600 hrs. Heavy rain, Unhealthy march – twenty miles. Unit billeted in Barracks.	Heavy rain
			Ref. Map GERMANY 1M. – 1:100,000	
EICHERSCHEID 10 M.	13th	1930	Unit left EISENBORN Barracks at 09.15 with 99th Inf.Bde. After very long stormy wet march arrived at EICHERSCHEID at 15.15. Men all very wet.	Heavy Rain
BOICH 7.J.	14th	1930	Unit left EICHERSCHEID at 08.45 and marched with 99th Inf.Bde. via SCHMIDT to BOICH arriving about 1600 hrs. 1 hour halt for dinner 3 K. E. of SCHMIDT. A long march, not much rain. Men of Unit billeted in School in Village. Boots getting very worn. 16 men of Bde. finished up on March. Very great improvement in Sobriety of Natives during last 3 days.	Rain

WAR DIARY
or
INTELLIGENCE SUMMARY

(Erase heading not required.)

Army Form C. 2118

Instructions regarding War Diaries and Intelligence Summaries are contained in F. S. Regs., Part II. and the Staff Manual respectively. Title Pages will be prepared in manuscript.

Place	Date	Hour	Summary of Events and Information	Remarks and references to Appendices
BOICH 7.J.	Dec. 15th	18.00	Ref. Map GERMANY 1:L. — 1:100,000. Unit resting, then getting Unit dried & cleaned. Civilian population behaving well — now ready to help.	Fine
"	16th	18.30	Unit resting.	Nil
"	17th	18.15	Unit resting. Very few sick from Brigade for last 3 days.	Nil / Nil / Cloudy
"	18th	17.50	Unit resting.	Nil
BIRKESDORF S.J.	19th	17.40	Unit left Boich with 99th Inf. Bde. at 08.00 hours today. Marched via DÜREN and arrived at BIRKESDORF about 12.00. A short march. No men of Bde. fell out on march. Unit well billeted in the village.	Showers cold.
"	20th	18.00	Unit resting.	Nil
OBEREMBT	21st	19.00	Unit left BIRKESDORF at 09.30 and marched via RATHAUSEN & NIEDERZIER to OBEREMBT arriving at 14.00. All other units of 99th Inf. Bde. remained in their former billets occupied on 19th inst. Unit billeted in village. Ambulance is now far away from units of Brigade & from CCS and great difficulty & delay in collection of sick is likely to be experienced.	Showers Nil

1875 W↑. W593/826 1,000,000 4/15 J.B.C. & A. A.D.S.S./Forms/C. 2118.

WAR DIARY or INTELLIGENCE SUMMARY

Army Form C. 2118

(Erase heading not required.)

Instructions regarding War Diaries and Intelligence Summaries are contained in F. S. Regs., Part II. and the Staff Manual respectively. Title Pages will be prepared in manuscript.

Place	Date	Hour	Summary of Events and Information	Remarks and references to Appendices
OBEREMBT I.J.	Dec. 22nd	18:30	Ref. Map GERMANY 1-4. 1/100,000. Unit settling down in winter Billets. Men very scattered, but very comfortable in most places.	Fine. Cold
"	23rd	19:00	Unit Resting. Major R.J. LANE MC leaves to temporary duty with HQXIs II Corps (In BERLIN.)	Very Rain
"	24th	19:30	Unit Resting. Leaving Men received for above translation on 27 inst. Chr. Interpreter (Mr. MARION M./s) was attached Units - very useful. Preparations being made for Christmas dinner.	Fine
"	25th		Christmas Day.	
"	26th	19:30	Unit Resting. Posters GIESSEN turned but will move tomorrow 27 Inst. Capt. TENNANT leaves temporary duty with 36th Bde R.F.A.	Fine. Cold
GIESSEN T.W.	27th	17:30	Unit left OBEREMBT at 09:15 and marched via BERGHEIM to GIESSEN arriving about 14:30. This is supposed the Units Final Billet. A small village, not too comfortable. Two thirds of Lieutenants, 99th Bde moving into new area in two marches. 4 Coalmines left unit today for Wupperal under Demobilization Scheme.	Cold. Rain
"	28th	18:00	Unit settling down into new billets	
"	29th	18:00	9 three Coal miners left unit to-day. Demobilized.	Rain

Army Form C. 2118

WAR DIARY
or
INTELLIGENCE SUMMARY
(Erase heading not required.)

Instructions regarding War Diaries and Intelligence Summaries are contained in F. S. Regs., Part II. and the Staff Manual respectively. Title Pages will be prepared in manuscript.

Place	Date	Hour	Summary of Events and Information	Remarks and references to Appendices
	Dec.		Ref. Map. GERMANY 1:L. — 1:100,000	
GIESSEN	30th	13:00	Routine. 1st Lieut. S.M. TROCKEY + 12 O.R. (Reinforcements) joined Unit from 2nd Dist. Reception Camp. & continued efforts for dispersal. Unit settling into Billets. Arrangements being made for Recreation & amusements. No football ground available in area — Wingfest drawback.	MC
I.N.				
"	31st	15:30	Routine: Capt. E.S. TENNANT MORC. reported from temp. duty with 35th Bde R.F.A. 1st Lieut. S.M. TROCKEY M.R.C. U.S.A. to temporary duty with 24th R. Fusiliers. A Small Red Station for Mild Sick of 99th Inf Bde. being formed in the school house GIESSEN.	

Mil₀ Newson
M/O. Shein
O.C. No. 100 Field Ambulance

Army Form C. 2118.

WAR DIARY
or
INTELLIGENCE SUMMARY
(Erase heading not required.)

2nd Div
Box 1012
Vol 32

149/5744

CONFIDENTIAL

WAR DIARY.

OF

No 100 FIELD AMBULANCE.

From January 1st 1919 to January 31st 1919

(VOLUME 39)

2098/31

CONFIDENTIAL

Army Form C. 2118

Instructions regarding War Diaries and Intelligence Summaries are contained in F.S. Regs., Part II. and the Staff Manual respectively. Title Pages will be prepared in manuscript.

WAR DIARY
No. 100. or FIELD AMBULANCE.
INTELLIGENCE SUMMARY

(Erase heading not required.)

Place	Date	Hour	Summary of Events and Information	Remarks and references to Appendices
GIESSEN I.N.	January 1919		Ref. Map GERMANY Sheet 1.L. - 1:100,000.	
	1st	1830	Routine. g.c. 99th Inf.Bde. visited unit & inspected billets etc	[signature]
"	2nd	1830	Routine. A.D.M.S. visited unit. Meeting of F.A. Commanders re Sports in the Field Amb. of the Division	[initials]
"	3rd	1800	Routine. 2 NCOs & 1 man left for different Horse of Christ Examined by Veterinary Board for Classification	[initials]
"	4th	1800	Routine. Regimental Courses of duties abolished	[initials]
"	5th	1800	Routine } Very few sick from 99th Inf.Bde.	[initials]
"	6th	1800	Routine }	[initials]
	7	"		
	8	"		
	9		Routine. Major P.J. LANE M.C. arrived from temporary duty with 3 Divs. II Corps (proceeding for British Prisoners of War in Germany)	[initials]
"	10		} Routine.	
	11			
	12	1700		
	13			
	14		Capt. C.S. TENNANT to U.K. on leave. Routine. Very little else. Investigation going very slowly.	[initials]

1875 Wt. W593/826 1,000,000 4/15 J.B.C. & A. A.D.S.S./Forms/C.2118.

Army Form C. 2118

WAR DIARY
or
INTELLIGENCE SUMMARY
(Erase heading not required.)

CONFIDENTIAL

Instructions regarding War Diaries and Intelligence Summaries are contained in F. S. Regs., Part II. and the Staff Manual respectively. Title Pages will be prepared in manuscript.

Place	Date	Hour	Summary of Events and Information	Remarks and references to Appendices
	1919 January		Ref. Map GERMANY sheet 1.L. — 1:160,000	
GIESSEN I.N.	15	1700	Routine, "Early Treatment Room" for Venereal Diseases has been established for some days in the Hospital, and is frequently in use.	NE
"	16	1700	G.O.C. 2nd Division inspected Billets & Institutes etc. of the Unit. "Revised Establishment" for a Field Ambulance received. Each Field Ambulance to consist of 2 Sections only.	NE
"	17			
"	18			
	19		Routine.	
	20			
	21			
	22			
	23			
	24			
	25			
	26			
	27			
	28			
	29			
	30			
	31			

Wifton Lieut. Col. R.a.m.c.
O.C. No. 1 N.Z. Field Ambulance

1875 Wt. W593/826 1,000,000 4/15 J.B.C. & A. A.D.S.S./Forms/C. 2118.

WAR DIARY
INTELLIGENCE SUMMARY

(Erase heading not required.)

Army Form C. 2118

CONFIDENTIAL

WAR DIARY

OF

No 100 FIELD AMBULANCE.

From February 1st 1919 To February 28th 1919.

(VOLUME 40.)

WAR DIARY
or
INTELLIGENCE SUMMARY

Army Form C. 2118

(Erase heading not required.)

Place	Date	Hour	Summary of Events and Information	Remarks and references to Appendices
GIESSEN I.N.	Feb.		Ref. Map. GERMANY – Sheet 1.L. 1:100,000	Wyton Lieut Col RAMC
	1.			
	2.			
	3.			
	4.			
	5.			
	6.		Major B.W. ARMSTRONG returned from leave to France.	
	7.			
	8.			
	9.			
	10.			Routine.
	11.		Lieut N.E. V NEWMAN to leave in France (10 days)	Sick now down to less than 75%. W.E. Stensitization therapy suspended.
	12.			
	13.			Many 1914 & 1915 men still left. Some distribution
	14.			at many 1916 & 1917 men in U.K. have been demobilised
	15.			
	16.			After cases of "Influenza" occurring
	17.			in 99th Inft Bde. His services
	18.		Capt. C.S. TENNANT ARMY to Temporary duty at No 17 C.C.S. DÜREN	cases.
	19.			
	20.			Wyton Lieut Col
	21.			RAMC

WAR DIARY
or
INTELLIGENCE SUMMARY

(Erase heading not required.)

Army Form C. 2118

Instructions regarding War Diaries and Intelligence Summaries are contained in F. S. Regs., Part II. and the Staff Manual respectively. Title Pages will be prepared in manuscript.

Place	Date	Hour	Summary of Events and Information	Remarks and references to Appendices
GIESSEN I.H.	Feb.			
	22		Map ref. GERMANY Sheet 1.4. ; I = 100,000 COLOGNE	
	23		One or two cases of Influenza have occurred lately in hosp. All substitutions	Routine
	24			
	25			
	26		New Convoy of Scabies amongst the troops extensive after trench. hostility due to repeated infected blankets.	
	27			
"	28		A few have Volunteered for Instructors service with Army of Occupation.	M/Maj. Lyons Kent Maj. ... ... O.C. No. 100 Field Ambulance

1875 Wt. W593/826 1,000,000 4/15 J.B.C. & A. A.D.S.S./Forms/C. 2118.

CONFIDENTIAL Army Form C. 2118

WAR DIARY
or
INTELLIGENCE SUMMARY

(Erase heading not required.)

100TH FIELD AMBULANCE.
No. 2096/39
Date 31/3/19

140/3001

Confidential

WAR DIARY

of

N° 100 FIELD AMBULANCE.

from March 1st 1919 to March 31st 1919.

(VOLUME 41.)

WAR DIARY
INTELLIGENCE SUMMARY

(Erase heading not required.)

Army Form C. 2118

Instructions regarding War Diaries and Intelligence Summaries are contained in F.S. Regs., Part II. and the Staff Manual respectively. Title Pages will be prepared in manuscript.

Place	Date	Hour	Summary of Events and Information	Remarks and references to Appendices
GIESSEN	March		Ref Map GERMANY. Sheet 14. — 1:100,000	Major Tyrone R.A.M.C.
	1st			
	2nd			
	3rd			
	4th	18.00	Visited Aytons to leave for Home personnel of units. Army Order 6 has not yet been received in the Division. 1 Case of V.S. (8 weeks old.) occurred in unit R.T.S.(H.T.)	Major Tyrone
	5th		Routine. Hospital trains being redistemperfiner. Scabies still occurring in Units.	Major Tyrone
	6th		1 case of Jaundice (Recurrence?) evacuated from Units today to C.C.S. Combined team from 3 Field Ambulances of Division defeated 24th Bn 4.4.9 in tapping of Final of Divisional Assoc. Football League. Visited H.Q. of 13th K.R.R. Corps - a Battalion just arrived in Division	Rain
	7th		Routine	Major Tyrone
	8th			
	9th		Capt (a/Major) N.W. ROYSTON R.A.M.C (T.F.) joined the unit for duty.	
	10th		Lieut. Col. R.E.V. NEWMAN M.C. R.A.M.C. departed on leave to U.K.	Wh Newman Lt.Col Administrative Major RAMC DDMS DMSA
	11th		Routine	
	12th			

1875 Wt. W593/826 1,000,000 4/15 J.B.C. & A. A.D.S.S./Forms/C. 2118.

Army Form C. 2118

Instructions regarding War Diaries and Intelligence Summaries are contained in F. S. Regs., Part II. and the Staff Manual respectively. Title Pages will be prepared in manuscript.

WAR DIARY
INTELLIGENCE SUMMARY
(Erase heading not required.)

Place	Date	Hour	Summary of Events and Information	Remarks and references to Appendices
GLESSEN	May 13		} Routine	MA
	14			
	15		R.A.M.C. combined team lost to Corps Heavy Artillery in semifinal of II Corps football competition at Deinze — Score 2-0. 2nd Division ceased to exist as such & the Light Division comes into being. Routine.	MA MA
	16			MA
	17		The G.O.C. 2nd Div. (Major General Pereira CB.) inspected the unit gave a farewell address referred in the highest terms to its continuous good service throughout the war.	MA
	18		Routine	MA
	19		Lt. Col. R.E.W. Newman M.C. R.A.M.C. dying under orders to report to the H.Q. The Dramis at Malta returned to the unit. To the purpose of "Handing over" to	MA
	20		Routine	MA
	21		Departure of Lt. Colonel R.E.W. Newman M.C. R.A.M.C. Major B.W. ARMSTRONG assumed temporary command	MA

Army Form C. 2118

WAR DIARY
or
INTELLIGENCE SUMMARY
(Erase heading not required.)

Instructions regarding War Diaries and Intelligence Summaries are contained in F. S. Regs., Part II. and the Staff Manual respectively. Title Pages will be prepared in manuscript.

Place	Date	Hour	Summary of Events and Information	Remarks and references to Appendices
GLESSEN	Mar. 22nd		Reorganisation of unit on a scale of two sections of three completed. Capt. P.J. LANE M.C. R.A.M.C. relinquished his acting rank of Major on ceasing to command "C" Section	MJF
	23		} Routine	
	24			
	25			MJF
	26			
	27			
	28			MJF
	29			
	30		Capt. C.S. TENNANT R.A.M.C. posted to 5-2nd Bn. Rifle Brigade is struck off the strength of the unit	MJF
	31		Routine	

W.W. Murchison
Major R.A.M.C.
O.C. 100 F.A.

1875 Wt. W593/826 1,000,000 4/15 J.B.C. & A. A.D.S.S./Forms/C. 2118.

Army Form C. 2118

WAR DIARY
or
INTELLIGENCE SUMMARY
(Erase heading not required.)

Confidential

WAR DIARY

of

N° 100 Field Ambulance (Light Division)
Rhine

from April 1st 1919 to April 30th 1919.

(Volume 42.)

Army Form C. 2118

WAR DIARY
or
INTELLIGENCE SUMMARY
(Erase heading not required.)

Instructions regarding War Diaries and Intelligence Summaries are contained in F. S. Regs., Part II. and the Staff Manual respectively. Title Pages will be prepared in manuscript.

Place	Date	Hour	Summary of Events and Information	Remarks and references to Appendices
GIESSEN	2/4/19		In accordance with D.G. Wire P.1921 dated 21/3/19 & D.D.M.S. IV Corps No 2/756/3 dated 23/3/19 I took over Command of No.100 Field Ambulance. Robert Ellis Capt. a/Major R.A.M.C.	
	3/4/19 to 8/4/19		Sanitary improvements & ordinary Routine Procedure. R.	
	9/4/19		Major B.W. Armstrong M.C. proceeded on leave to UK. R. Capt. P.T. Lane M.C. returned from leave to UK	
	12/4/19		In accordance with Detached wire D.M. 34154 A.M.D.1, dated 5th inst I proceeded to U.K. for service in India having handed over command of unit to Major N.W. Kidstone R.A.M.C. W.	

Robert Ellis
Capt a/Major R.A.M.C.

Army Form C. 2118

WAR DIARY
or
INTELLIGENCE SUMMARY
(Erase heading not required.)

Instructions regarding War Diaries and Intelligence Summaries are contained in F. S. Regs., Part II. and the Staff Manual respectively. Title Pages will be prepared in manuscript.

Place	Date	Hour	Summary of Events and Information	Remarks and references to Appendices
GLESSEN	12/4/19		Major R. Ellis MC Reeve having proceeded to England, unit D.M. 34159 A.M.O. dated 5th inst. Conference on [illegible]. Canteens Reinforcement arrangements to engine Sanitary Improvements to engines and latrines carried out.	[illegible] Major Reeve G
"	13/4/19		"	
"	14/4/19		"	
"	15/4/19		"	
"	16/4/19		"	
"	17/4/19		Capt. P.J. Lane MC Reeve proceeded to 5th Battn Royal Irish Regiment to [illegible] duty under instructions from H.D.M.S.	
"	18/4/19		Appointment to Hon. Capt. L.B. Shardlow returned from leave to U.K.	
"	19/4/19		Sanitary inspections & ordinary routine carried out.	
"	20/4/19		General duties	
"	21/4/19		General duties	
"	22/4/19		Conference to C.O. unit D.M.S. 2 Army re. Cholera inoculation of all units.	
"	23/4/19		Sanitary improvements & ordinary routine carried out.	
"	24/4/19		"	
"	25/4/19		"	
"	26/4/19		[illegible] duties Major R Reeve G	

Army Form C. 2118

WAR DIARY
or
INTELLIGENCE SUMMARY
(Erase heading not required.)

Instructions regarding War Diaries and Intelligence Summaries are contained in F. S. Regs., Part II. and the Staff Manual respectively. Title Pages will be prepared in manuscript.

Place	Date	Hour	Summary of Events and Information	Remarks and references to Appendices
Gheen	April 27		Major B.W. ARMSTRONG R.A.M.C. rejoined unit from leave in U.K. took on command from Major N.W. RIDSTON R.A.M.C. (T.F.)	M/Armstrong Major RAMC
	28			
	29		Routine	M/Armstrong Major RAMC
	30			

1875 Wt. W593/826 1,000,000 4/15 J.B.C. & A. A.D.S.S./Forms/C. 2118.

Army Form C. 2118

WAR DIARY
or
INTELLIGENCE SUMMARY
(Erase heading not required.)

CONFIDENTIAL

WAR DIARY

OF

No. 100 FIELD AMBULANCE

FROM 1ST MAY, 1919 TO 31ST MAY, 1919.

(VOLUME 43)

Instructions regarding War Diaries and Intelligence Summaries are contained in F. S. Regs., Part II. and the Staff Manual respectively. Title Pages will be prepared in manuscript.

Place	Date	Hour	Summary of Events and Information	Remarks and references to Appendices
	1 may 1919			

1875 Wt. W593/826 1,000,000 4/15 J.B.C. & A. A.D.S.S./Forms/C. 2118.

Army Form C. 2118

WAR DIARY
INTELLIGENCE SUMMARY
(Erase heading not required.)

Instructions regarding War Diaries and Intelligence Summaries are contained in F. S. Regs., Part II. and the Staff Manual respectively. Title Pages will be prepared in manuscript.

Place	Date	Hour	Summary of Events and Information	Remarks and references to Appendices
GIESSEN	May 1		Routine	
	2		Notification received from A.D.M.S. that the appointment of Capt. E. Percival	A/Armstrong Lt Col
	3		D.S.O. M.C. R.A.M.C. to command No. 10.0 F.A. has been approved by D.M.S. Army N. Major R.A.M.C.	
	4		Routine	M.A.
	5		Routine D.M.S: Attended conference at Cologne for Administrators officers & O.C. units	M.A.
	6			
	7			
	8			
	9		Routine	
	10			
	11			M.A.
	12			
	13		Capt. E. PERCIVAL D.S.O. M.C. joined & assumed command of the unit	Armstrong Major R.A.M.C.

1875 Wt. W593/826 1,000,000 4/15 J.B.C. & A. A.D.S.S./Forms/C. 2118.

Army Form C. 2118

Instructions regarding War Diaries and Intelligence Summaries are contained in F. S. Regs., Part II. and the Staff Manual respectively. Title Pages will be prepared in manuscript.

WAR DIARY
or
INTELLIGENCE SUMMARY
(Erase heading not required.)

Place	Date	Hour	Summary of Events and Information	Remarks and references to Appendices
GLESSEN	13-5-19		Capt. E. PERCIVAL. DSO. MC arrived today & took over command of the unit.	Forwarded Separately
"	15-5-19		Quiet - five patients in Hospital. Eight infantry men (3 6th London, 3 12 R.I.R & 2 Q.V.R) arrived today for a course of instruction in sanitation at this unit. Weather very fine.	CP
"	16-5-19		Capt P.J. LANE MC RAMC rejoined the unit today from temporary duty with 5. Rgnl Fld Amb. Rate of Demobilization of unbearable men accelerated from two men per week at two per day.	CP
"	19-5-19		Capt P.J. LANE MC. RAMC proceeded today to take over temporary medical charge of the 18th Batt King's Royal Rifles at NOERINGEN. He meter to take place of Demobilised RAMC. 34 infantrymen arrived today for study (10 9th London Rgt - 10 12th R.I. Rifles - 1 Q.V.R & 13 men 6" London Rgt.) & billeted in consort hall at eastern end of village - fitted to various duties, clerks, dressers etc on unit under instruction.	CP
	20-5-19.		Medical inspection of all men of unit for lice, scabies & venereal disease, & afterwards for syphilis infection.	CP
	21-5-19.		Quiet - fine day. Orders received that unit is to be taken up - rebounds men demobilised & rebounds sent to other ambulances.	CP

Army Form C. 2118

Instructions regarding War Diaries and Intelligence Summaries are contained in F.S. Regs., Part II. and the Staff Manual respectively. Title Pages will be prepared in manuscript.

WAR DIARY
or
INTELLIGENCE SUMMARY

(Erase heading not required.)

Place	Date	Hour	Summary of Events and Information	Remarks and references to Appendices
GIESSEN	22-5-19		Visited ADMS reference demobilisation of unit. Lt. Col. ____ & MM appointed acting before without Pay	EP
	23-5-19		All returnable men posted to 5 & 6 Field Ambulances – 1 NCO & 10 men to N°3 & 1 NCO & 10 men to N°2 Field Ambulance. 8 men arrived from Regiments of 2nd Light Brigade for instructions in sanitary duties. Ten men as usual paraded today for demobilisation.	EP
	24-5-19		Returns received from ADMS to close down unit forthwith. Cases in Hospital evacuated to CCS. Stores now being packed for demobilisation next day.	EP
	25-5-19		Sunday. Sick collected from units of 2nd Light Bde. & taken to N°5 Field Ambulance. SINNERSDORF for admittance. Hospital being closed & equipment gradually being collected together. 34 infantry men sent away, 17 to N°5 F. Amb & 17 to N°6 F. Amb.	EP
	26-5-19		Routine. Strength of unit today RAMC 59 ORs & 5 Officers, ASC MT 24, ASC MT 11.	EP
	27-5-19		Routine. Unit four men sent off for demobilisation. Surplus material stores returned to 11 ADM Stab BONN.	EP
	28-5-19		All cars & motor cycles with personnel returned to DIV MT at BEDBURG – leaving only two MAC cars with unit. One MAC car reported for duty from 5 & 6 F. Ambulances. Four men demobbed.	EP
	29-5-19		In accordance with authority from DIV (Q 19/207/10/Q/29/5/19), OC & F. ambulance closed for 2 nominal from 5 & 6 Field Ambulances.	EP

Army Form C. 2118

WAR DIARY
or
INTELLIGENCE SUMMARY
(Erase heading not required.)

Instructions regarding War Diaries and Intelligence Summaries are contained in F. S. Regs., Part II. and the Staff Manual respectively. Title Pages will be prepared in manuscript.

Place	Date	Hour	Summary of Events and Information	Remarks and references to Appendices
GIESSEN	30-5-19		Strength of unit - 4 officers & 47 other ranks RAMC - ASC HT 24 & ASC MT 1.	GP
"	31-5-19		Rate of demobilization unimproved to five per day from tomorrow onwards. Sure unprofitous posts of transport distance to retain ASC personnel due for demobilization. Actual strength of same 43 ORs & 4 officers - ASC HT 24 - ASC MT 1.	GP
	1/6/19.			

E Spencer
Capt RAMC
OC 100th Field Ambulance

1875 Wt. W393/826 1,000,000 4/15 J.B.C. & A. A.D.S.S./Forms/C. 2118.

Army Form C. 2118

WAR DIARY
or
INTELLIGENCE SUMMARY

(Erase heading not required.)

CONFIDENTIAL

WAR DIARY.

OF

No. 100 FIELD AMBULANCE.

FROM JUNE 1ST TO JUNE 22ND 1919.

VOLUME 45.

23 MAR 1920

Army Form C. 2118

WAR DIARY JUNE 1919
or
INTELLIGENCE SUMMARY FIELD AMBULANCE

(Erase heading not required.)

Place	Date	Hour	Summary of Events and Information	Remarks and references to Appendices
GLIESSEN	1.6.19		Rate of demobilization caused from today to five men per day. Five signalmen attached today to this unit from DIV TRAIN for transport duties.	EP
"	2.6.19		Ordnance equipment men & some authorization equipment sent to DADOS' Lgt Barren. Interview under DMS at 64 CCS COLOGNE at 10.30 am. Five men demobilized.	EP EP
"	3.6.19		General holiday in honour of Birthday of H.M. the King.	EP
"	4.6.19		Medical equipment of Field Ambulance forwarded to Army Medical Store, Worwick. Kept MFO Brown Sor, Cologne.	EP
"	5.6.19		Strength of unit RAMC ORs 23. - ASC MT 14. Men & to rest for demobilization on Wednesdays & Saturdays neg in future.	EP
"	6.6.19		Strength of unit — Officers 5 RAMC. RAMC ORs nil for demobilization & two RASC. RAMC ORs nil. ASC MT nil - ASC MT 14. Attached to unit 3 MAC car with driver, — 11 ORs RAMC. — ASC MT nil - 1 Sgt. ASC from N°2 Gy Train. Five PB men with unit. 14 infantry for transport duties.	EP
"	8.6.19		Under ADMS N°220/a/19 d/3/6/19 Capt a/Major H.W. WINSTON proceeded to U.K. on company medical charge 12 Royal Irish Rifles STOMACH.	EP

WAR DIARY or INTELLIGENCE SUMMARY

Army Form C. 2118

Place	Date	Hour	Summary of Events and Information	Remarks and references to Appendices
SLESSEN	10-6-19		Quiet.	EP
"	13-6-19		One man of ASC sent to Demobilisation.	EP
"	14-6-19		Strength of unit - namely Officers 6, ORs - 13. RASC HT 13 - PB attached 5. 2 orderlies 3 MAC drivers, 14 infantrymen from ASC drivers & 15ft from DIV Train attached	EP
"	15-6-19		Officers posted to units as follows - Capt E. PERCIVAL RAMC (temp attached 100th F Ambulance) & Major MIDSTON to 5th Field Ambulance — Capt ARMSTRONG & Capt LANE to 6th Field Ambulance. Capt ARMSTRONG proceeded to 6 Londons for temporary duty.	CP
"	16-6-19		2 orderlies with Light DIV Q 19/303. 13 L.D. horses & 11 H.D. horses handed over to 24th Veterinary Hspl. Meemscheg - Cigare.	EP
"	17-6-19		10 RASC HT personnel, 1 PB attached & 11 infantrymen attached HT posted to Light DIV Train. Strength of unit now - Names / Officers - 6, ORs - 18, PBs - RASC HT No 2, 6 on account of production of horses. Strength of unit now - Names / Officers - 5, FAmb (Capt PERCIVAL), 3 MAC drivers, & 3 infantrymen. 3 PBs now 4, — attached 1 Officer 5 FAmb (Capt PERCIVAL) Horses & riders to 5 H.D. for transport duties & 1 Sergt N°2 by other Train. Horses & riders on arrival & orders received these on 2 - 3 day on connection with same journal. S.C.S collected on arrival & for Field Ambulance wagon park to Brigade at POUCHEIM, 1st 2nd Light BRIGADE.	EP

WAR DIARY or INTELLIGENCE SUMMARY

Army Form C. 2118

(Erase heading not required.)

Place	Date	Hour	Summary of Events and Information	Remarks and references to Appendices
GLESSEN	18-6-19		J-2 day. Sick collected & sent to No 5 Field Ambulance SINNERSDORF from ① Artillery at NIEDEREMPT, KIRCHTROISDORF & KIRCHERTEN ② M&C-Eisighoven ③ 6th Londons at EHRENFIELD – 9th Londons & 1/2 R.I. Rgt at BICHENDORF near COLOGNE. Orders received from ADMS to withdraw ambulance wagons from 2nd Light Bde.	CP.
	19-6-19		J-1 day. Sick collected from Artillery as above – from 6th Londons at EHRENFIELD & from 9th Londons & 1/2 R.I. Rgt in their arrivals in Phil Barracks. Wire received from ADMS that all further moves of Divisional stopped until further orders.	CP.
	20-6-19		Orders received from ADMS for reduction of No 10 Ambulance to move to SINNERSDORF tomorrow 21st. Ambulance Wagons returned from 2nd Light Bde. Sick collected from Artillery only.	CP.
GLESSEN TO SINNERDORF	21-6-19		Unit moved to No 5 FA at SINNERSDORF. Two lorries reported at GLESSEN at 10 am – all equipment of unit taken on them. Horses from 5 Ambulance reported at 9.30 am to transport moved to SINNERSDORF at 10 am – empty. Personnel arrived in lorries & cars. On arrival unit billeted with No 5 Field Ambulance. Strength of unit – RAMC Officers 1, OR 13. HTASC 3. Horse pickers 5 – HD 5 attached "PB" men 4 – 3 infantrymen as ASC drivers – 1 Sgt ASC from No 2 Cav Train – 3 MAC drivers with cars – one officer No 5 Field Ambulance. All equipment packed & ready for shipment. On arrival personnel attached to No 5 Field Ambulance.	CP.

Army Form C. 2118

WAR DIARY
or
INTELLIGENCE SUMMARY

(Erase heading not required.)

Place	Date	Hour	Summary of Events and Information	Remarks and references to Appendices
SINNERSDORF	22-6-19		Handed over vehicles & equipment of unit to Capt SNOWDEN RAMC- Quartermaster. This being the right hours handed over to 70 Corps Heavy Artillery. Unit disbanded on from 16-5-19 (Authority DMS Rhine Army N° DM 245/19 of 16-6-19) & all outgoing post & officer cases from that date. Capt A/major ARMSTRONG reverted to Captain from 16-5-19. Last Entry in War Diary. 22/6/19.	E.P.

E. Stewart
Capt RAMC
OC 100th Field Ambulance